I0810050

IMAGES
*of America*

# EDUCATION IN ALBUQUERQUE

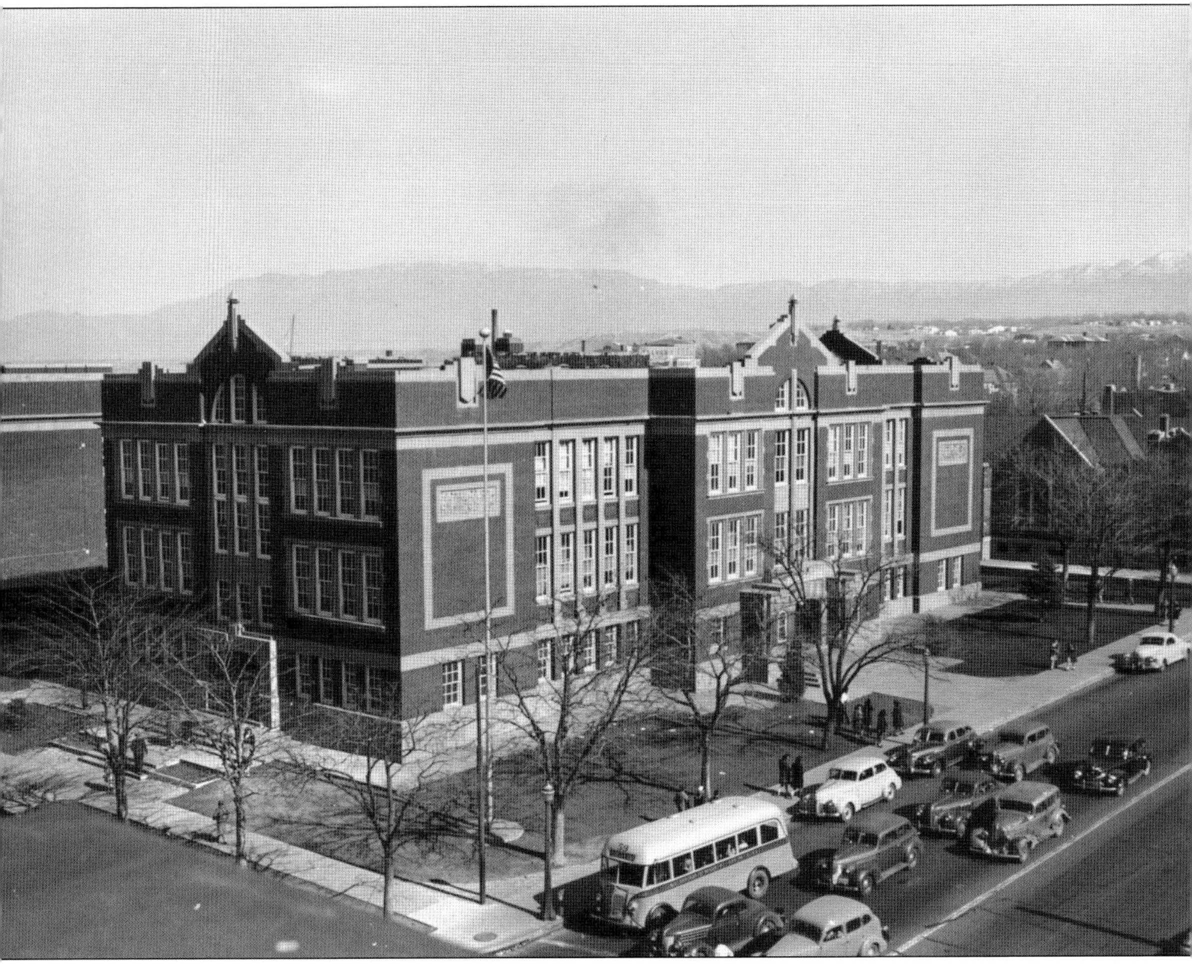

Albuquerque High School, the city's only comprehensive public high school for over 60 years until Highland High opened in 1949, has operated out of several locations since 1879. Located on the northeast corner of Broadway and Central, today the building still echoes voices of thousands of Albuquerque High alumni, living and past. Visible here, this older AHS was erected in 1914. While additions to this building were made many times, it remained in continuous use until a new AHS was opened north of this location in 1974. The old AHS stood nearly vacant for over two decades and came close to being razed, but a concerted community effort resulted in the building being renovated and converted into loft apartments in 2003 with a total revitalization of the neighborhood underway. (Courtesy APS.)

**On the Cover:** Built in 1931, Monte Vista Elementary served the new heights area of Albuquerque near the University of New Mexico. Just blocks from the Nob Hill Business Center, Albuquerque's first shopping center, Monte Vista's neighborhood population exploded after World War II. (Courtesy APS.)

IMAGES
*of America*

# EDUCATION IN ALBUQUERQUE

Ann Piper
Foreword by Dr. Ernie Stapleton

ARCADIA
PUBLISHING

ISBN 978-1-4671-3103-2

Published by Arcadia Publishing
Charleston, South Carolina

Printed in the United States of America

Library of Congress Control Number: 2013952338

For all general information, please contact Arcadia Publishing:
Telephone 843-853-2070
Fax 843-853-0044
E-mail sales@arcadiapublishing.com
For customer service and orders:
Toll-Free 1-888-313-2665

Visit us on the Internet at www.arcadiapublishing.com

*I dedicate this book to the students, teachers, parents, and community of Albuquerque's learning institutions, past and present, whose passion burns from a belief that by educating our youth and ourselves, we continue to create a better world for all.*

# Contents

# Acknowledgments

Gratitude goes to my husband, Blair Kaufman, who supported this project I jumped into within weeks after finishing my doctorate—yet another stint in front of the computer. I also thank my children who long ago gave up the idea that my—or their—learning is ever finished.

The support of my mentors is greatly appreciated: that of Dr. Alicia Chavez, who helped me grow wings to achieve a big goal; Dr. Ernie Stapleton, who was steady and standing by when we lost our dear Dr. John Mondragon; Jim Hulsman, historian extraordinaire; and Jane Mahoney, who steered me to Arcadia. Also, thanks to John Dufay of Albuquerque Public Schools and Dr. Robert Milne, who aided me in accessing so many fabulous photographs.

I sing thanks to my girl friends, constant pillars of strength to me. I give untold gratitude to my school friends in Albuquerque who team with me to support students and families, build up dreams, and achieve our own goals. Thanks, also, to the Albuquerque Public Schools Foundation that does great things for kids.

Photographs appear in this book courtesy of a variety of sources. Commonly used sources are (and will be abbreviated as shown here): Albuquerque Public Schools Archives (APS), *Albuquerque Progress Magazine* (APM), University of New Mexico Center for Southwest Research and Special Collections (CSWR), and Dr. Robert Milne's personal collection of Eldred R. Harrington photographs (ERH).

# FOREWORD

A rich portion of New Mexico history is revealed when examining the educational record of the Land of Enchantment that stretches across centuries. New histories and stories about our schools are very welcome. Maude Crosno, an Albuquerque educator, penned these words: "The past ever needs capturing." Albuquerque's schools constitute the lion's share of New Mexico's educational journey, and in her admirable and scholarly history of education in Albuquerque, Dr. Piper invites us to share "those school days." We welcome her excellent retrieval of Albuquerque's schooling and its share of great accomplishments and challenges.

The story of Albuquerque's educational institutions offers a parallel view of the growth of the city. The legacies of the Native American, Spanish, and frontier periods; the tumultuous struggle for statehood; the population explosion after World War I; and all the major changes occurring after World War II have all impacted the city and its schools. Dr. Piper's narrative traces the convergence of historical, cultural, social, religious, economic, and educational forces that set the stage for their coming of age.

Significant changes occurred in the complex power structure of education in the Albuquerque area. Albuquerque's school systems gradually morphed from rural/urban to urban. Dr. Piper creatively captures these dramatic developments as well as the positive presence of our religious institutions and their schools. The author depicts people of diverse backgrounds working in concert. She shows Albuquerque's leaders, members of the Board of Education, professional organizations, and others historically strong and committed to building and maintaining a successful and inclusive educational community—one with its share of heroic men and women making major contributions. Additionally, Dr. Piper brings to life the remarkable legacy of Supt. John Milne.

This book combines many community and educational voices, and it includes a fortuitous collection of photographs tracing Albuquerque's colorful educational history. The book is an essential read for all persons interested in Albuquerque's journey from the early mists of New Mexico's human birth to the 21st century. Dr. Piper's informed work helps us to understand and appreciate the humanity of our schools. *Education in Albuquerque* will help educate the public about public education.

—Dr. Ernie Stapleton
Emeritus, University of New Mexico
Albuquerque Public Schools Superintendent, 1971–1977

# INTRODUCTION

Albuquerque glitters in the high desert mesa of New Mexico, reflecting a unique history in American education. For centuries, Pueblo Native Americans in the area transmitted their ways of knowing to their young, emphasizing oneness with the land and universe. In the mid-1550s, sun-blinded Spaniards stumbled into the region bringing their ways of education. In 1821, Mexico gained rule of the Albuquerque area and feebly attempted to establish public schools across the great divide of desert and dust that separated the Albuquerque area and Mexico City, the seat of Mexican rule. People, time, and money were scarce, and therefore most education took place in homes of well-to-do citizens who could pay the local priest to teach children to read and write.

In 1821, the newly annexed Mexican citizens in the Albuquerque area witnessed thundering wagons, footsteps, and hooves from the northeast beginning to carve the Santa Fe Trail north of Albuquerque. A vibrant mix of cultures, religions, and languages ported systems of education into the Rio Grande Valley. Spurred by the passion of Manifest Destiny, in 1846 the Mexican-American War caused Gen. Stephen Kearney and the Army of the West to occupy New Mexico and lay claim for the United States. In early 1848, Albuquerque and New Mexico awoke to find themselves suddenly a territory of the United States, and these former Mexican citizens were offered full citizenship and rights as Americans. Ninety percent of New Mexico's surprised populace remained in the area and flourished under the terms of the Treaty of Guadalupe-Hildalgo. But New Mexico struggled to develop a cohesive public school system, battling challenges of mixed languages, cultures, and resources. When the iron horse rolled into New Town Albuquerque in 1880, a tax base sprang up and public schoolhouse doors opened. By 1912, New Mexico won hard-fought entry to the union as the 47th state, but concerns in the East about schooling in the area are tallied as one major delay to entry into the union.

As growth exploded in the Albuquerque area post World War I and, more markedly, post World War II, unique situations impacted the Albuquerque area's evolving educational systems. The tuberculosis recovery industry in the early to mid-1900s affected Albuquerque unlike any other major city. New Mexico was coined "Heart of the Health Country," and Albuquerque garnered a leading role as a destination for tuberculosis patients flocking to seek a comfortable hospice and hope for a cure. Albuquerque's high altitude (5196 feet above sea level); the sunny, dry climate; and relatively temperate conditions year-round made Albuquerque a Mecca nationwide for tuberculosis patients. While overall records of the number of tuberculosis patients were not kept, it is estimated that between 1880 and 1940 the numbers were in the thousands. Well-known people who came to Albuquerque and New Mexico to chase the cure for tuberculosis for themselves or their family, and then went on to contribute to the area include Albert and John Simms, Hugh A. Cooper, William R. Lovelace, Clinton P. Anderson, John Gaw Meem, Clyde and Carrie Tingley, Chester T. French and his brother, Kathryn Kennedy O'Connor, and the family of future long-term public school superintendent John Milne. The economic and human influence of this influx uniquely impacted education in Albuquerque.

Another phenomenon unique to the evolution of education in Albuquerque is the city's location on the north–south singular waterway in the area, the Rio Grande. Additionally, the city perched along the major highway in the southwest for most of the 20th century, Route 66, as well as along the major railroad arterial connecting Chicago/Kansas City, Denver, Phoenix, and Los Angeles. During World War I, World War II, and the Korean War, Albuquerque served as a major goods, troops, and transport hub. Also, with the post–World War II explosion of individual family automobile ownership, tourism as an industry evolved. Albuquerque flourished as a result—motels, tourist courts, small businesses, and restaurants sprang up throughout the Albuquerque area, and schools were hard-pressed to meet the ensuing explosive enrollments.

Similarly unique to the Albuquerque area, and therefore to the schools, was the demand to serve the influx of residents resulting from the post–World War II nuclear and scientific research industry that mushroomed after the design in nearby Los Alamos, and the testing of the resulting nuclear bomb south of Albuquerque at White Sands Missile Range. Sandia Labs was established at the Air Force base located on Albuquerque's southern perimeter. The nearby airport grew to serve as a major transportation artery, and Lovelace research hospital sprang up as a partial result of new scientific research going on in the area.

This singular combination of social and political forces in the Albuquerque area coalesced to crate a unique combustion of educational development reacting to the needs of the ever-growing Albuquerque residents and their children. Governing the Albuquerque area, in chronological order, were Native American tribes, Spain, next Mexico, then the United States as a territory, and finally—not until 1912—winning statehood. This governmental blending simmered up an educational evolution like nowhere else. The story of education in the Albuquerque area is a fascinating one of history, economics, people, places, personalities, and faces that color the alternating dusty and lush landscape with a unique palette.

# *One*

# A Collision of Cultures in Albuquerque and New Mexico

The indigenous people of the Albuquerque area held long-established traditions for educating their youth before the European invaders forever disrupted their ways in the 1500s. Education for Native Americans, like all societies, served the purpose of uniting one generation to the next and creating the collective consciousness of a people. However, traditions utilized by Native Americans to educate their youth differed sharply from those brought by the Europeans. In fact, there is no word for "education" in most indigenous languages.

Varying reasons motivated most Europeans who were resettling in the Americas, but chief among them was the opportunity to practice religious freedom and to better their economic situations. Spain ruled the New Mexico area for nearly 300 years, and the crown was intent on converting the American Natives to Christianity. The Albuquerque-area Natives nurtured a Pueblo culture—not a nomadic one—with established permanent communities, thus making them easy targets for Spanish attempts at conversion. Missionaries believed teaching the Natives to read scripture would hasten the process. Five Catholic "schools" for Natives operated in the Albuquerque area by 1598. Missionaries in New Mexico, by and large—though not exclusively—worked toward converting Natives rather than eradicating or relocating them.

In 1821, Mexico broke free of Spain and took on the government of New Mexico. Mexico attempted to bring public schooling to New Mexico, but the vast distances proved daunting. Additionally, the Santa Fe Trail penetrated the territory in 1821, opening a conduit for diverse traders and settlers from the center of the United States to enter New Mexico. American occupation of New Mexico (1846–1848), and its subsequent American territorial status (1848–1912) still did not establish widespread public education, and little progress was made through the 1850s and 1860s.

In 1873, William Ritch—appointed territorial secretary—oversaw public funds to both nonsectarian and religious schools. In 1879, Colorado College opened Albuquerque Academy on the east side of the city plaza for grades 1 through 12, and within three years 242 students were paying tuition. The school relocated several times in the next few years, but city schooling was underway. Meanwhile, steel rail lines inched toward sleepy Albuquerque.

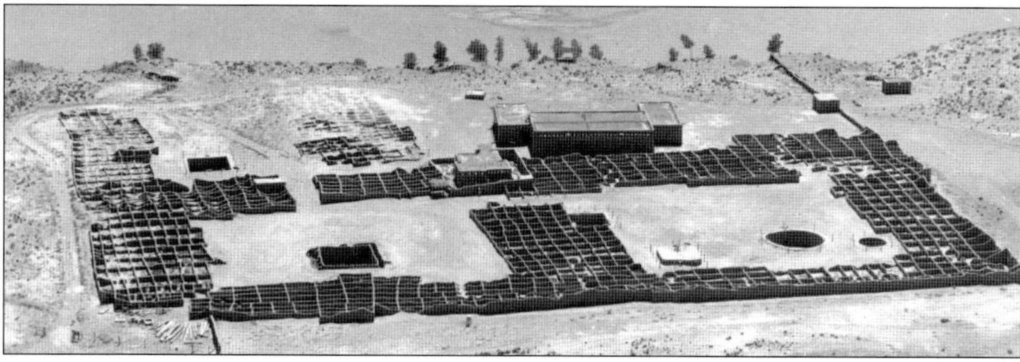

The Spaniards' economic and overtly religious interests in the New Mexico area began in 1540 with Juan Vasquez de Coronado's invasion. Pictured in the 1950s are the remnants of the giant native Pueblo civilization Coronado violated during his march north at what is now Coronado State Monument. Accompanying Coronado were Franciscan friars Fray Juan de Padilla and Fray Luis de Escalona, who are often dubbed the New Mexico area's "first teachers," as they attempted to establish schools for converting Native peoples to Catholicism. (Courtesy CSWR, PICT 000-461-0198.)

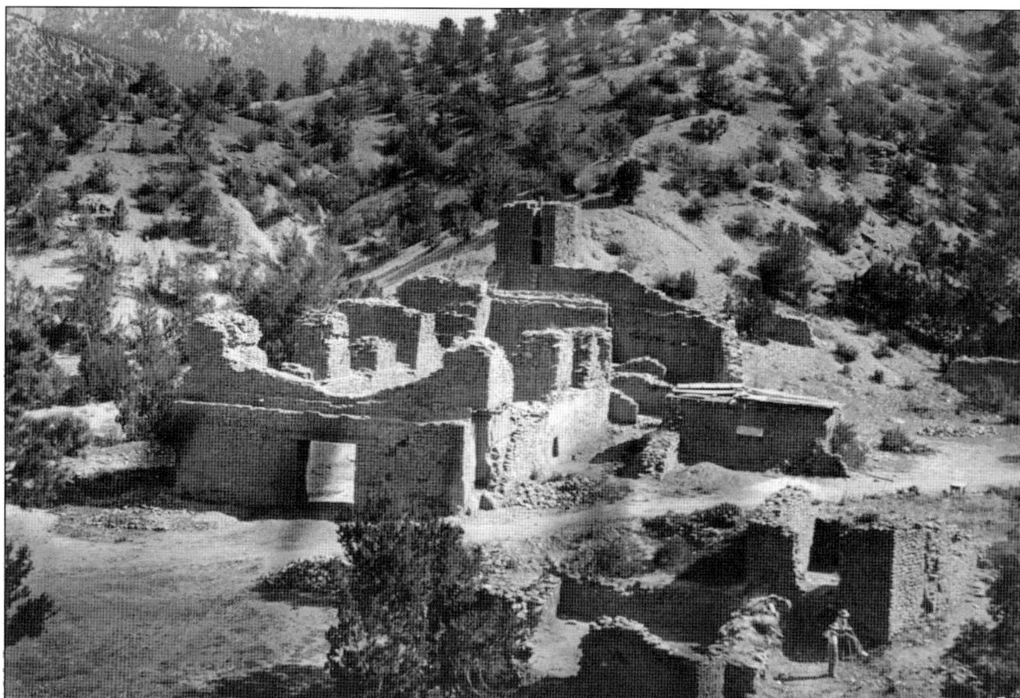


In 1598, Juan de Onate was charged by the Spanish crown to explore, expand, and colonize the Mexico and New Mexico area. Onate was a ruthless and aggressive invader, and with his large expedition parties came more friars set on establishing schools to convert Natives to Christianity in order to rid them of their demonic and "heathen" ways. It was common practice for the friars, backed by the king's soldiers, to force the native population to construct the schools in which they would be educated. Pictured above are the ruins of the Jemez mission church, built around 1625 with forced labor. The friars abandoned the Jemez mission around 1640, and all of the Spanish were driven out of the New Mexico area in 1680 in a violent coup. (Courtesy CSWR, PICT 000-003-0159.)

In 1822, the Mexican government passed a law that all of its provinces should establish public schools, but they did not provide funding. By 1829, the New Mexico area reported only 18 schools and 18 teachers. When Mexican rule of the New Mexico area ended in 1846, the bishopric of Durango, Mexico, transferred its authority to that of Cincinnati, Ohio, and the French Jesuit John Baptiste Lamy, whose c. 1870s portrait is at right, swept into Santa Fe. Immediate conflict erupted between Lamy and the area Franciscan priests. The respected Padre Martinez of Taos (who had established a renowned school there and published the first textbooks in New Mexico) eventually was excommunicated by Lamy. Bishop Lamy acted on schooling, establishing several Catholic schools including the Loretto Academy for Girls and St. Michael's College in the Santa Fe area. (Courtesy Archdiocese of Santa Fe.)

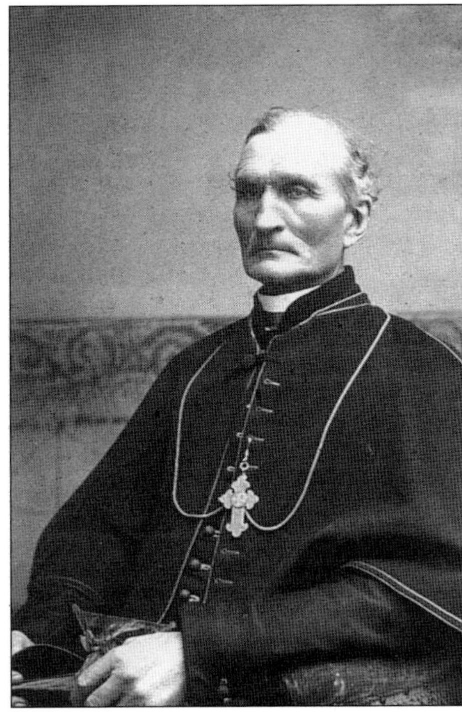

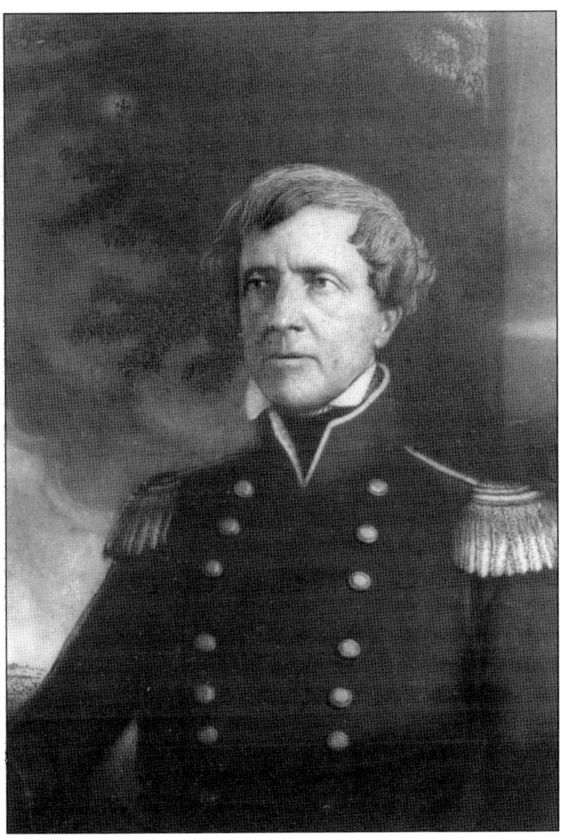

Stephen W. Kearney led the United States Army of the West into New Mexico in August 1846, and in a bloodless take-over, New Mexico became a territory of the United States. Overnight, people who had been citizens of Mexico became those of the United States. The ensuing "Kearney Code" and the laws of the United States mandated public schools, but little changed in the New Mexico area concerning the establishment of schools. Challenges continued along the lines of financial support, distances, language, religion, politics, and issues around ethnic differences. (Courtesy CSWR, PICT 000-742-0067.)

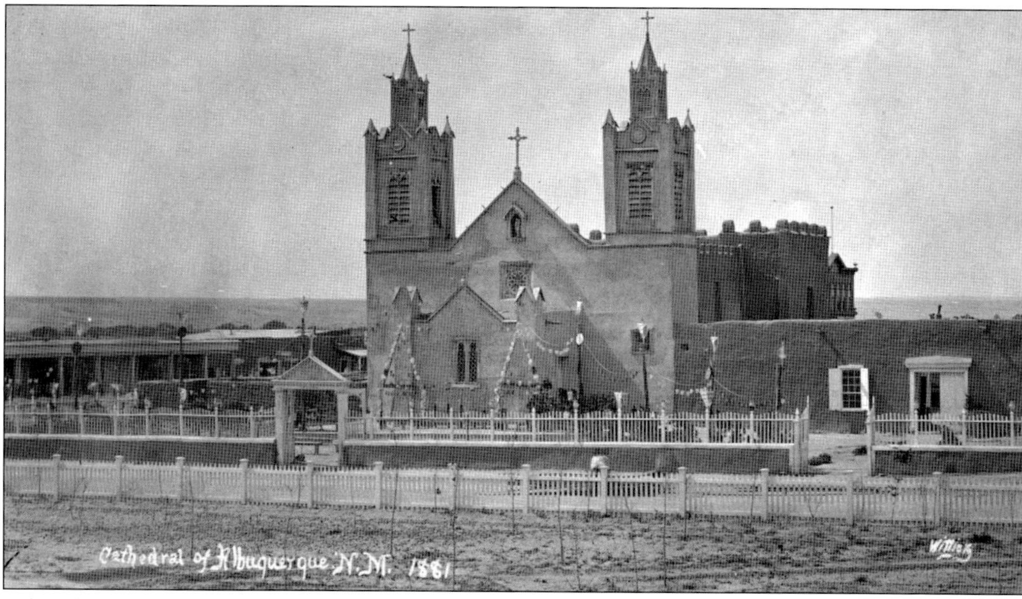


After the American occupation of New Mexico and the subsequent territorial status beginning in 1848, an 1875 report counts 138 schools in the territory with 147 teachers. San Felipe de Neri "Old Town" Church, pictured above in 1881, formed the north side of Albuquerque's Old Town Plaza. In 1879, Colorado College in conjunction with the Congregational Church founded Albuquerque Academy on the east side of the plaza (reportedly at the location of today's Hacienda restaurant), a tuition school for children of all ages. This school is not to be confused with today's private school Albuquerque Academy. The school soon moved to the Perkins Building in New Town, at the site of today's Edith and Central Public Library. (Courtesy CSWR, PICT 000-742-0795.)

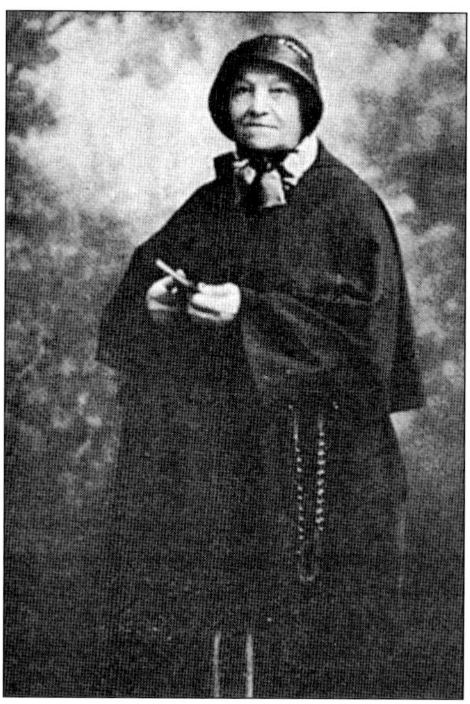

Sister Blandina (Rose Maria Segale) arrived from Trinidad, Colorado, to Albuquerque's Old Town in 1881. The Sisters of Charity convent, attached to the north side of Old Town's San Felipe de Neri church, received public funds to open a school that became known as Sister Blandina's School. Formally, the Sisters of Charity operated Our Lady of Angels, and the Jesuit priests ran Old Town Public School, both in the same convent building.

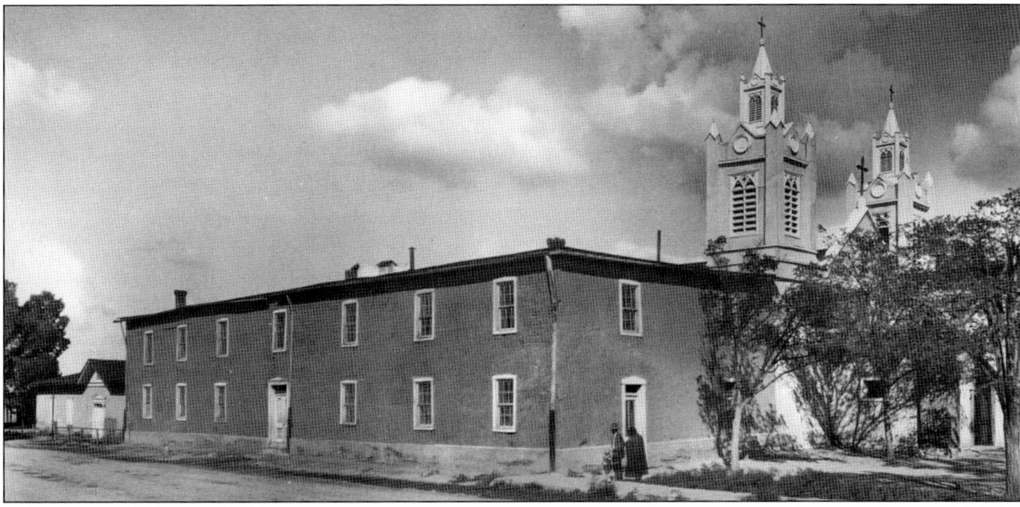

Sister Blandina's school and convent, pictured above (date unknown), still stand in Albuquerque as the San Felipe de Neri's gift shop attached to the church in Old Town. In addition to the Old Town schools she opened in 1881, Blandina reportedly oversaw the opening of the Immaculate Conception School, other area schools in the Barelas and Duranes neighborhoods, and St. Vincent's Academy in Albuquerque's downtown (near present day Sixth Street and Lomas Boulevard). St. Vincent's was built on land donated by brothers Perfecto, Mariano, and Jesus Armijo. (Courtesy CSWR.)

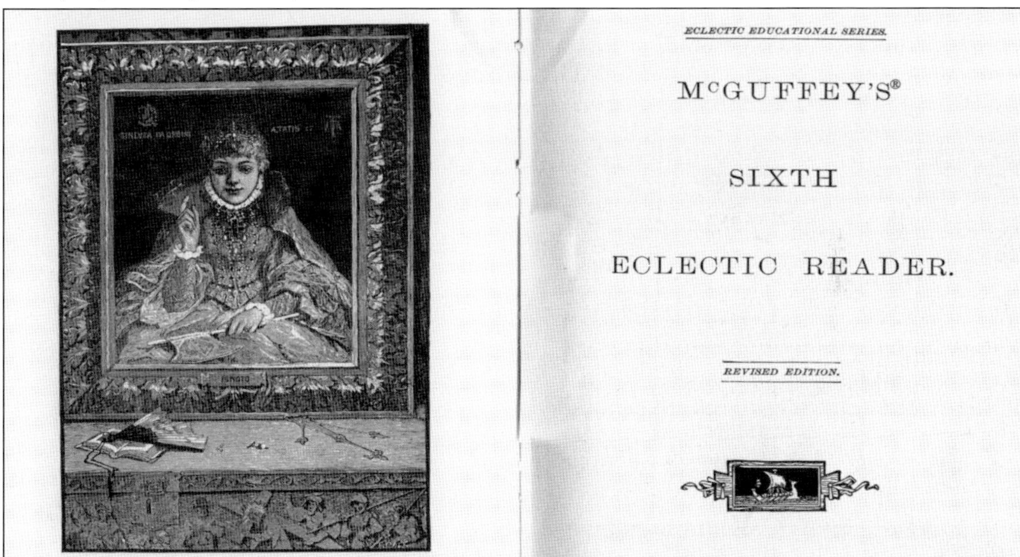


No other textbook in America has enjoyed such widespread use as the *McGuffey Reader*, the first text designed to become progressively challenging as the student moved through levels one through four. Right, a version of the *First Reader* that utilized a phonics approach to reading. The readers were used in New Mexico's schools to some extent. William McGuffey and his brother James infused the early readers with Presbyterian Calvinist values, even including—some say—anti-Semitic beliefs. The readers were revised in the 17th century to reflect the melting pot assimilation idea that became the perceived American way. (Author's collection.)

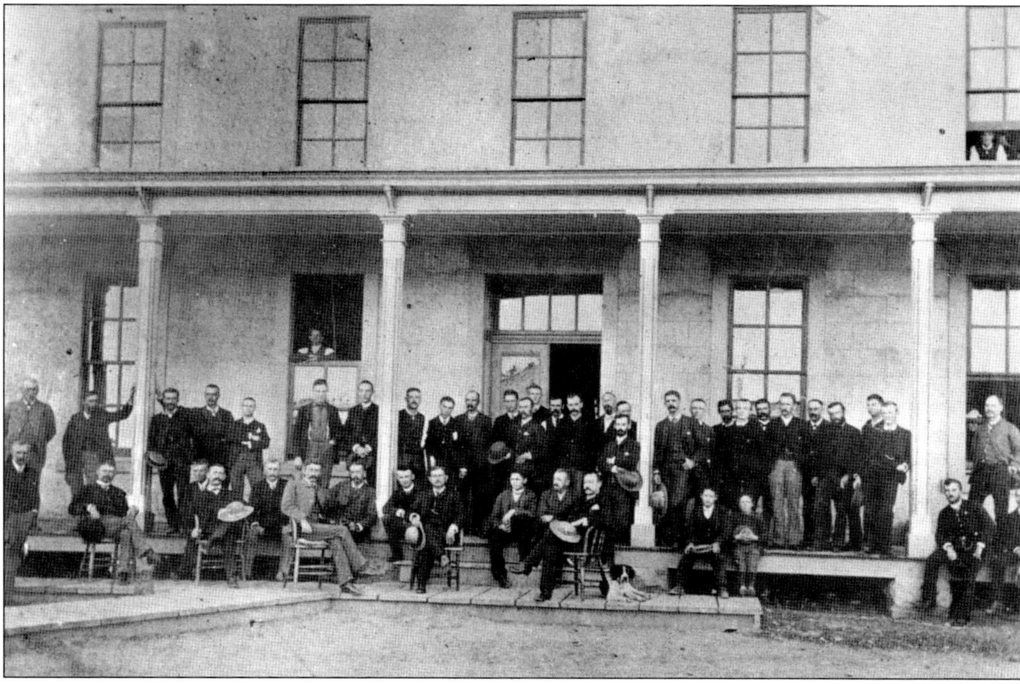

The railroad came in April 1880 and forever changed the educational, social, economic, and cultural fabric of Albuquerque. Shown above are some of the Atlantic & Pacific Railroad employees that churned into the area. New Town sprang up east of the Old Town Plaza, pulling thousands of European immigrants into the area to establish shops, work on the railroad, open churches, and serve the population of this burgeoning town which surged from a few hundred people before 1880 to a metropolitan area of over 17,000 by the turn of the century. (Courtesy CWSR, PICT 000-742-0214.)

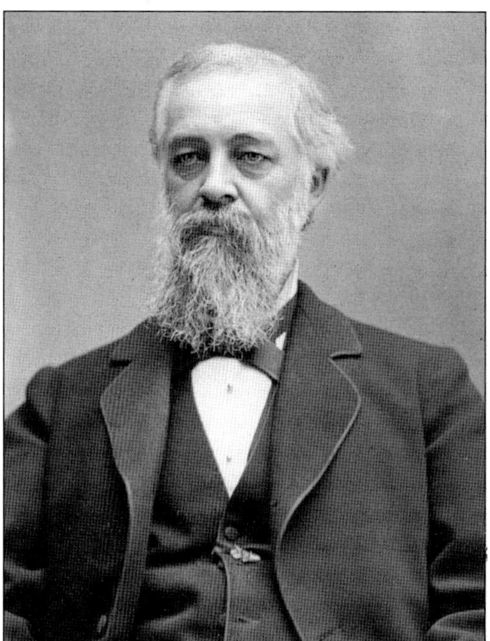

William G. Ritch, left, served as New Mexico's territorial secretary and governor from 1873 through 1885. Ritch saw to fruition a measure passed in early 1891 by the territorial legislature allowing local municipalities—in addition to counties—to levy taxes in order fund schools. Albuquerque incorporated as a city, and funds going to schools such as St. Vincent's and the Albuquerque Academy were transferred to the Albuquerque city school board. In April 1891, the board named the Albuquerque Academy's principal Charles E. Hodgin as the first superintendent of city schools. That fall, Albuquerque Academy closed and leased its building, Perkins Hall, at the corner of Edith and Central Avenue to the city. (Courtesy CSWR, PICT 000-742-0124.)

# *Two*

# Public Schools Evolve in Albuquerque

New Mexico's lack of a cohesive public school system hampered the continuing bid for New Mexico statehood. Politicians, corporations, merchants, immigrants, farmers, and others poured into New Mexico and the Albuquerque area once the steel railroad lines reached the high ground east of old Albuquerque in 1880. Civil engineer Colonel Marmon built a depot and laid out streets named Central Avenue, Broadway, First, Second Third, and more.

By 1886, the tuition-funded Albuquerque Academy (not to be confused with the present day Academy) had swelled in enrollment, and by 1890, the school had 385 students. A new three-story building was erected at Central and Edith (the site of the Edith public library that was built there in 1925). The University of New Mexico opened on the far-east mesa hills above New Town in 1889 with a single imposing four-story building.

After much political wrangling and drama, the New Mexico territorial legislature passed a bill establishing common schools in New Mexico in 1891 and set up a state superintendent of public instruction. Two important differences were established by the legislation: a means by which communities could raise funds to build school facilities (taxation), and a requirement unique in the United States that teachers be able to speak English, yet honor children who could only speak Spanish. Formal school districts were formed in New Mexico following this 1891 legislation.

Albuquerque lost no time establishing a school system. The principal of Albuquerque Academy from 1886 to 1991, Charles Hodgin, became the first superintendent of the city schools, and elementary schools were constructed. Albuquerque High School (AHS) opened on the third floor of the Albuquerque Academy building at Central and Edith with 30 class members and three graduates in the class of 1892. In the fall of 1893, AHS moved to a frame building in the 200 block of South Edith, and in the fall of 1900 the school moved again to the Central School Building at Third Street and Lead Avenue. Soon after, a site was selected for a permanent AHS structure on the northeast corner of Broadway and Central Avenue.

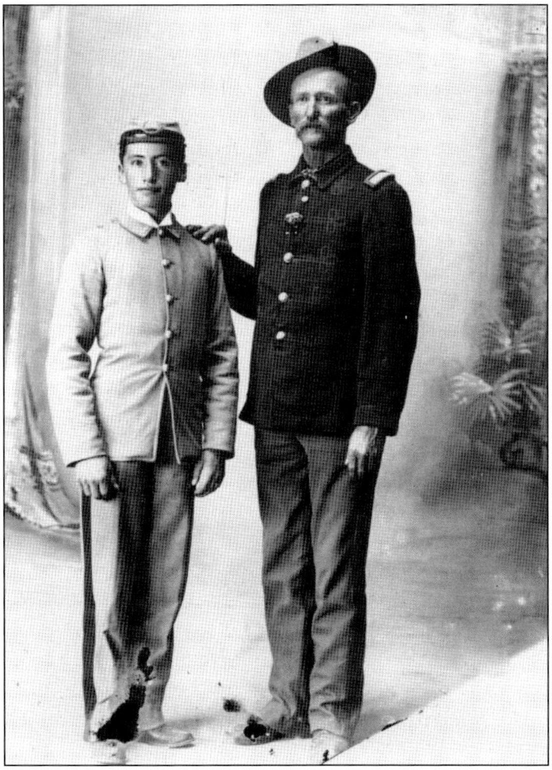

Col. Walter Marmon, a civil engineer for the Atlantic & Pacific Railroad, platted out streets in New Town Albuquerque in the 1880s and named the east–west main street Central Avenue. Along and west of the railroad tracks came First, Second, Third Streets, and so on. East of the tracks, New Yorker Marmon named Broadway, Arno Avenues (after New Town developer Franz Huning's son), then Edith and Walter Streets after Marmon's own two children, and finally High Street—named so because it was as far west as the town was envisioned to grow, on high ground above any chances of flooding. Marmon (pictured here with son Walter) was a visionary in his day to lay wide streets, easing traffic flow as the years progressed. (Courtesy CSWR, PICT 000-742-0083.)

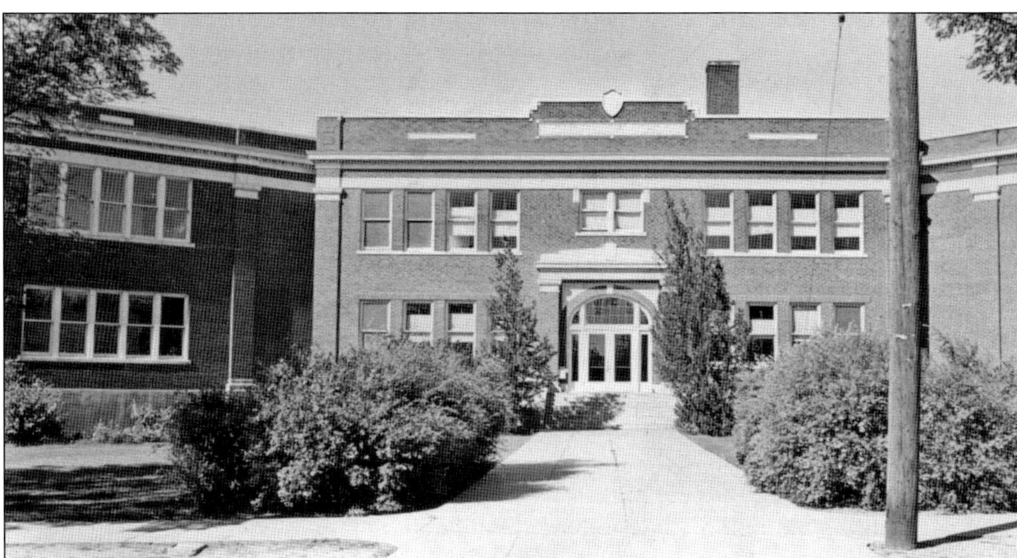

Longfellow School, pictured above around 1944, embodies the oldest "moving target" public school in old Albuquerque. Undoubtedly an existing home or church school in the area, Longfellow came into the formal Albuquerque city schools system by 1891. Older Albuquerque High graduates today remember to old Longfellow situation north of Hopewell Field near Tijeras and Broadway—later to become the United Services Organization Building. Today, this proud dual-language school serves a diverse sector of Albuquerque's student population. (Courtesy APS.)

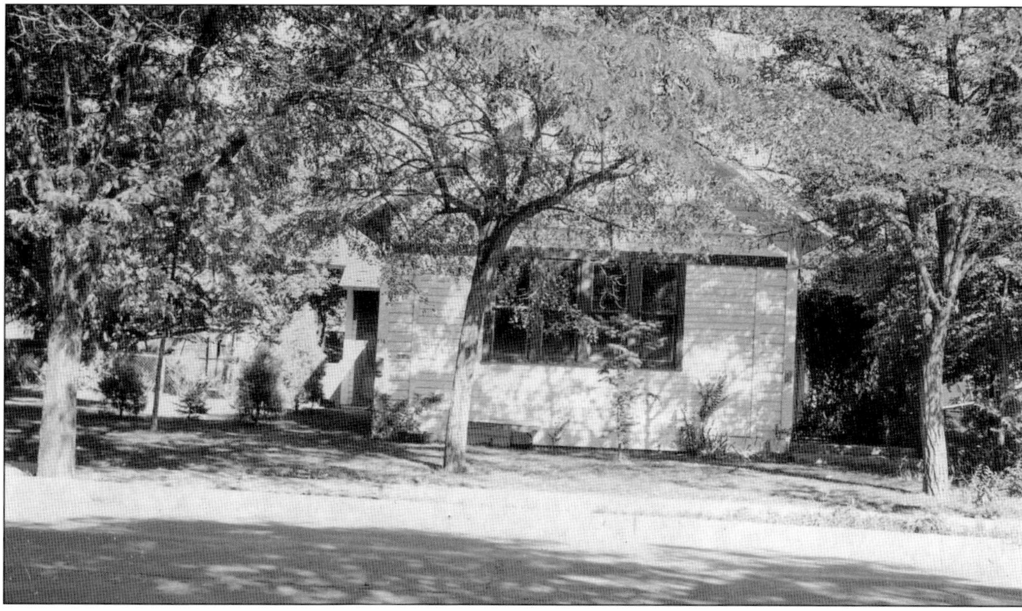

In 1891, with the birth of the city schools as an entity, Albuquerque High had moved into Perkins Hall at the northwest corner of Edith and Central that was abandoned as Albuquerque Academy went out of business. This wood-frame building, above, was the site of Albuquerque High School from 1893 until about 1900. It was located at 214 South Edith Street, and 35 students attended it in that first year. (Courtesy ERH.)

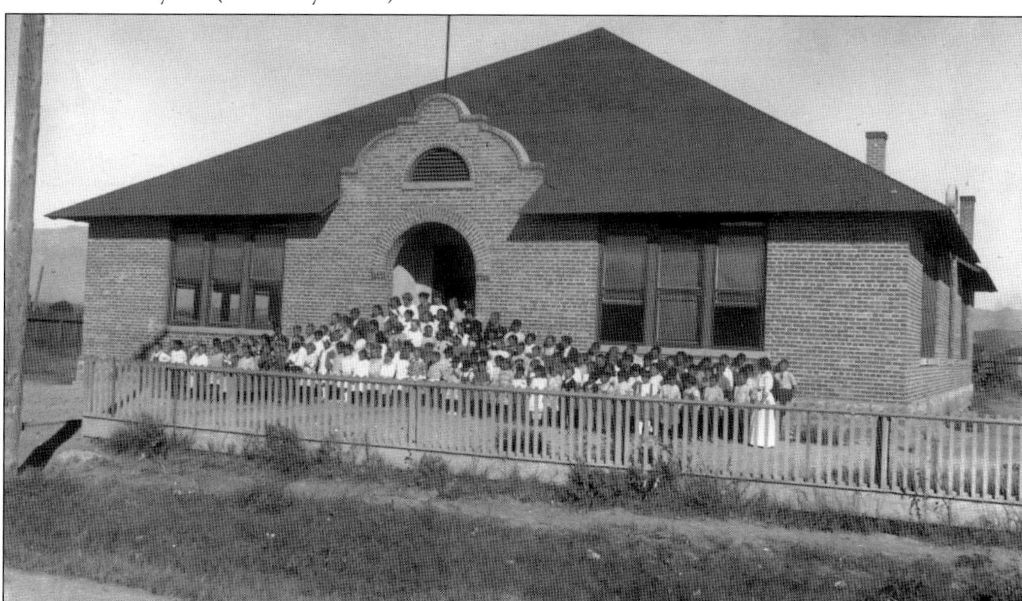

San Jose Elementary School has a cloudy and muddled history because it is one of the oldest continuously used schools in the Albuquerque area. East San Jose School is well known at 415 Thaxton Southwest, and reports circulate of West San Jose School, which perhaps became River View Elementary at 1700 Barelas Southwest. The library area of the National Hispanic Cultural Center is said to have swallowed up West San Jose. Pictured above are students and staff of what is reportedly one of the San Jose schools in the south Albuquerque area. (Courtesy APS.)

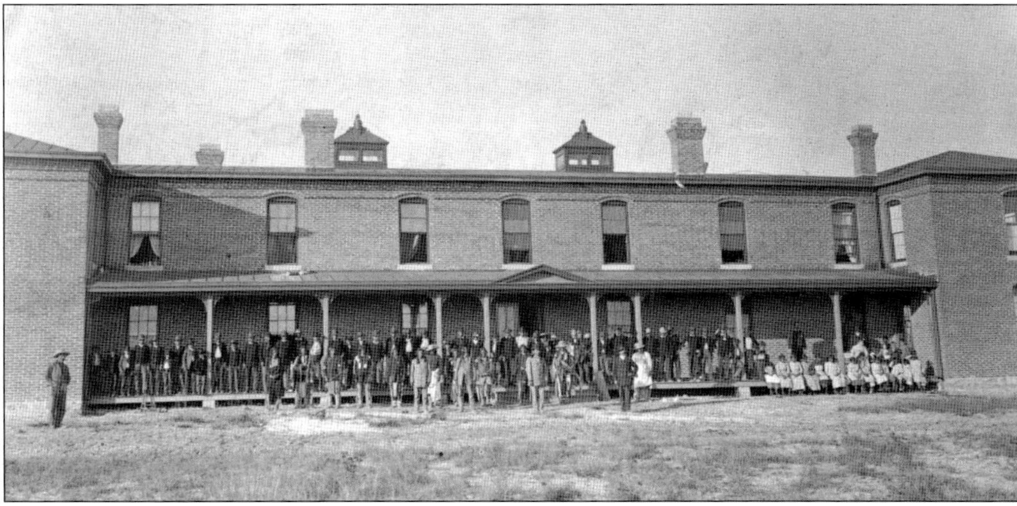

The tilted light of history reflected by the European invaders', the Mexican government's, and the ensuing United States government's attempts to "educate" Native Americans shines a sordid spotlight that exposes shameless and inexcusable abuses cloaked in many motives. The issue is too complicated and extensive to explore in these pages. However, pictured above around 1890 is a group on the portico of the Albuquerque Indian School. Presbyterian missionary Sheldon Jackson arrived in the city by 1880 to advance the cause of "assimilating" Natives to Eurocentric ways, and to additionally, Christianize them. (Courtesy CSWR, PICT 000-001-0027.)

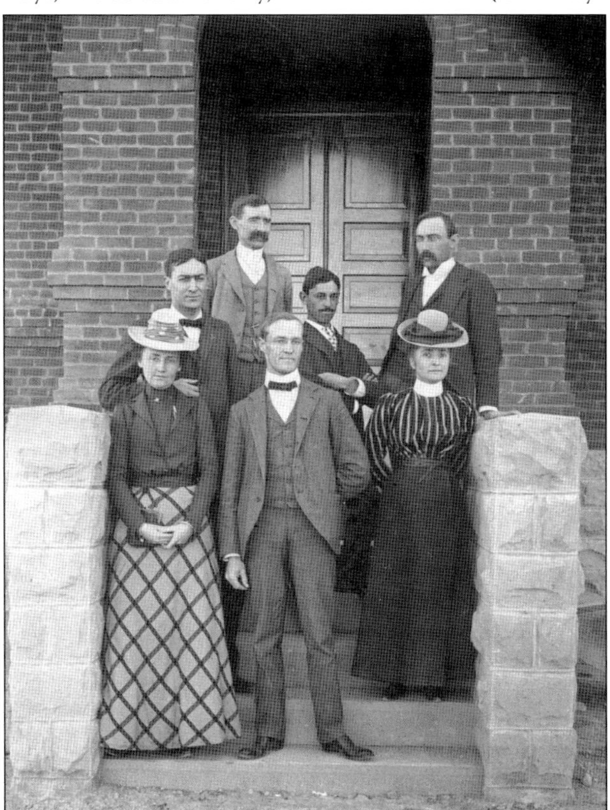

On the left stands C.E. Hodgin with a group of educators who misguidedly believed eradicating the Native American culture was right and true to advance "civilization." Hodgin, however, became an active civic leader in Albuquerque, the first superintendent of city schools, a secondary teacher, and a scholar in his own right. (Courtesy CSWR, PICT 000742-0242.)

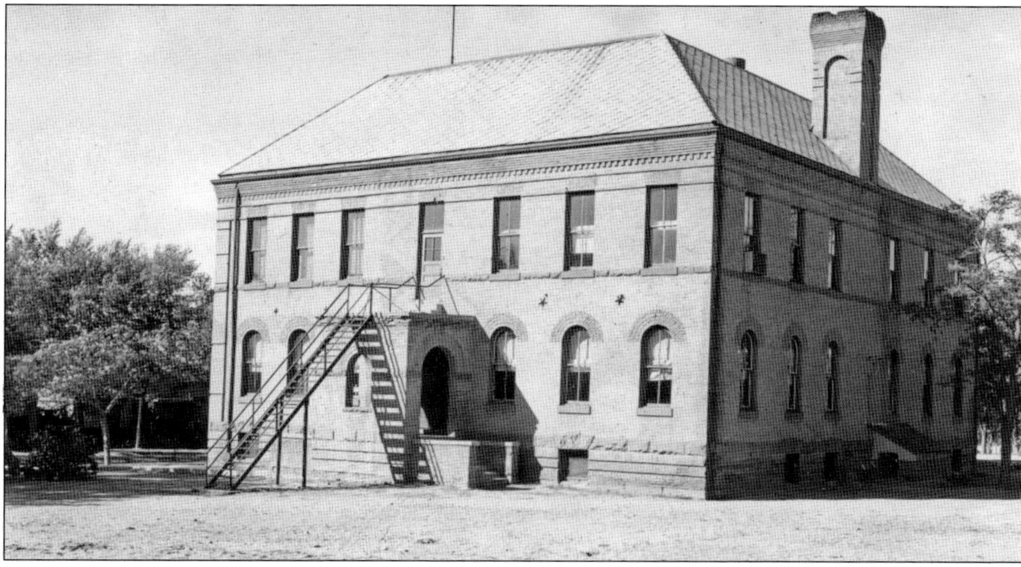

The First Ward School building, above, no longer standing at its long-established corner of Edith and Grand, proudly opened its door in 1882. The school emerged as one of four of the city's "ward schools" after a bond issue passed in 1883 to fund a school for each of the four city political wards that elected representatives to the City Commission. First Ward School housed 12 sturdy classrooms and was the site, according to Albuquerque High teacher E. R. Harrington, of many an Albuquerque citizen acquiring "character education" by "having a yardstick laid across the seat of his trousers." (Courtesy ERH.)

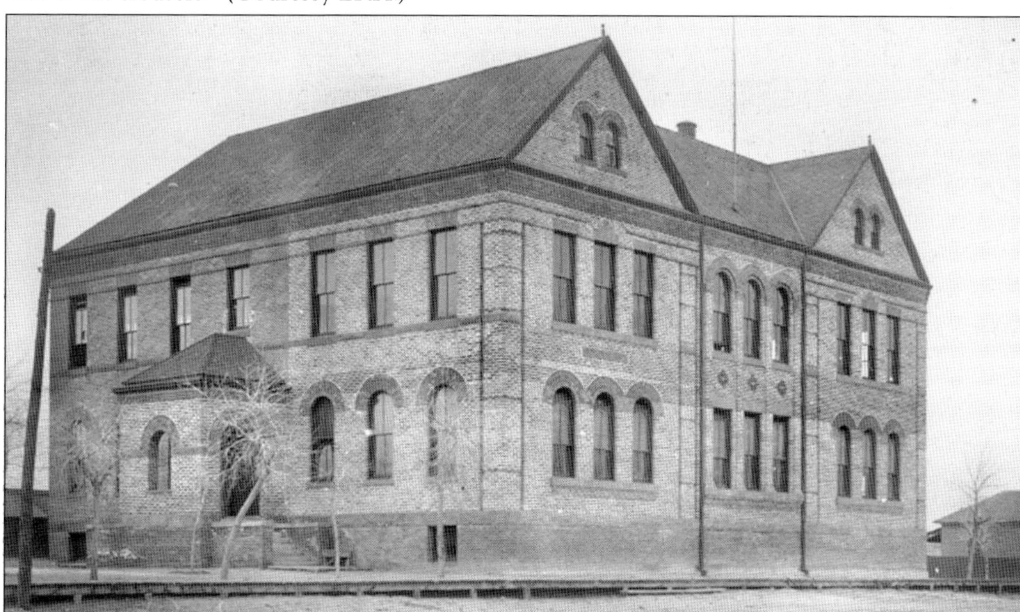

Albuquerque's political Second Ward built its school at 900 Edith Southeast. The solid structure housed all of the ward's elementary students until a population boom in the 1920s spurred the building of Eugene Field (just two blocks north of the Second Ward School), followed by the John Marshall School southeast of Eugene Field, and then Lew Wallace School that replaced the Fourth Ward School. (Courtesy APS.)

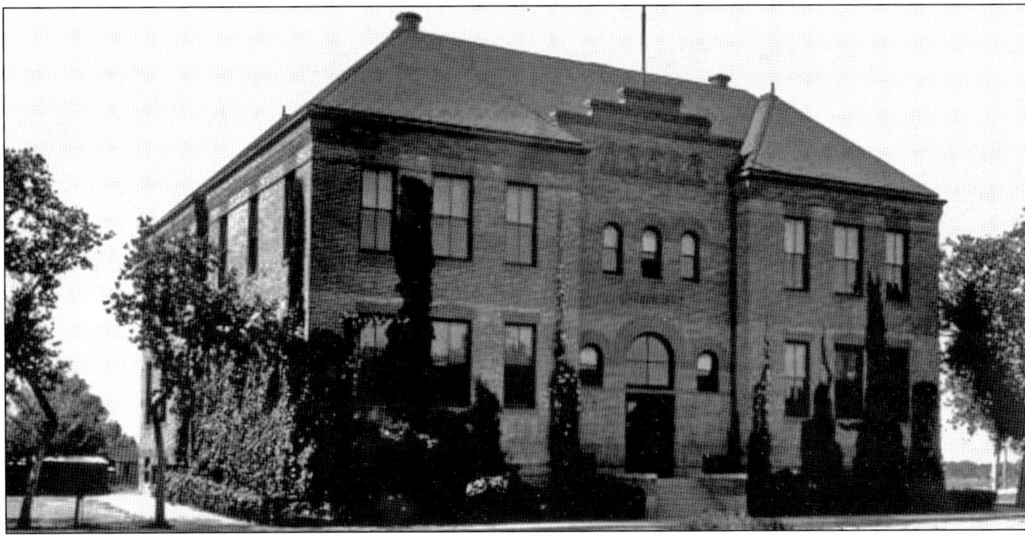

The school that served Albuquerque's political Third Ward children was located near Fourth Street and Iron. Like the other three ward schools, it stood imposingly high, bricked, and strong. In 1935 this school was renovated to become Coronado Elementary. Other currently APS schools believed to have opened prior to 1911 in some fashion include Los Padillas, Griegos, and Mountain View. (Courtesy APS.)

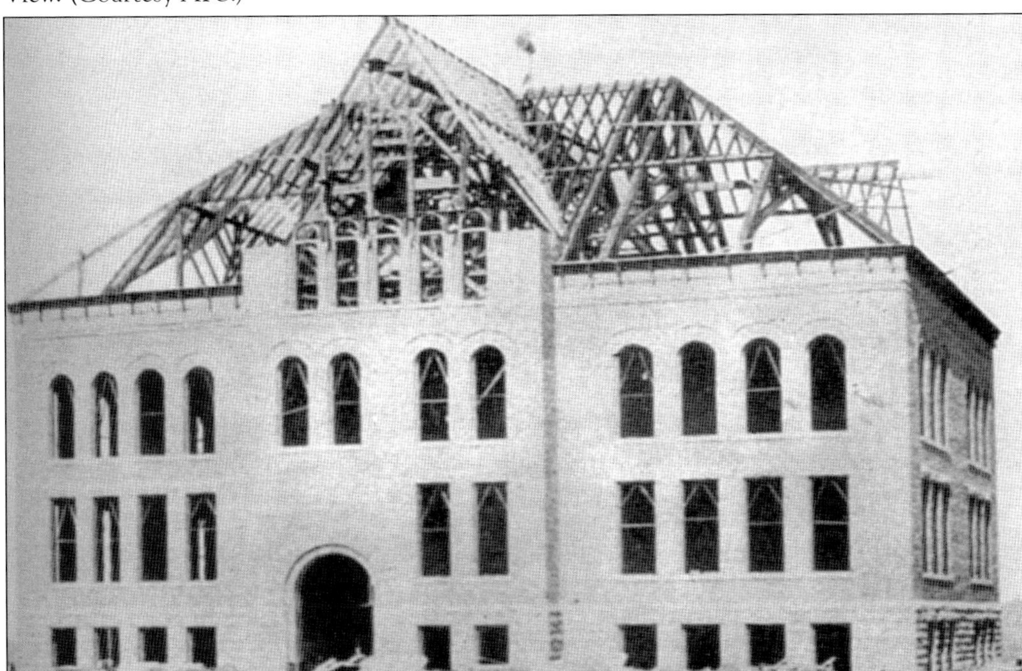

In 1889, Bernard Rodey spearheaded a move in the territorial legislature to authorize the opening of the University of New Mexico in Albuquerque, the School of Mines in Socorro, and the Agricultural School in Las Cruces. The first permanent building of the university opened in 1892, and is visible above boasting redbrick walls with light-colored stone trim and proud arched doorways. Elias Stover and Hiram Hadley led the institution through 1897. Stover, a businessman, served as president while Hadley was in charge of academics. (Courtesy CSWR.)

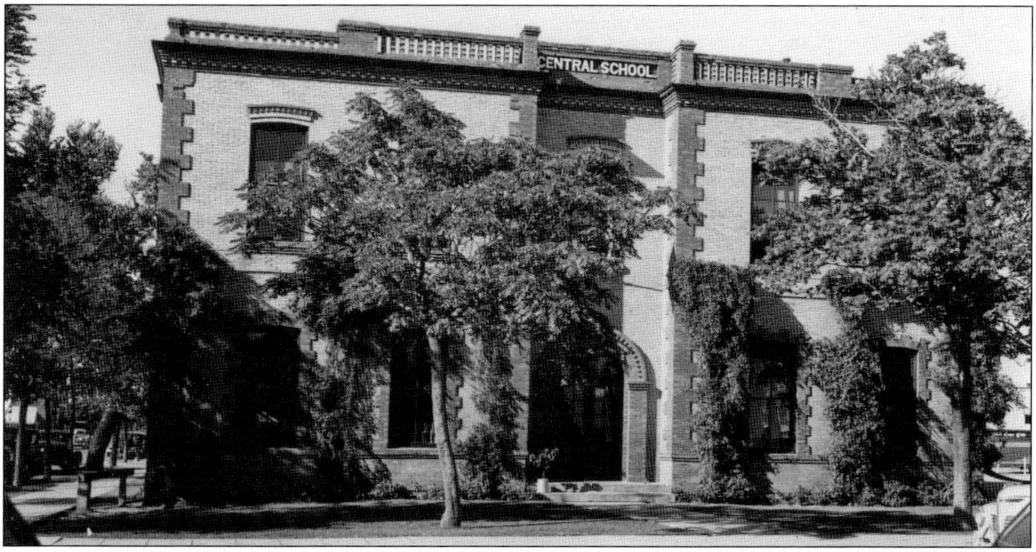


In the fall of 1900, Albuquerque High moved from its wood-framed Edith and Central location to the building visible above. The first floor housed grades 6–8, and the upper floor was home of the high school. Later used as the Central School, located at Central Avenue and Third Street, the building housed the Albuquerque Public Schools' administrative offices from the 1930s until after World War II. The building was converted to become the central administration offices and many teachers reported to this building to be interviewed and hopefully hired by longtime superintendent, John Milne. In 1952, the Board of Education sold this building to the New Mexico Department of Public Welfare. (Courtesy ERH.)

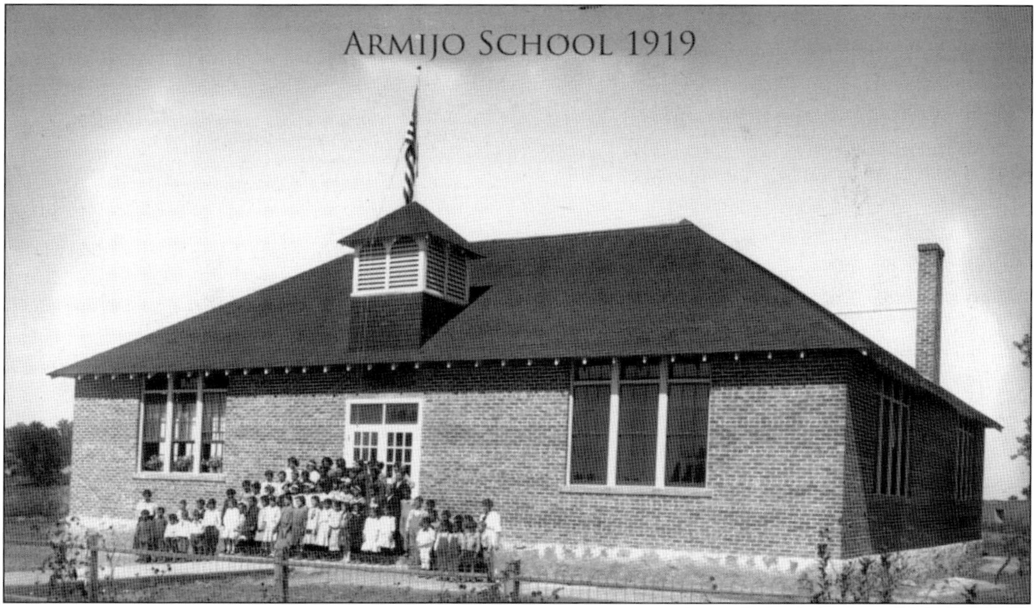


Armijo School, located in the south valley of Albuquerque, has served a diverse and wide-ranging population of rural and urban students and families. Visible above, around 1910, students pose with staff in the brush outside the school. An extensive remodel of Armijo took place in 1957, and the school is currently being remodeled to house a portion of Robert F. Kennedy Charter School. (Courtesy APS.)

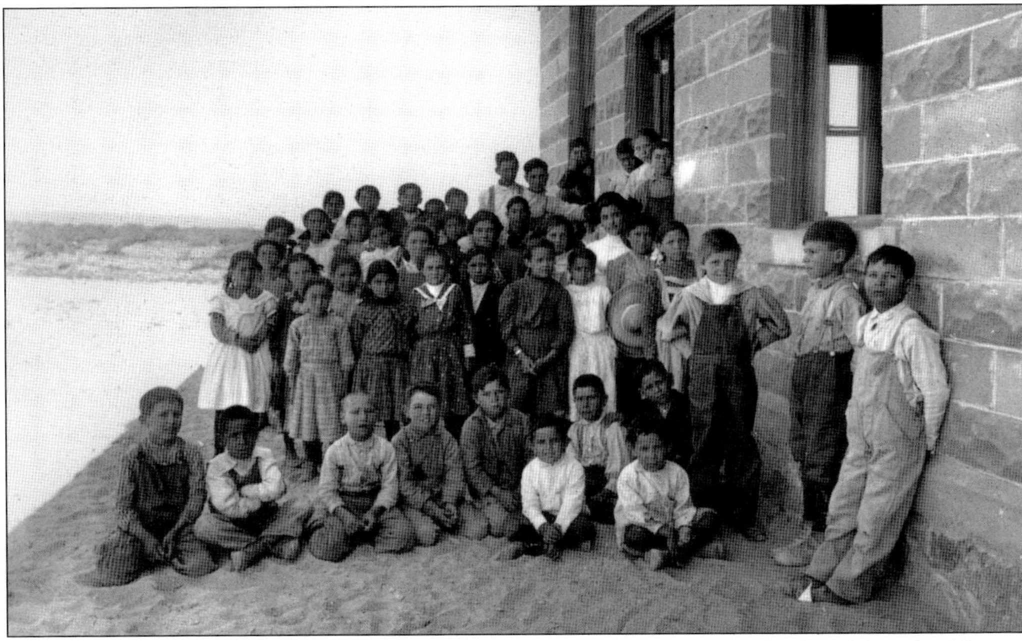

Children from San Jose School, pictured around 1900, cluster in the shade of their building to be photographed. The school served students and families from the culturally diverse south end of Albuquerque. As the railroad gained importance as an economic force in Albuquerque, many African American families settled near the rail yards and San Jose School. (Courtesy APS.)

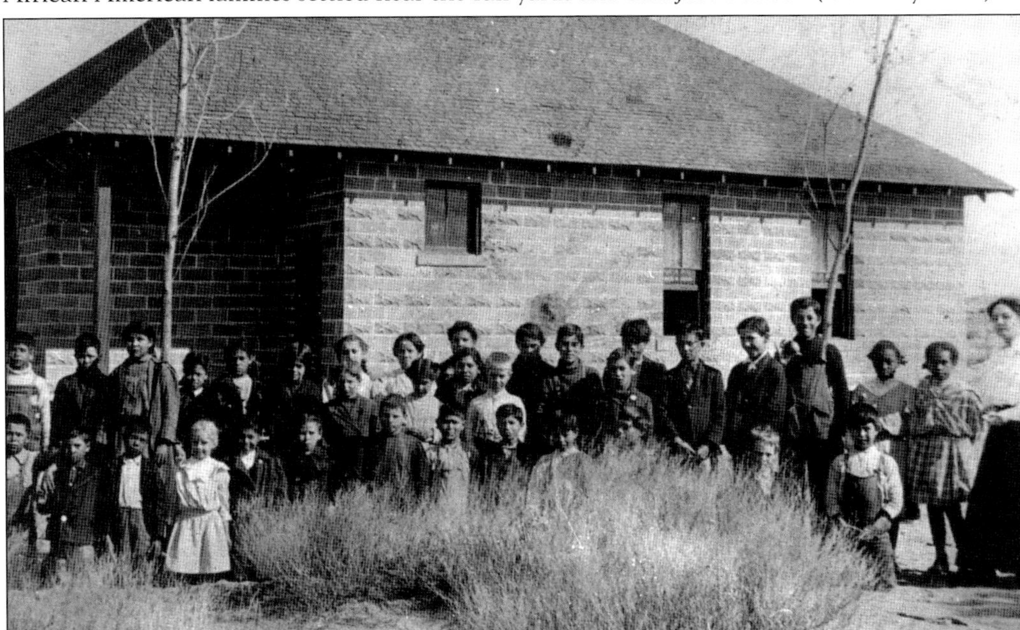

Above, San Jose School students and their teacher pose outside their school. Today's East San Jose School was officially opened in 1958, but the school was a part of the Bernalillo County Schools for decades before the county and city consolidated in 1949. Before 1950, a West San Jose School existed, went dormant, and was eventually swallowed up by the National Hispanic Cultural Center's library. (Courtesy APS.)

# *Three*

# Parochial Schools in Albuquerque

The history of publicly funded education by governments under the jurisdiction of the United States does not span a long time line in Albuquerque, nor much of the western United States. Albuquerque High formally opened its doors in 1891 and was fueled with newly authorized public funding. Home and church-based schooling had filled a gap in years stretching back for centuries in the area, and the presence of church schools is delicately intertwined with publicly funded schools.

Children and families of European and Mexican descent settled in the New Mexico area beginning in the 1500s, opening small widely scattered and isolated schools. Motivations varied, and the available church of the immigrants was often the educational vehicle—Spanish, Mexican, and many European faiths and cultures mixed in Albuquerque, including Greeks, Moors, and Jews.

The lack of widespread public schools and the unresolved Protestant/Catholic conflict concerning who should educate hampered the continuing bid for New Mexico statehood. Even though schools in New Mexico after 1891 had access to local and state funding, many of New Mexico's public schools employed Catholic nuns as teachers, and this issue was not resolved until 1951 when a lawsuit was filed (*Zeller v. Huff*), resulting in the Archbishop removing all nuns from public schools. Also, the isolated nature of many of New Mexico's rural communities—often with hundreds of miles separating localities—added an extra challenge to delivering education to children. However, in United States history, New Mexico carved out a unique position by educating children in both Spanish and English languages, a practice not often implemented elsewhere in the Southwest.

Church schools—staffed by educated lay community and church members—have been a vibrant and contributing feature to Albuquerque's educational landscape for hundreds of years, bringing the varied values, assumptions, cultures, and beliefs of many diverse people to a common schoolhouse desk in order to positively impact children.

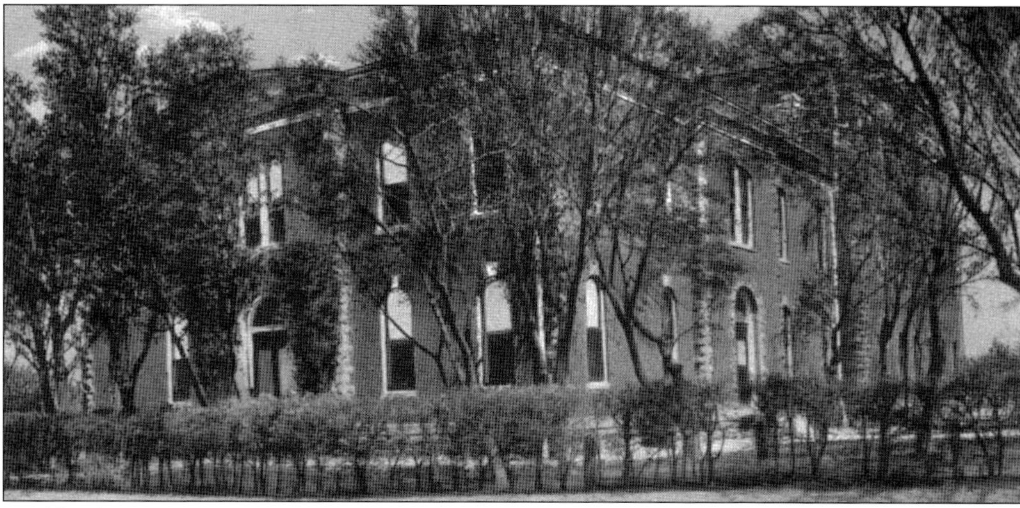

Visible above is St. Vincent's Academy around 1888. Founded in 1881 as Our Lady of Angels School near the Old Town Catholic Church, the Sisters of Charity from Ohio received public funds to begin Number 12 School by 1883. Soon, the school relocated to Sixth and Lomas, and later broke with the public system, eventually closing in 1969. In the heyday, nuns found dates for the girls from nearby St. Mary's, and parents hosted summer barbecues for the girls and the teaching nuns. There are rumors of spiked sodas unbeknownst to the sisters who enjoyed the events. Other legends state that St. Vincent students Nancy Hebenstreit and Carla Singer got a kiss from Elvis Presley when he visited the area in 1956, sending Albuquerque Academy into a scandalized spin that spring.

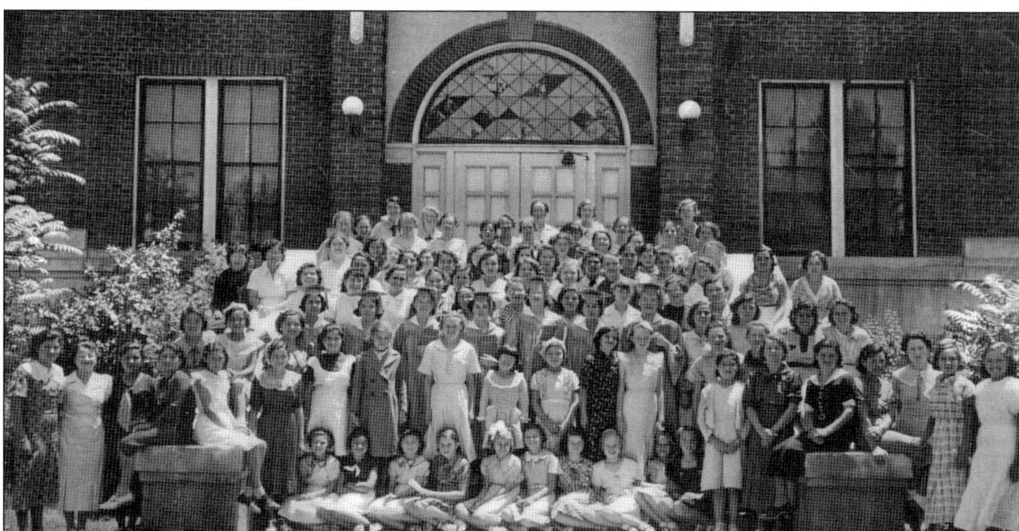

Harwood Schools was founded by Thomas and Emily Harwood, who were Methodist missionaries arriving in the area in the 1880s. The boys' school grew up on Fourth Street and San Lorenzo and burned down in the 1920s. The girls' school opened at the corner of Seventh and Mountain in 1925. Funded with public works funds, a new building was added in 1935, followed in 1940 by the brick edifice, Hudd Hall, that stands today. Regretfully closing in 1976, (pictured that year, above) the Harwood School building has housed many community groups and, most recently, the Escuela del Sol and Harwood Art Center. (Courtesy Harwood Art Center.)

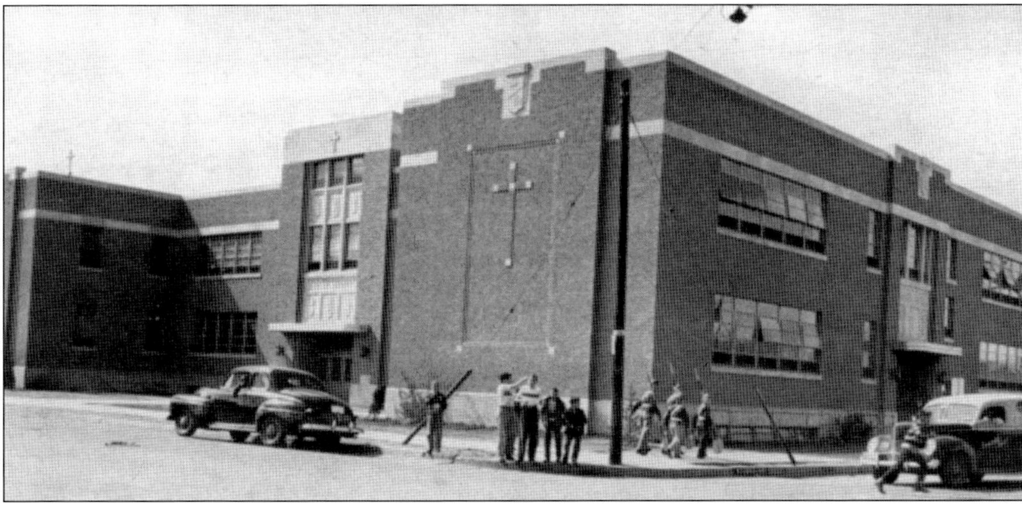

Father Alfonso Mandalari arrived in 1884 to head Immaculate Conception Church, which later took the name of St. Mary's. The school began in 1892 to serve boys in New Town, Albuquerque, opening in the Garcia home at Sixth and Central (Railroad Avenue). By 1893, a two-story, four-room school rose at Sixth and Tijeras, pictured here in 1951. (Courtesy APM.)

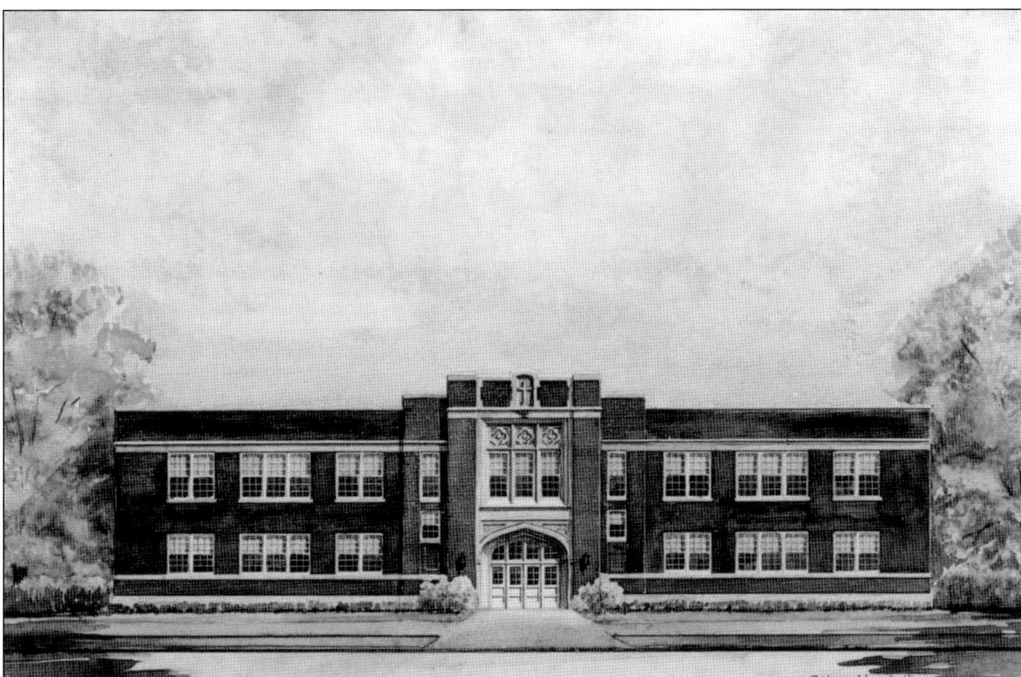


After a large, two-story building was erected, St. Mary's school out-paced the needs that edifice could provide. By 1940, architect Louis Hesselden designed a larger building (his sketch is above) that stands today joined to more expansions. The sister of New Mexico's longtime senator Pete Domenci was the principal of the school that both she and her brother attended. St. Mary's is vibrant and utilizes a powerful brush to paint a bright picture of academics, athletics, and service in Albuquerque education. (Courtesy CSWR, PICT 000-742-1046.)

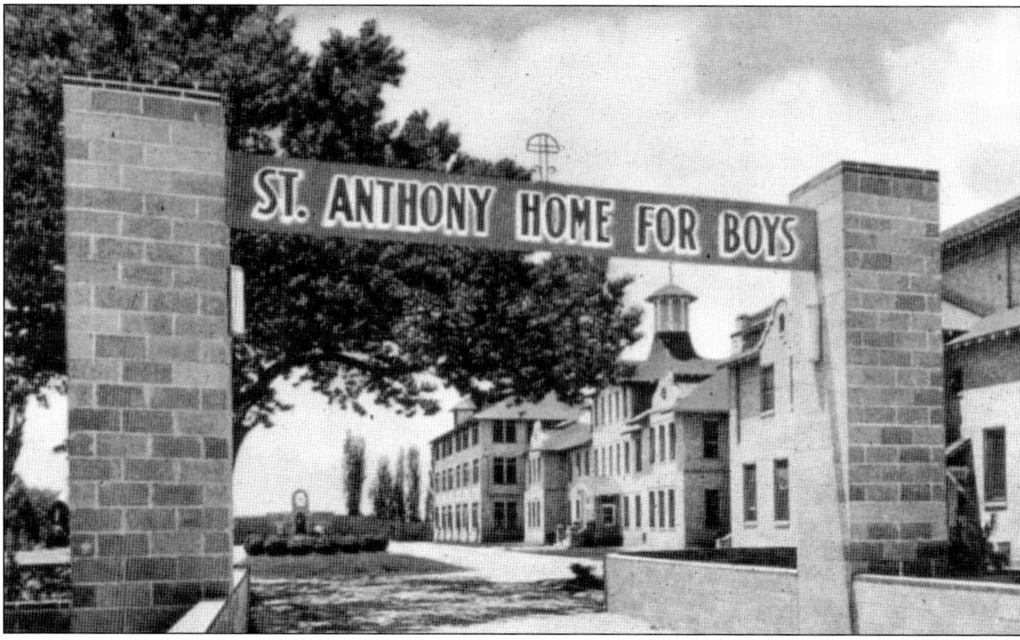


Father Mandalari of Immaculate Conception Church (later St. Mary's) commissioned nuns from Indiana to open a much-needed orphanage for boys in the area located on irrigable land in near northwest Albuquerque in 1913. A community-based effort led by the city, the Jewish temple, and Father Madalari's parish raised buildings that housed nearly 200 boys who planted, farmed, and harvested from the school lands, garnering trades and education. In 1971, the school sold its lands, engulfed by the expanding Albuquerque north valley, to the US Department of Labor. (Courtesy APM.)

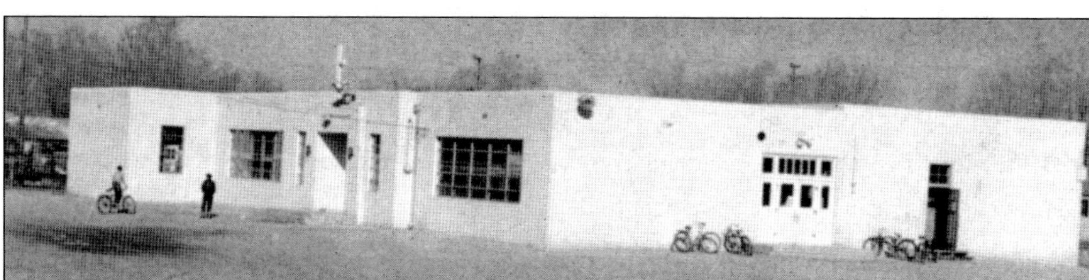

In the fall of 1947, St. Therese Catholic School opened under the direction of Catholic nuns to bring education to children of Albuquerque's north valley. With minimal facilities, a garden hose reportedly brought water to the students, and desktops were hinged to the backs of the church's pews to form writing surfaces for the school's new students. Still in existence, St. Therese is a well-known landmark and respected educational institution, resting along North Fourth Street. (Courtesy APM.)

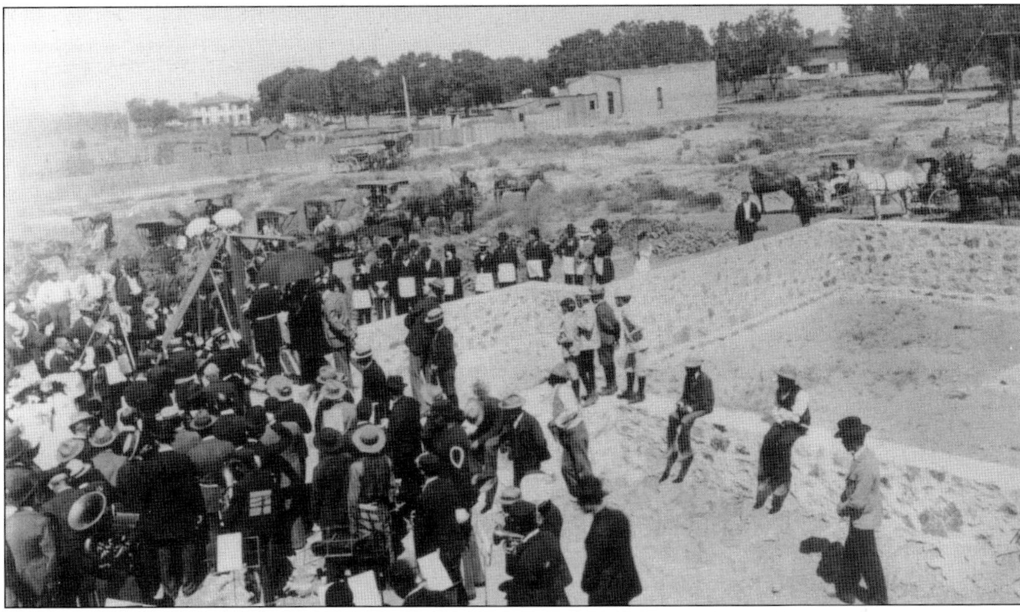

Erected at Seventh and Gold in 1897, Congregation Albert embraced members and strongly cemented the cultural mix that young Albuquerque began to build. Progressive, forward-thinking, and involved, Albuquerque Jews were—by and large—welcomed by the larger community, embraced in, and strongly contributed to the economic growth of the area. (Courtesy of CSWR, PICT 000-742-0467.)

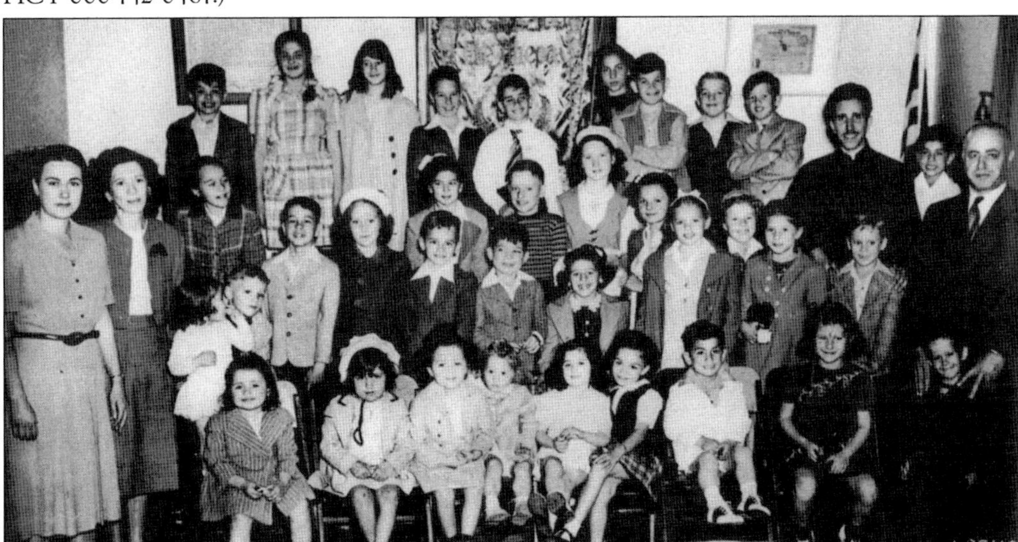


In the early 1900s, nearly 200,000 Greeks entered United States' shores to better their lives in hopes of escaping war and poverty. Looking for opportunity, a growing group of Greek immigrants seized on Albuquerque's potential in the restaurant business, mining, construction, the coming railroad, and more. During the 1920s–1930s and beyond, popular Greek-owned restaurants included the Court Café, Liberty Café, Pigs in Calf, and the Pig Stand. Establishing the only Greek-based tuberculosis sanatorium in the United States in Albuquerque, the Greek community was and continues to be vibrant. Above, students from the St. George Greek school are pictured. (Courtesy William Laskar via Katherine Pomonis.)

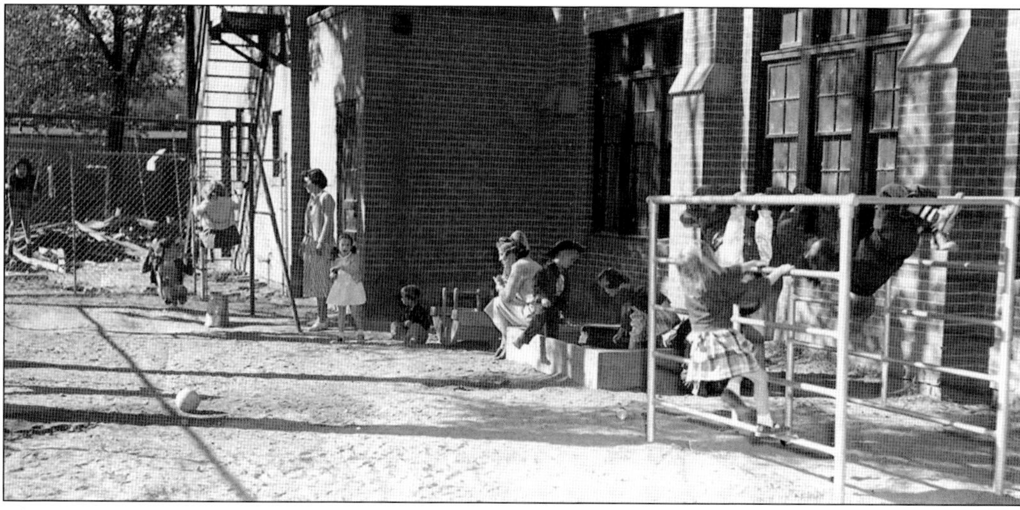

The Episcopal Church in the United States holds a fascinating evolution, entwined with both British and American politics. New Town Albuquerque sprang from the steel rails that came to town in 1881. By late 1882, Bishop George Dunlop held services to celebrate the new building at Fourth and Silver. St. John's and other area Episcopal churches continue to thrive. Pictured above is a scene from St. John's Day School that served many, many young students in Albuquerque, regardless of denomination. (Courtesy St. John's Cathedral and Cindy Davis.)

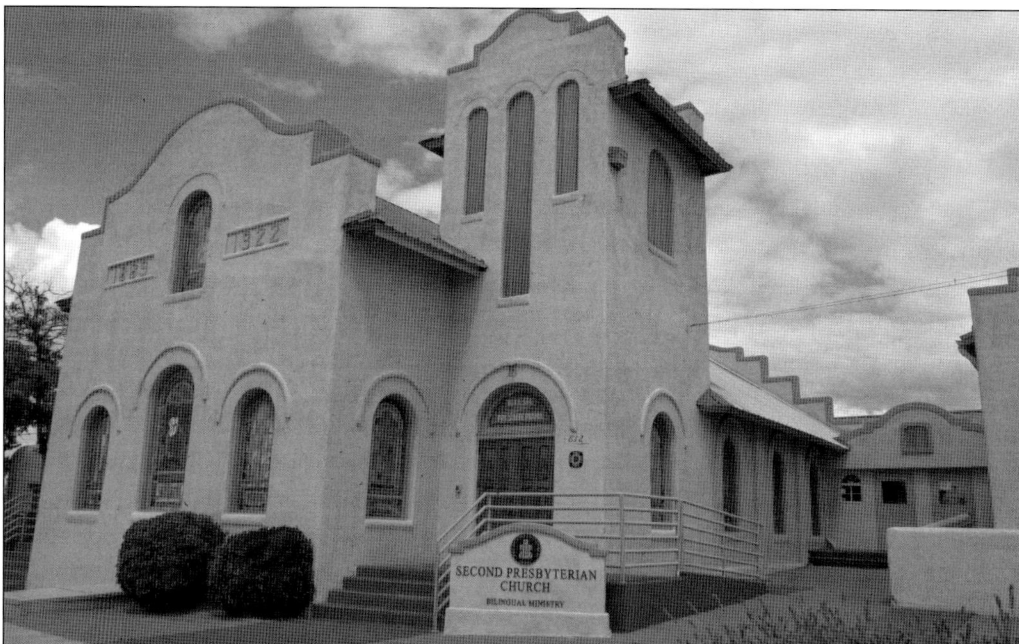


Still located at the northeast corner of Lomas and Edith, Second Presbyterian lends a strong hand to educational history in the area. Manuel and Anna Maria Martin, leaders of the Martinez Town area of the city, broke with the Catholic Church in the late 1800s, and joined with James Menaul (founder of Menaul School) to erect a church that became supported by a branch of Presbyterians dedicated to spreading religion bilingually. This effort branched to support numerous educational efforts throughout the area. (Author's collection.)

Located on Albuquerque's then upper mesa near the university, the doors of St. Charles Borromeo School swung open in 1952 to serve the expanding heights community. Father Hogan petitioned to open a school, and the respected Bishop Edwin Byrne approved. Right, the procession dedicating the opening of the gym parades to ceremonies with the church proper in the background. (Courtesy St. Charles Borromeo School.)

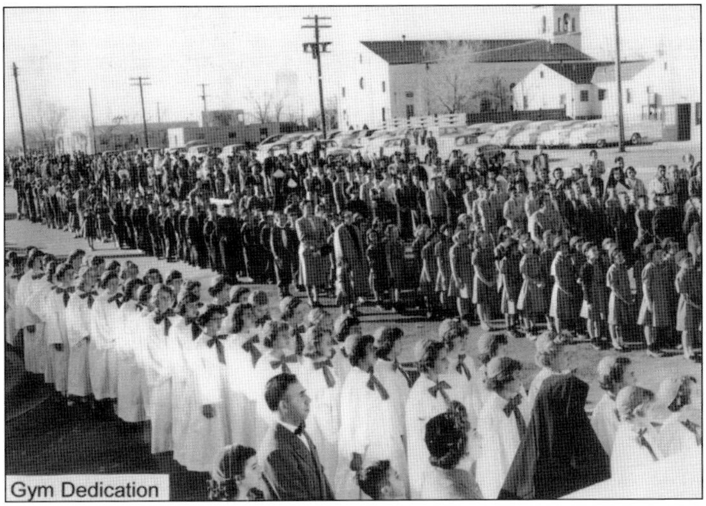


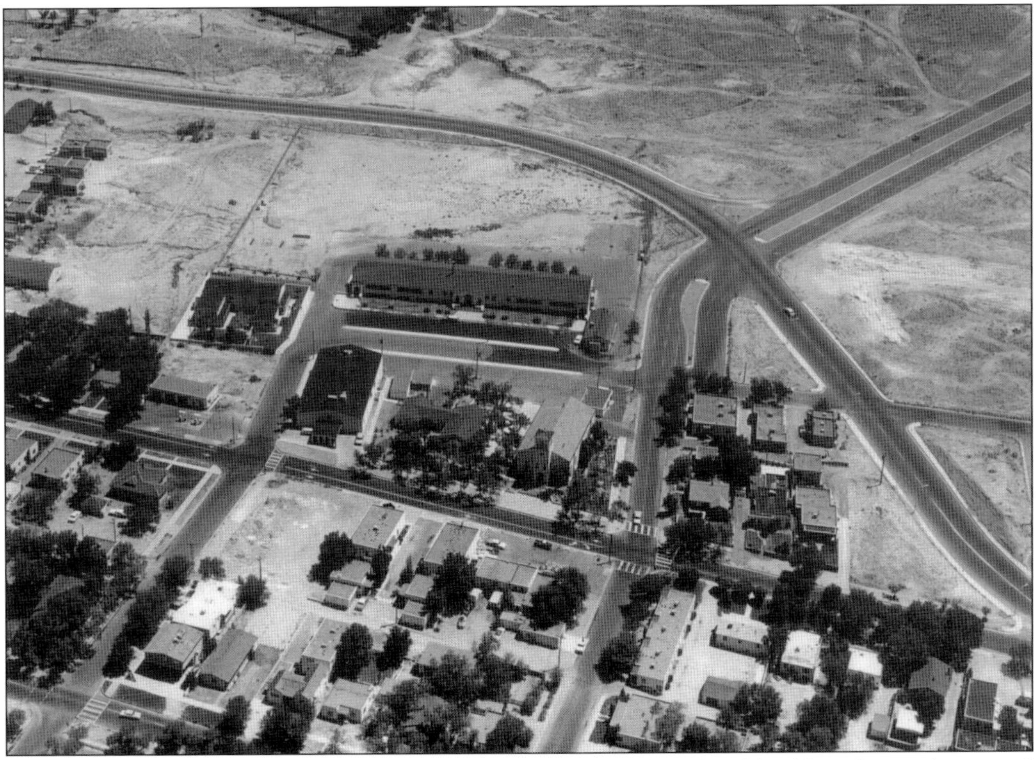

This aerial view of the St. Charles complex, center, shows the school building facing downward (north) with the sweep of what would become Coal Avenue curving in the top of the photograph east to west. University Boulevard runs to the right and above the church complex, as it does today, south toward what then was a lonely beginning of a burgeoning airport. The empty property at the top (south) of the school building would morph into today's Central New Mexico Community College. (Courtesy St. Charles Borromeo School.)

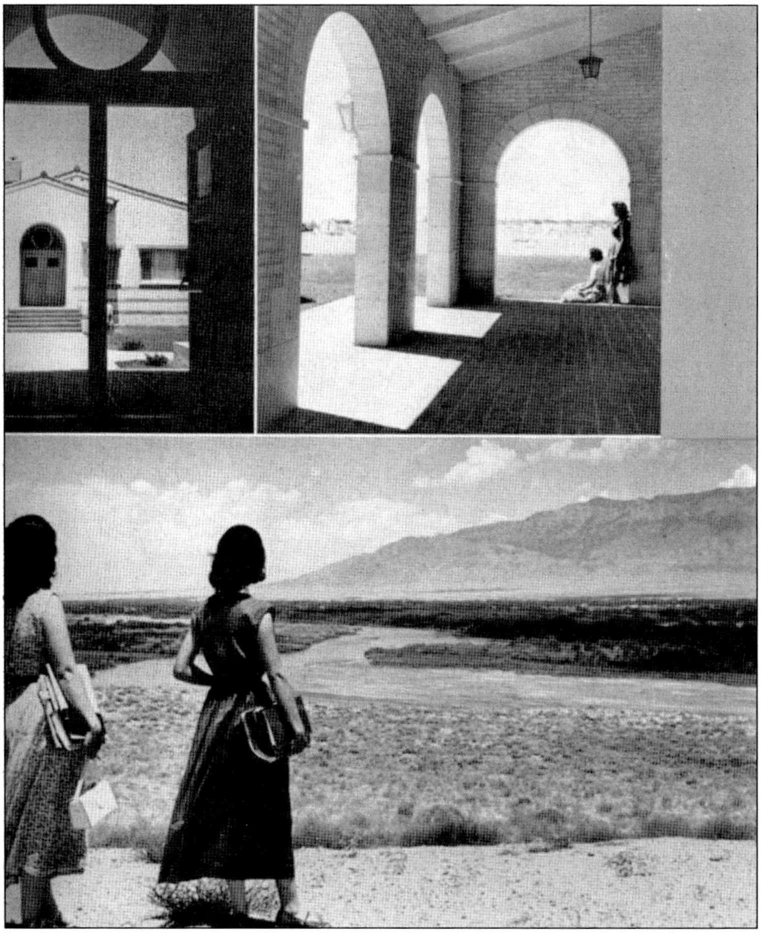

In 1950, Bishop Edwin Byrne and others turned the first shovel full of sand to begin a mission of formally spreading Catholic secondary education west of the Rio Grande in the Albuquerque area. The campus flourished and then became the home of the Catholic supported University of Albuquerque, which closed in 1986. The Catholic high school of St. Pius, then crowded in its coveted corner near Louisiana and Indian School, spread its wings to relocate to the University of Albuquerque's site in 1988. Left, excited students attend classes in October 1952. (Courtesy APM.)

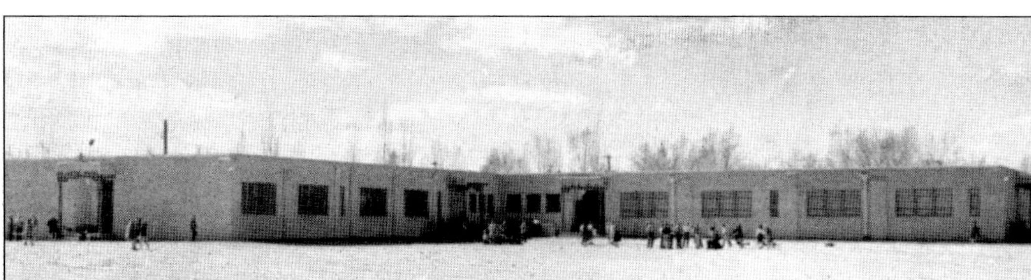

Shown above, in 1951a few years after opening in 1948, Fatima school sprang from Our Lady of Fatima Catholic Church located at Morningside and Lomas. Built on a land gift from Mr. and Mrs. Harry Owen, Archbishop Edwin Bryne helped break ground in July 1949 for the school, with support of the nearby resource-stretched sister Catholic school, St. Charles. (Courtesy APM.)

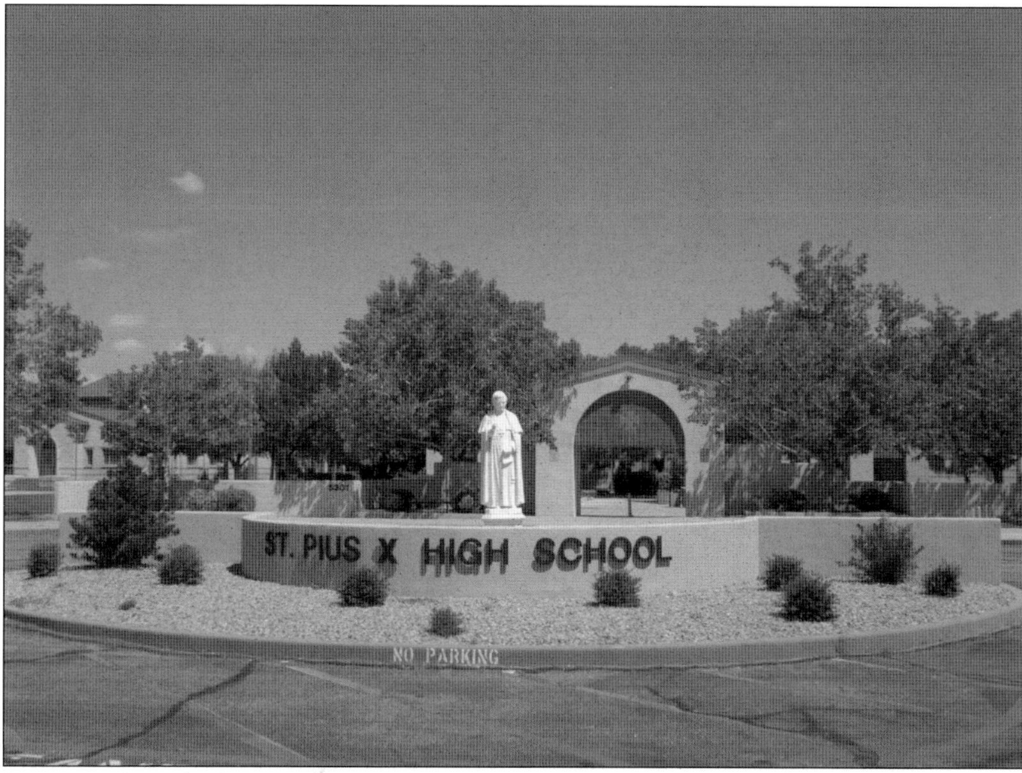


Sprouting from the basement of St. Charles Borromeo School to serve the needs of high school aged students, St. Pius charged forth. In the fall of 1959 it opened classes in its new buildings located at Louisiana and Indian School—the shopping area that Albuquerque Uptown inhabits today. When in 1986 the Catholic-run University of Albuquerque closed on the west bluffs of the Rio Grande, St. Pius took its campus to the university's location and continued to expand. A vibrant school, St. Pius contributes to the educational and athletic fabric of Albuquerque today. (Both, courtesy Blair Kaufman.)

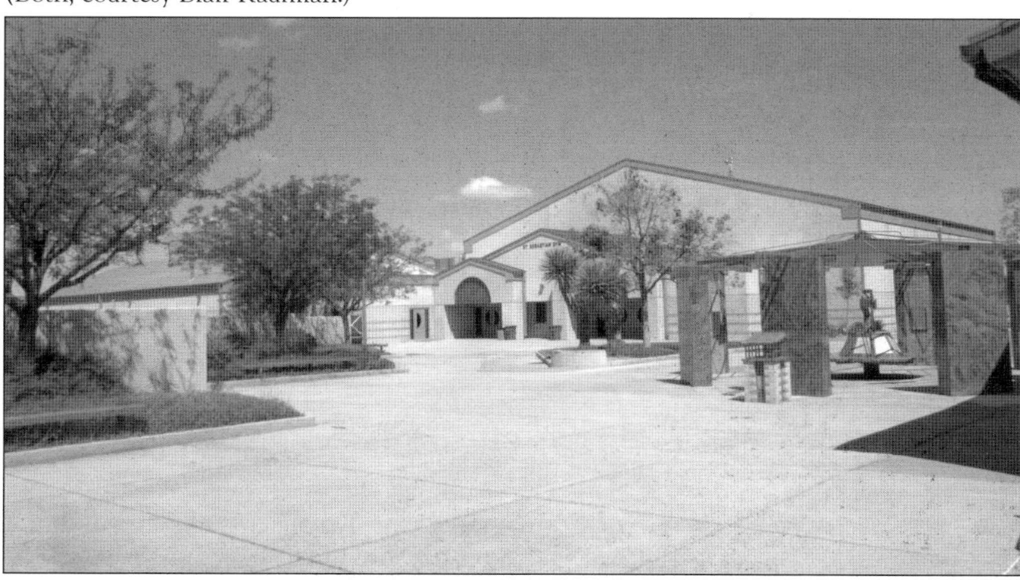

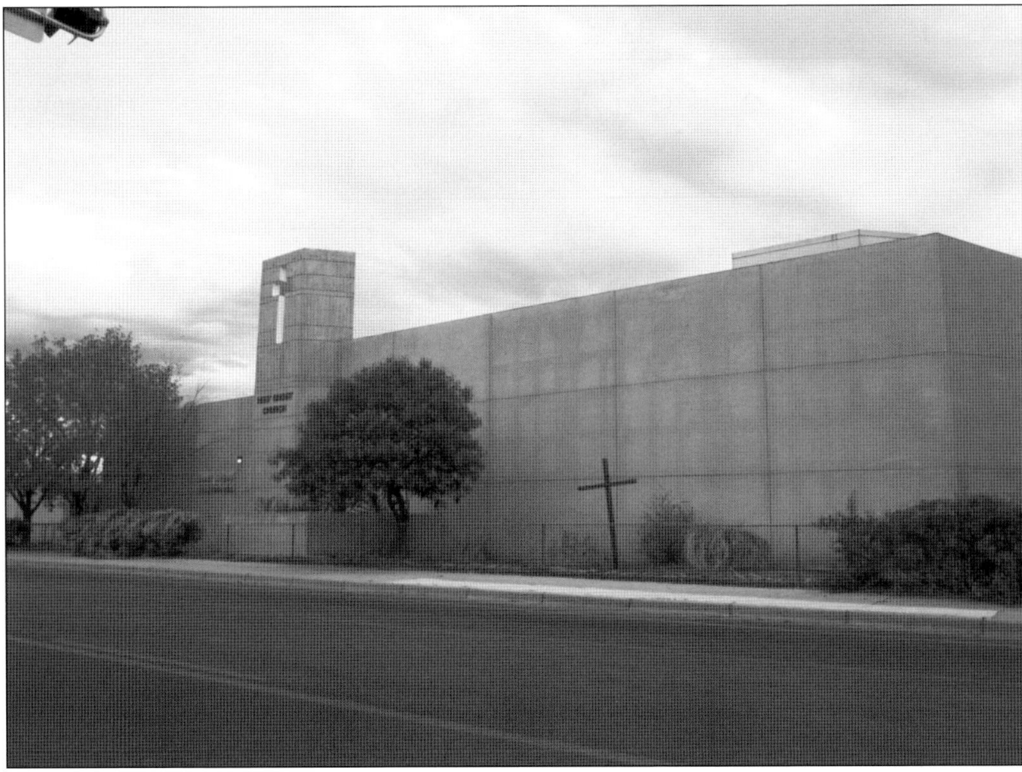

Founded in 1953, Holy Ghost School evolved to be agile in adjusting to the service learning, community-based needs of Albuquerque's southeast heights. The two campuses that were located just east of Wilson Middle School, along with the Native American Charter School (that relocated to the west), have formed a community-based learning "center" for the area. (Author's collection.)

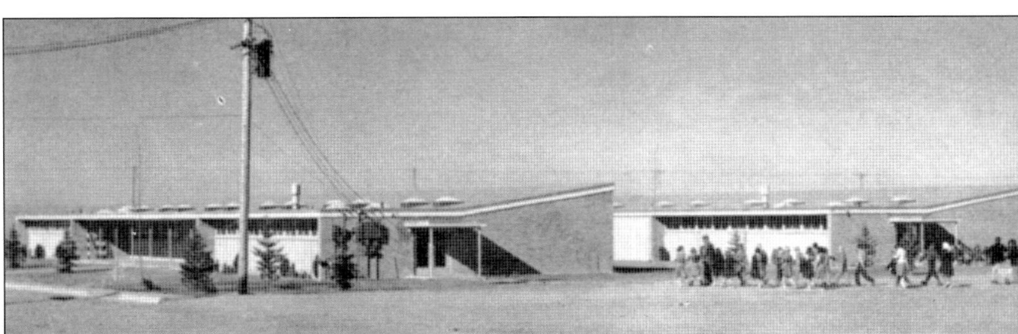

Above, Queen of Heaven School is pictured in 1953 after the exploding church community finished building the first structures and grounds. The tradition of Catholic schools in New Mexico blossomed as Albuquerque grew to the north and east after World War II. (Courtesy APM.)

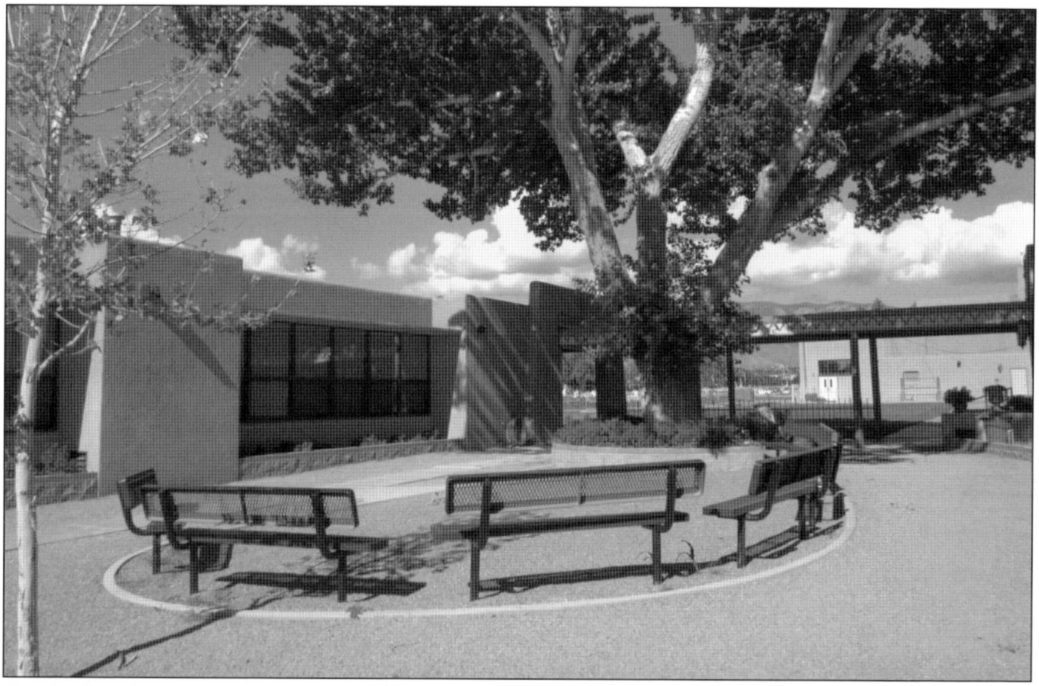

Our Lady of Assumption parish and school were established in 1955. Both were built to serve the increasing demands of the northeast heights of Albuquerque after World War II. Still thriving, above, Assumption is an inviting and inclusive campus. (Author's collection.)

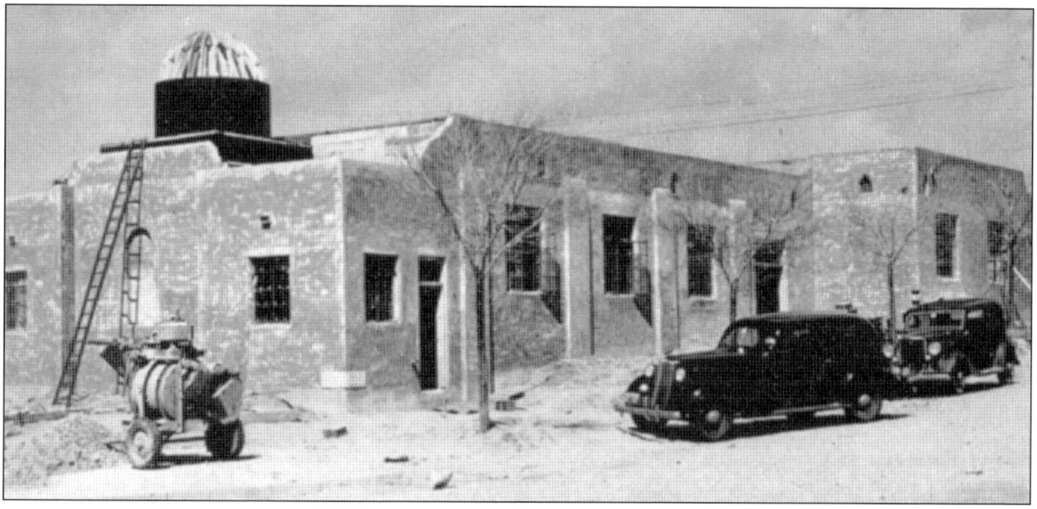

As strong and consistent leaders and agents of change in the Albuquerque area, Jewish settlers were welcomed as forceful contributors to the cultural, economic, and social climate of Albuquerque. Congregation Albert laid its building's cornerstone in 1899. Springing from its 1883 roots, B'nai B'rith was formally founded in 1941 at Coal and Cedar (pictured above). It was primarily Eastern European Jews that populated the temple of B'nai Israel, a more conservative congregation than the existing Congregation Albert. A friendly rivalry ensued, and prominent names such as Seligman, Ilfield, Mandell, Maisel, Goldstein, Jaffa, and many more cemented the solid Jewish community in Albuquerque that was relatively embraced and welcomed, and continues to thrive and contribute today. B'nai Israel still has a flourishing school for young children. (Courtesy APM.)

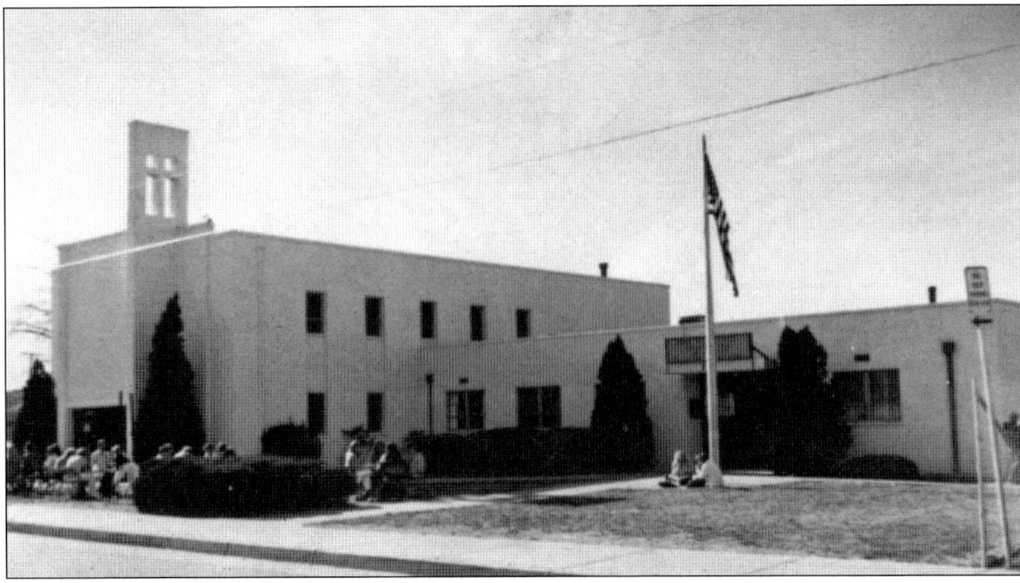

In this image from the 1980 Hope Christian School yearbook, students reflect focus and determination to achieve academically. Founded in 1976 by C. Wayne Ehlert and Howard Stansell, Hope has continued to expand its mission as a nondenominational Christian school. Now serving nearly 1,500 students grades prekindergarten through twelve, Hope is located in the city's northeast heights.

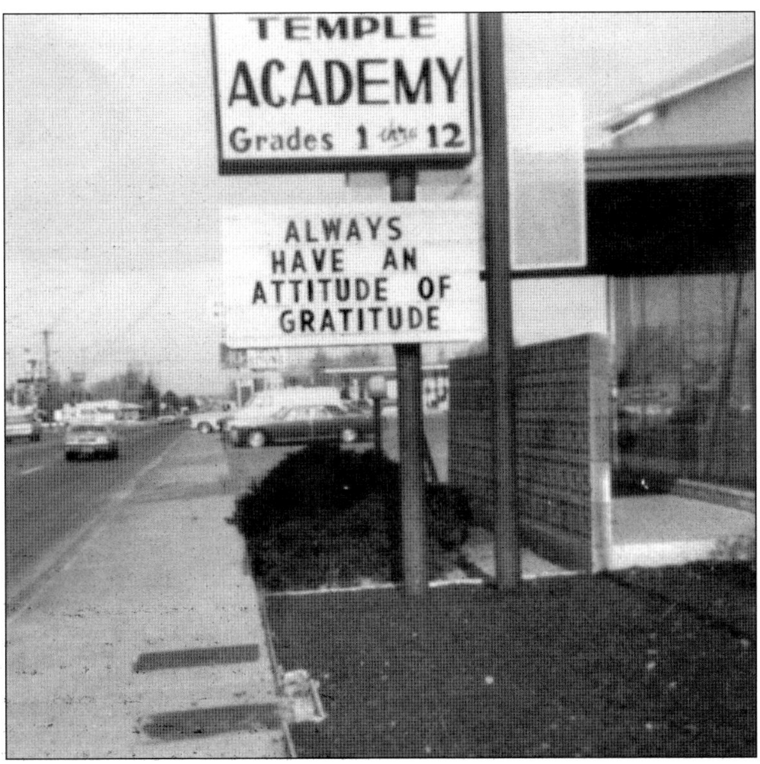


Pictured at left in 1971, Temple Baptist spans a history since 1971 of serving students and families who look for a quality Christian education, grades kindergarten through 12. Located in the heart of uptown Albuquerque, Temple has housed many younger and older graduates. Pictured around 1981, the marquee of the school sends a positive message. (Author's collection.)

# *Four*

# PRIVATE SCHOOLS IN ALBUQUERQUE

Schools open—public or private—fostered by a desire to transmit a culture's knowledge, beliefs, traditions, and values to the next generation. For hundreds of years, New Mexico and the Albuquerque area provided no cohesive public education. From the mid-1550s when Europeans invaded the New Mexico area, churches filled the void by offering schooling in homes or in the parish, taught by a religious figure. It was not until 1891 that the territorial government of New Mexico organized means to fund public education.

Several entities chose to open their own schooling system, some charging tuition and some not, and that tradition of private education has continued in the Albuquerque area along side of public schooling.

Albert and Ruth Hanna McCormick Simms greatly influenced the private education sector in Albuquerque. The Simms arrived in Albuquerque in 1932 after completing two-year terms serving in the US House of Representatives and opened the Sandia School on land that is now on the Air Force base. Ms. Simms enlisted architect John Gaw Meem to design a campus that would prepare girls for excellent educational and career opportunities in a secular environment. While waiting for the school to open, Sandia School operated out of La Glorietta, the Huning-Fergusson home that now houses Manzano Day School. The Sandia opened for boarders and day students, but World War II caused the transportation for boarders to be tenuous, and the school closed. The land the Simms had donated was held and sold, and by 1958 Barbara Young Simms was instrumental in opening a new Sandia Prep with a nondenominational, college preparatory mission. Sandia Prep today continues to be a vital and important private school in the city.

Between 1955 and 1964, the Simms deeded a massive tract of land to form the Boys' Albuquerque Academy. The school has grown from serving 12 boys in the 1955 school year to now housing more than 1,000 day students, both boys and girls.

The passion of Peggy Ann Findlay at Bosque Prep sprang to life in 1995 with 72 sixth and seventh graders in attendance in a northeast heights makeshift facility. By 2000, Bosque Prep moved to its current 100-acre site near Coors and Montano, and began building. Today Bosque's enrollment is around 500—both boys and girls—and the school is a presence in the city's private school community.

Another large footprint stamped on private education in Albuquerque is the Menaul School. Begun as an outreach of the Presbyterian Church in 1881, the mission of Menaul was to train Native American children in trades. It was called the Pueblo Training School in 1882 and was connected with the federal government for funding. The government ended its contract with Menaul in 1891, but the school continued in its faith-based mission to educate boys of need in trade skills. By 1934, girls were admitted, and in 1972 the Presbyterian Church stepped back and Menaul became an independent private school "respecting the Christian tradition" and serving nearly 200 students each year.

By no means is a comprehensive inventory of private school options presented here, but an overview of major influences in the private school development are highlighted. It is important for our city to offer a variety of educational options for students and families, and private, church and public institutions have committed to doing so.

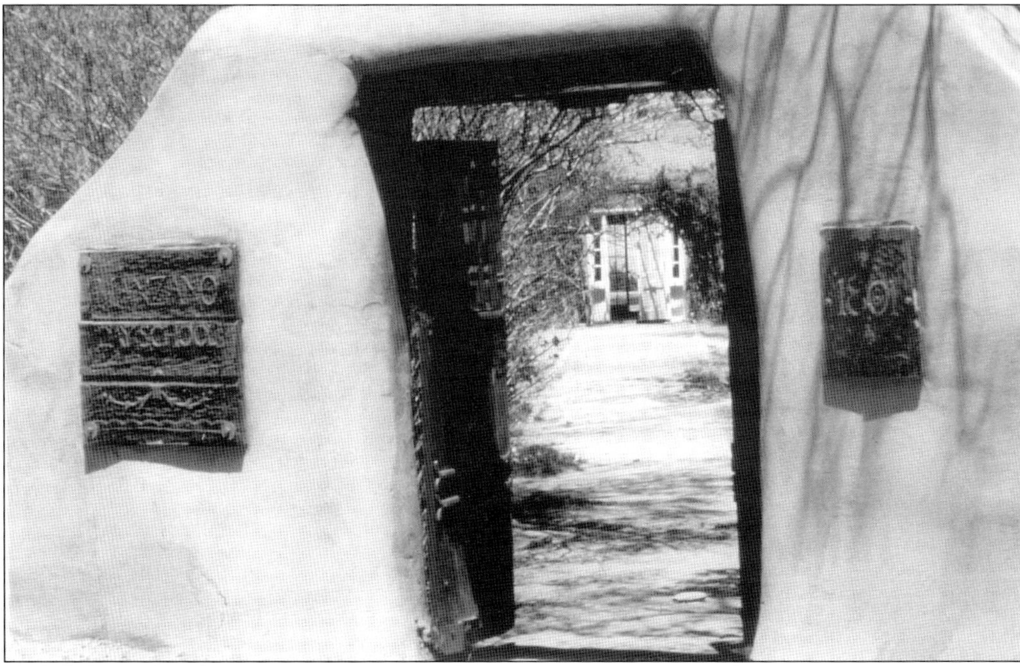

Above is the 1942 gate to Manzano Day School, which started in the spacious (Franz) Huning Castle in 1938, a project spearheaded by Ruth Hanna McCormick Simms. Simms also opened the private Sandia School for girls in 1932. In 1942, with roughly 100 pre-kindergarten through eighth grade students, Manzano Day relocated to its current campus: 1801 Central Avenue Northeast, the former (Clara) Huning (H.G.) Ferguson home (La Glorietta). (Courtesy Manzano Day School.)

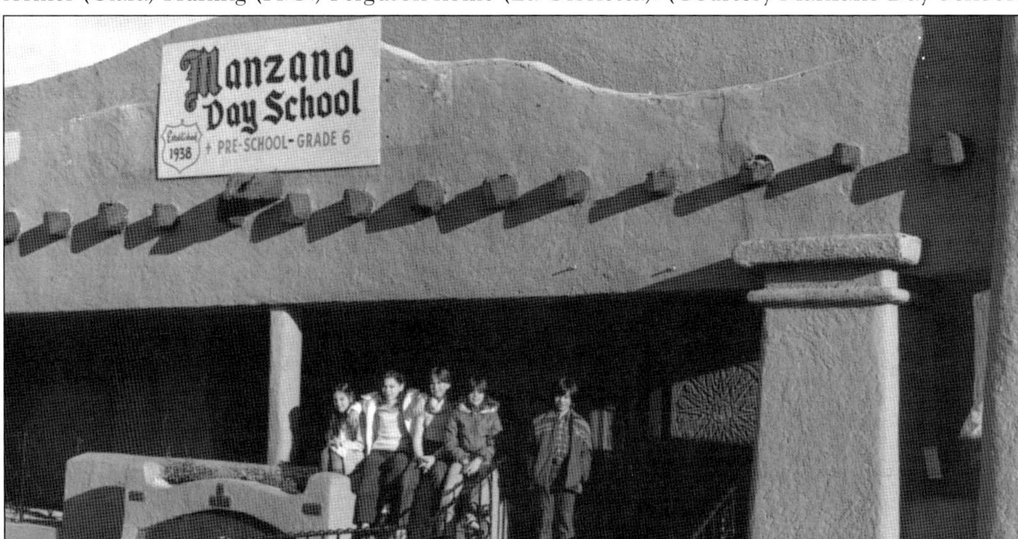


In this undated photograph are students outside Manzano Day School. Ruth Hanna McCormick Simms swept into Albuquerque with her second husband, Albert, just after she served in Congress representing Illinois from 1928 to 1930. Albert Simms and his brother John each contributed greatly to Albuquerque's community. Albert and John served in Congress and John became New Mexico's youngest governor at that time from 1955 to 1957. (Courtesy Manzano Day School.)

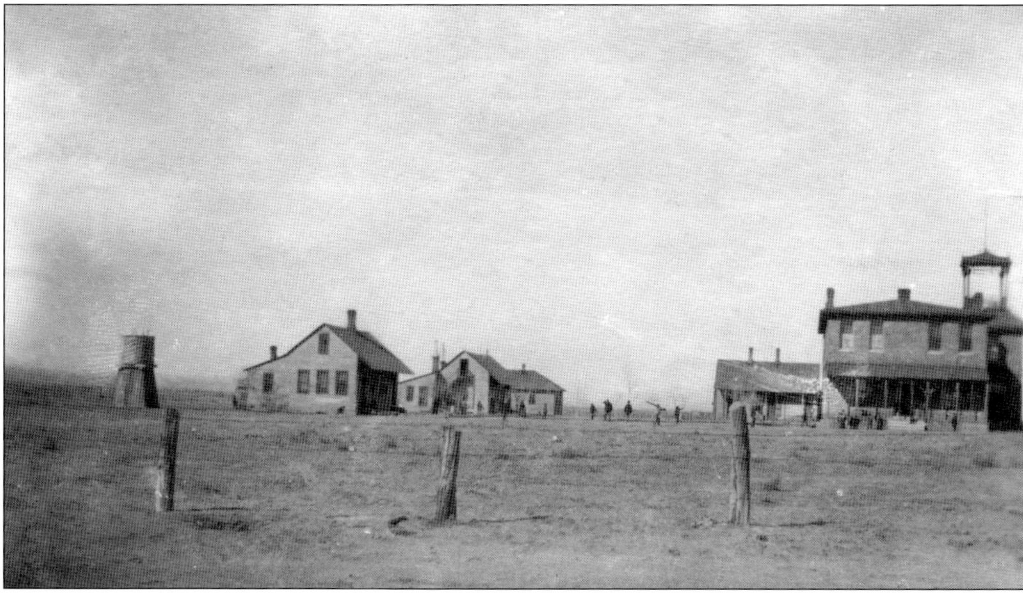

The Pueblo Training School opened in 1881 near what today is the Indian Pueblo Cultural Center. Founded by Presbyterian Reverend Sheldon Jackson, political shifting caused the federal government to take over Native American education. The Presbyterians purchased a large tract of land near today's Broadway and Menaul. Above are early buildings standing lonely in the desert in 1887—"Old Brick" is on the right. (Courtesy Menaul Historical Library of the Southwest.)

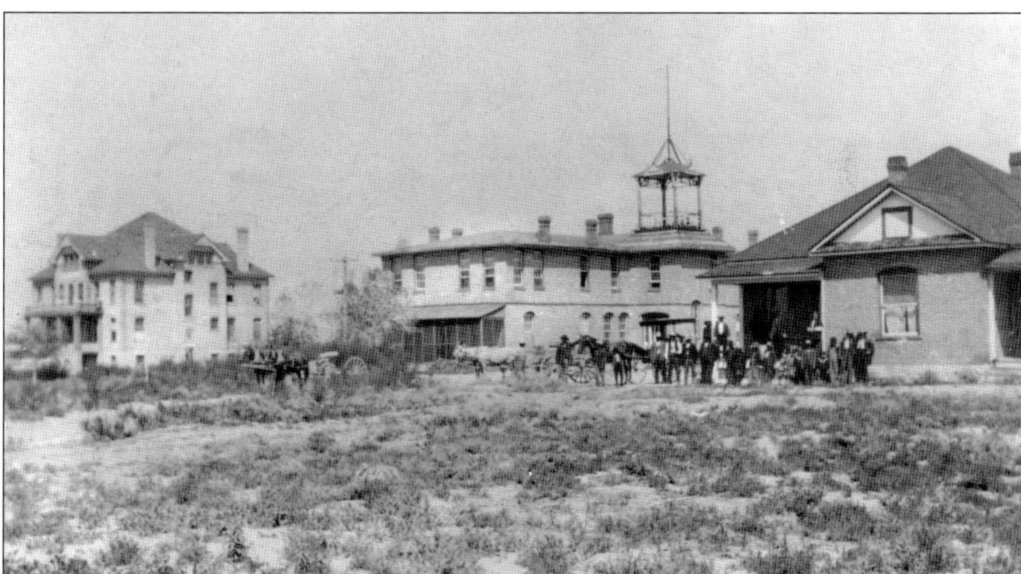

Menaul, pictured above around 1908, became a boarding school and farm, first serving boys from a wide area including northern New Mexico and included girls in 1934. The school was dedicated to teaching trades, a strong work ethic, and life skills. (Courtesy Menaul Historical Library of the Southwest.)

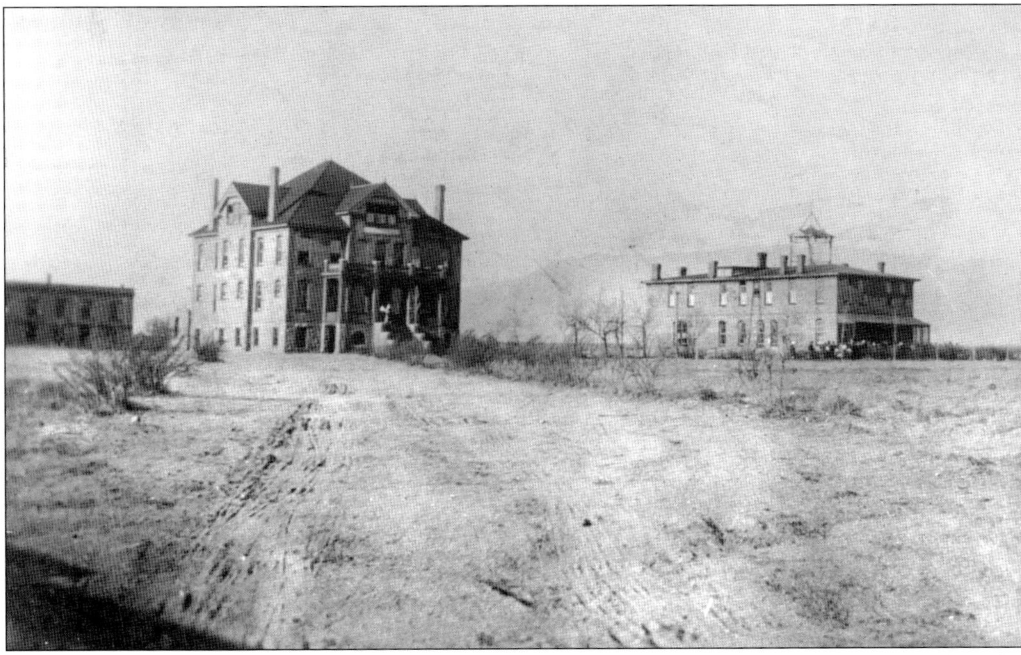

The hardscrabble determination of the Presbyterians to bring life out of the dry ground and to deliver education to needy students of New Mexico and Colorado drove the founding of Menaul School, pictured above. Pierson Hall is on the left. "Old Brick," on the right, still stands today. (Courtesy Menaul Historical Library of the Southwest.)

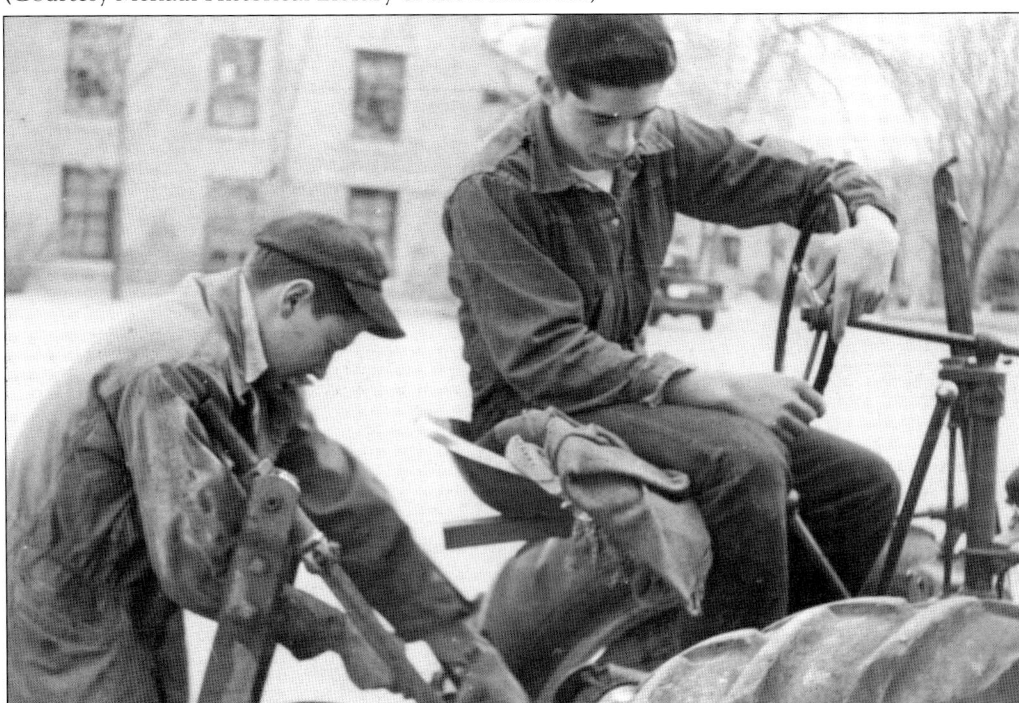

Above, students of Menaul School are preparing to work the school farm around 1942. (Courtesy Menaul Historical Library of the Southwest.)

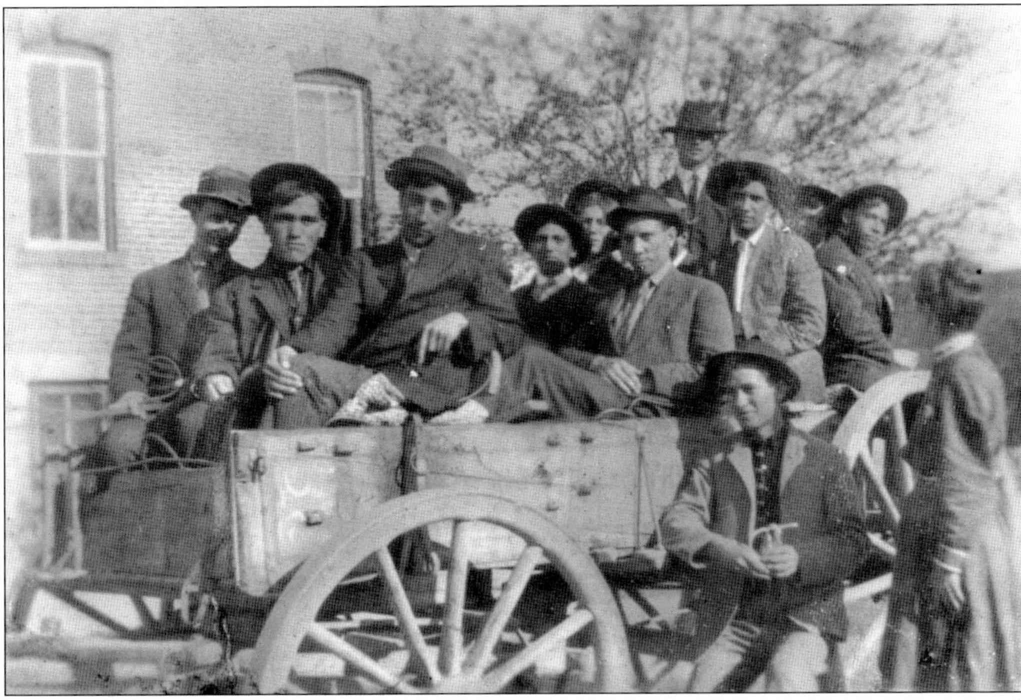

Students pile into a wagon as they prepare to tend Menaul School's farm around 1910. A female teacher is seen on the right. (Courtesy Menaul Historical Library of the Southwest.)

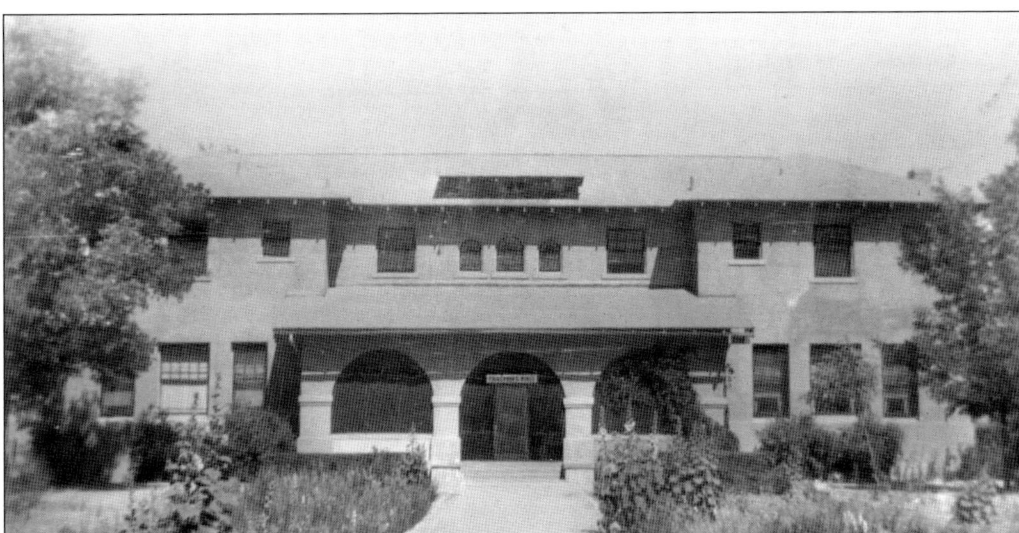

Visible above before 1930, the Menaul School's Teachers' Hall stands today appearing much the same and now houses school administration. By 1972, very few students boarded at Menaul, and by 2000 Menaul served solely day school students. However, with a change in mission, Menaul reinstituted boarding as an option in addition to its day school in 2010. Today's school serves approximately 180 students, grades 6 through 12, and centers on a college preparatory curriculum. (Courtesy Menaul Historical Library of the Southwest.)

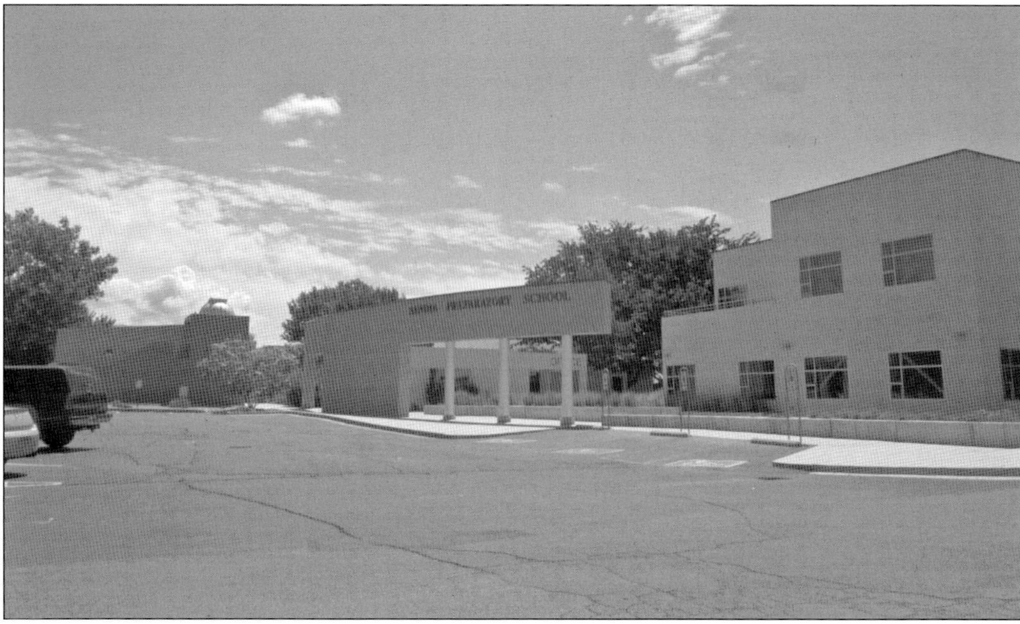

Sandia Prep, springing from the impetus of Ruth Hanna McCormick Simms's desire to have a high quality school option for her daughter and other girls, opened first as Sandia School in 1932 on Albuquerque's east mesa, and then reopened by 1966. Still in operation today, "Prep" is a known force on the educational scene of the city. Pictured above is the school's entry arch; below is one of the gym areas. (Both, courtesy Blair Kaufman.)

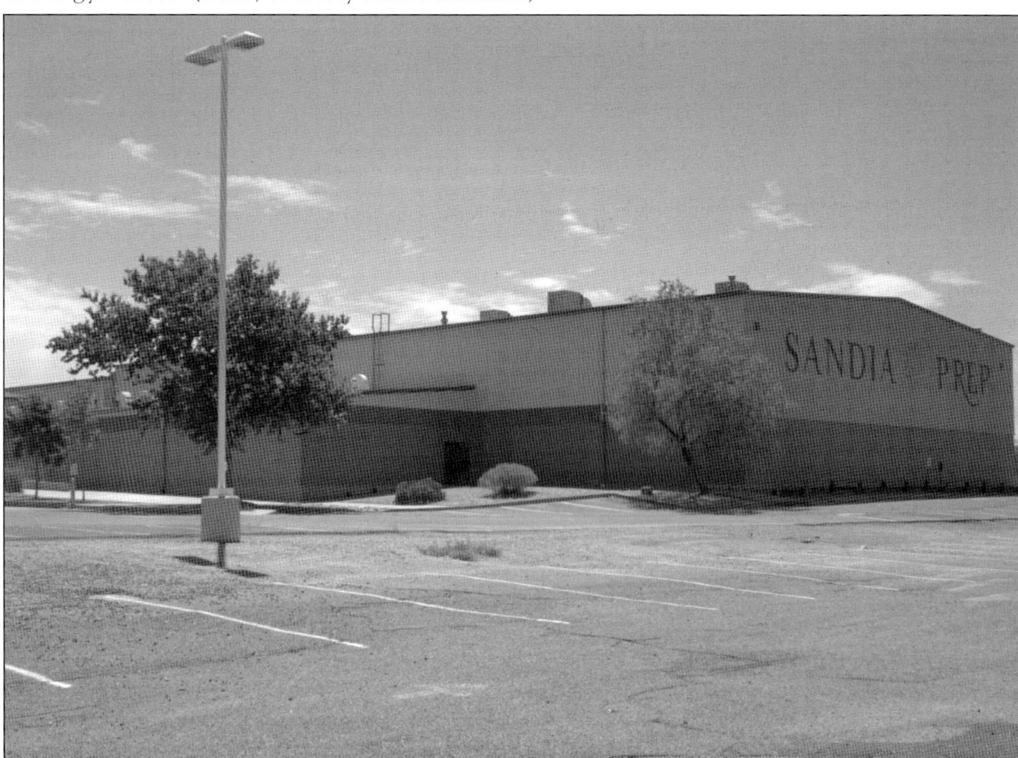

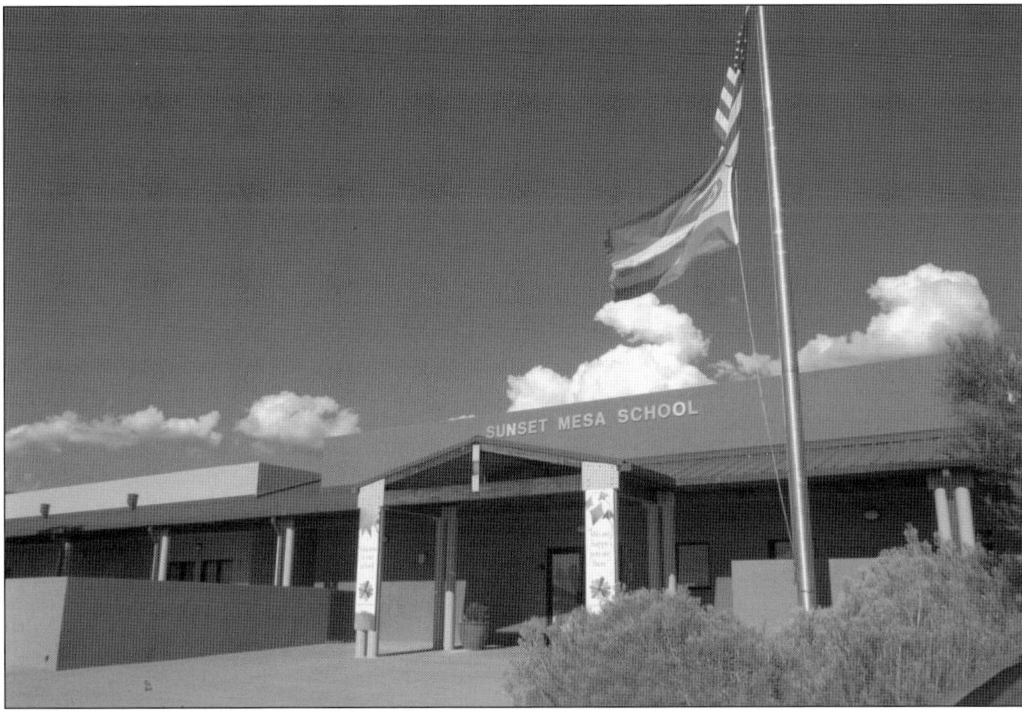


Sunset Mesa School, above, opened in 1948 near Girard And Lomas Boulevard Northeast in the university area by Mrs. Atkins of Ohio, and the school is reported to be one of the first kindergartens in the city. In 1957, the school changed hands to Eulene Sheriff. By 1962, Sunset Mesa relocated to Morris and Candelaria Northeast, still concentrating on early-childhood grade-level education. In 1970, grades one through four were added, and in 1975, John and Wynona Ratliff purchased the school. In 1985, the campus became a Montessori school, and by 1998, the Ratliff's daughter Deborah Mask was operating the school. In 2003, a south campus was added, and the school continues to thrive today with an enrollment around 450 students. (Author's collection.)

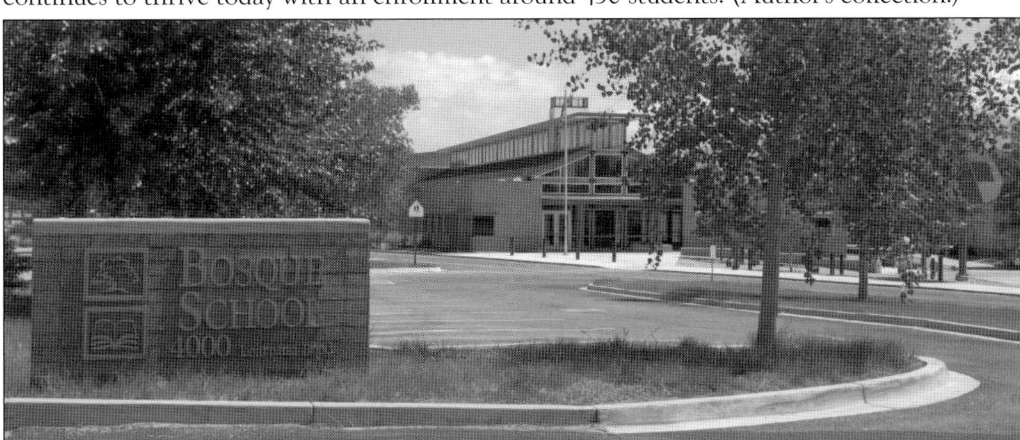


Bosque School—opened in August 1995—is home to around 500 private school students. Operating a middle school and a high school campus, Bosque emphasizes different ages interacting and cooperating, along with a grade-level team approach. The curriculum at Bosque emphasizes an understanding of environmental science and utilizes the nearby river area as a living lab. (Courtesy Blair Kaufman.)

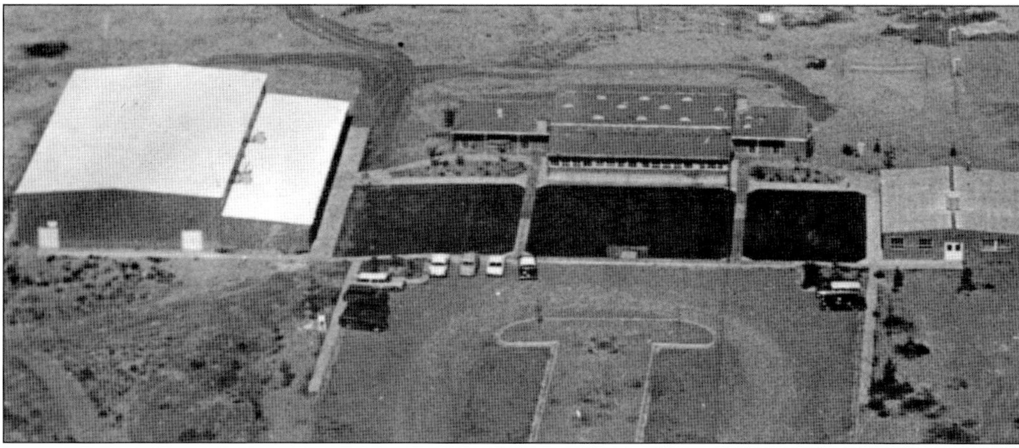

The above c. 1964 photograph shows Albuquerque Academy's campus. Below is a contemporary view of the well-known arches near the lower gym. Albuquerque Academy was made possible through an unimaginable land grant bequest given by Albert and Ruth Hanna McCormick Simms, one of the wealthiest couples in New Mexico, who wanted to make a lasting donation that would benefit the education of young people. News of Ruth's passing after acute pancreatic failure hit Albuquerque on January 1, 1945, and in her honor at their scheduled meeting January 2, the Albuquerque City Commission closed all city offices the morning of January 4. Today, Albuquerque Academy serves around 1,000 boys and girls in the school year and hosts a wildly popular summer program open to the public, offering academics and a wide spectrum of arts and athletics. (Both, author's collection.)

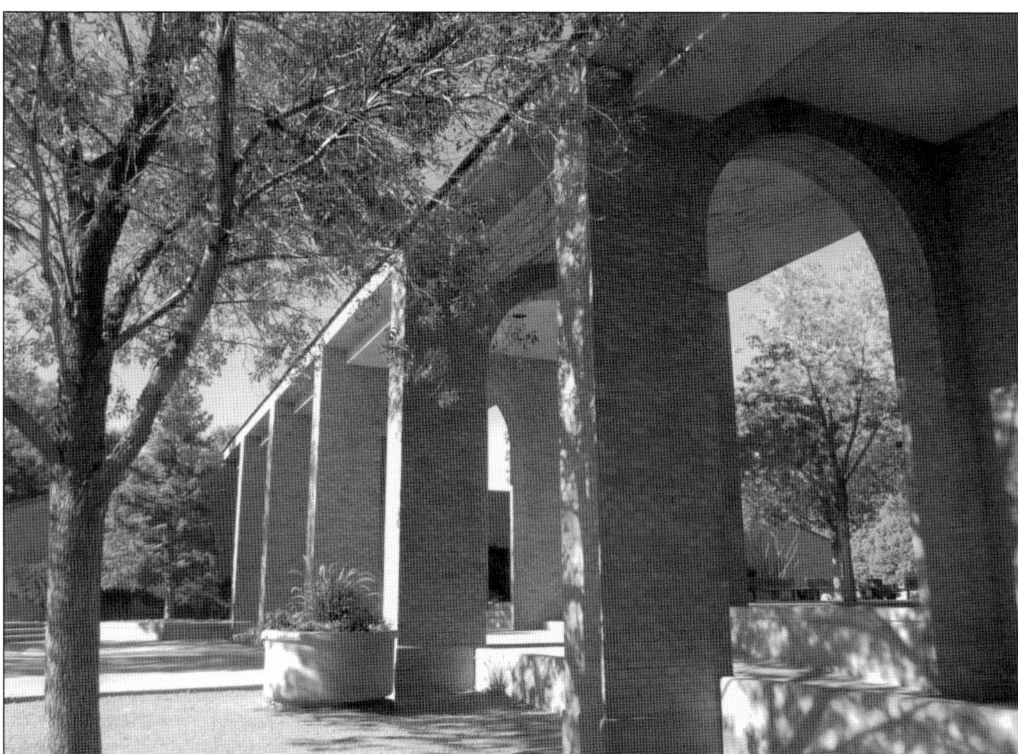

# *Five*

# Superintendent John Milne and the APS Journey

Just as Albuquerque's mix of turquoise skies, golden sands, and green sage are unique against the backdrop of the rose-colored Sandia Mountains and the shimmering, shifting Rio Grande, so is the shining story of John Milne unique in the United States. Born in Scotland, Milne graduated from the Wisconsin State Normal School and found his way to Albuquerque. He was named principal of the Third Ward School in 1907, and by 1911, Milne was superintendent of the city schools—a tenure he held for a nationally unprecedented 45 years.

Milne, while small in stature, was a giant in foresight. He became a master of planning ahead, shrewdly acquiring vast tracts of lands (most on the far outskirts of town) for the city schools and he likewise gathered people who were able, supportive, and stable around him. Milne could negotiate with multiple governors, the vitriolic long-term Albuquerque politician Clyde Tingley, and numerous prominent citizens—many of whom served for long terms on the city's school board. Milne himself volunteered for membership in many civic groups including the Rotary Club and the Shriners. Milne's forte was obtaining vast sums of federal dollars for the city schools through a myriad of means.

Gathering to his circle school business manager John Varney and school architect Louis Hesselden, Milne began a march stretching across both the east and west mesas of Albuquerque culminating in the post–World War II years when 18 new schools opened, more than doubling the city school district, followed soon by a boom of 13 more schools before Milne retired in 1955. *Time Magazine*, in a 1955 story, quoted a young Albuquerque student who was amazed that the reporter was unfamiliar with Milne, stating, "You don't know who Mr. Milne is? Why, Mr. Milne is the boss of the whole world!"

John Milne's foresight, team building, and exceptional planning shaped a school district that grew from 1600 students in 1904 to over 38,000 in 1955 over his tenure as superintendent.

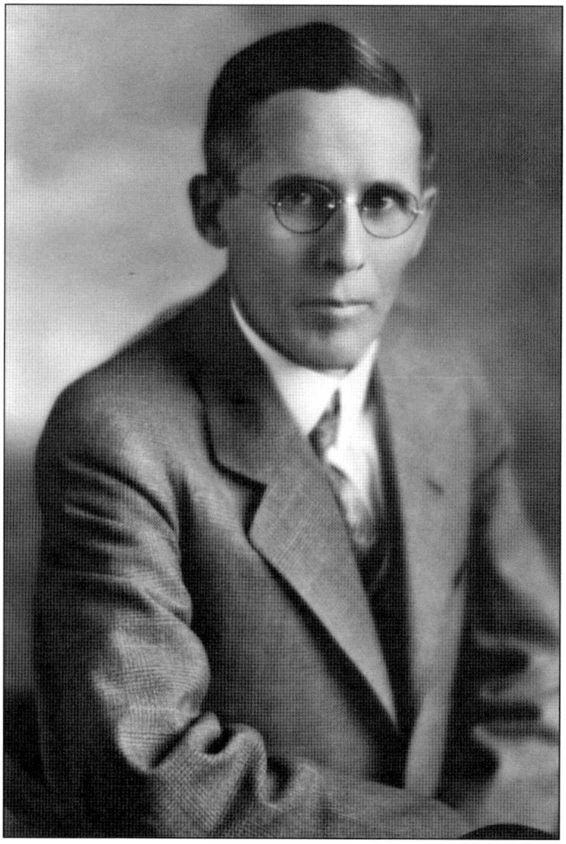

John Milne served an unprecedented and still-unrivaled tenure as a public school superintendent: 45 years of uninterrupted and fairly tranquil service. Brought on board in 1911 to serve as the leader of APS, he gathered around him wise business manager John Varney, skilled architect Louis Hesselden, and a remarkably stable board that serve with little change of membership during the 1940s and 1950s. A native of Scotland, Milne came west with family who were members seeking a cure for tuberculosis. He was named the principal of the Third Ward School in 1907. Following this he became principal, coach, and math teacher (all at once) of Albuquerque High in 1908. Milne championed public service, and he walked his talk, serving as president of the Rotary Club and Potentate of the New Mexico Shriners. (Courtesy APS.)

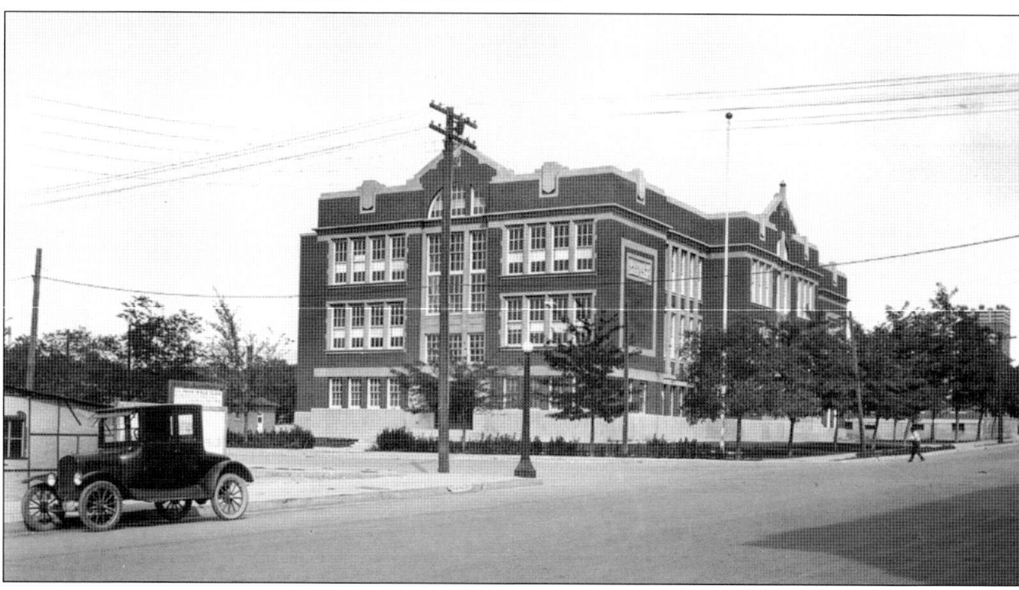

Pictured above is the Albuquerque High School around 1920. The original building, erected in 1914, stands alone in this image. The Manual Arts Building flanked it in 1927, with the gym and cafeteria joining the complex in 1938. To the right and behind the trees is the steeple of the Central Methodist Church that would later relocate to University and Central. (Courtesy APS.)

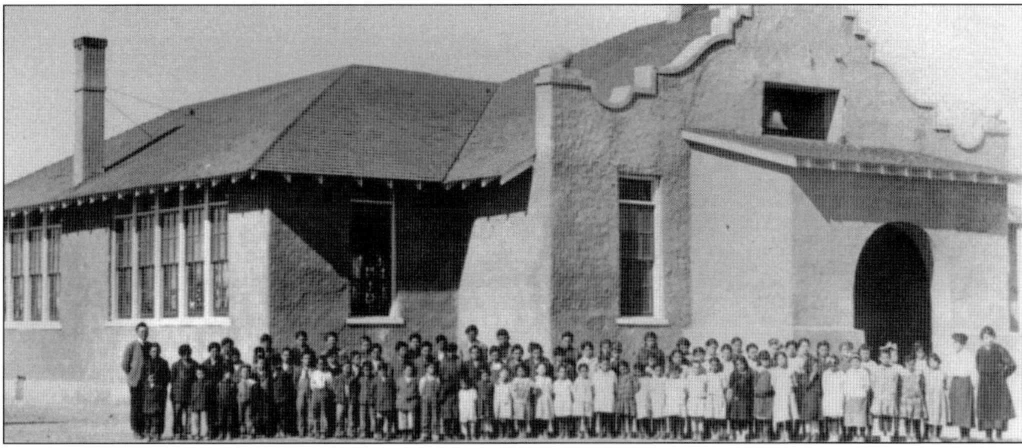

Los Padillas emerged from the work of Father Padilla, who, around 1880, began teaching at the school for students whose parents had been killed by Indians or other misfortunes. Presumably funded by county money, the school grew to six classrooms by 1912. Visible here around that time are a large group of students and several staff members. The male teacher is said to be Frank Gonzales. The principal, Adolph Gonzales, is not pictured. (Courtesy CSWR, PICT 999-045-0019.)

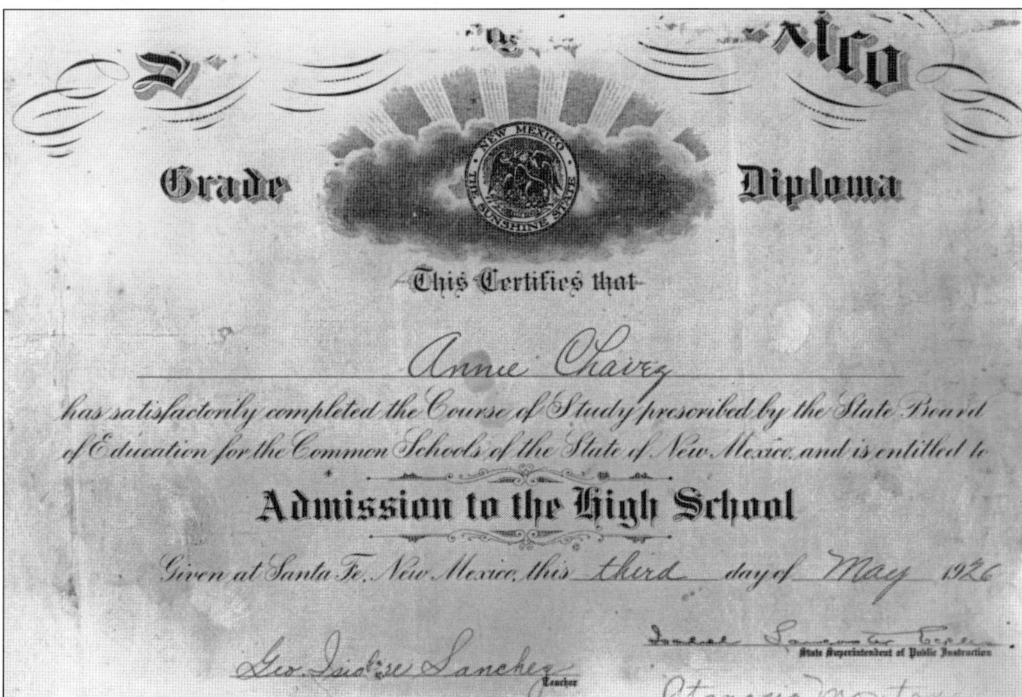

Grade Diploma

This Certifies that

Annie Chavez

has satisfactorily completed the Course of Study prescribed by the State Board of Education for the Common Schools of the State of New Mexico, and is entitled to

Admission to the High School

Given at Santa Fe, New Mexico, this third day of May 1926

Geo. Isidore Sanchez
Teacher

State Superintendent of Public Instruction

This important paper allowed an 1926 eighth grader named Annie Chavez Sanchez admission to high school from Los Padillas Elementary. The teacher whose signature appears in the bottom left corner, George I. Sanchez, went on to become a champion scholar and activist for civil rights educational equality for Chicano, African American, and Native American students. Dr. Sanchez was on the faculty at the University of New Mexico and at the University of Texas, Austin, where a building bears his name. Additionally, he led the fight in several landmark civil rights cases pertaining to educational equity during his term as president of the League of United Latin American Citizens in the 1940s. (Courtesy CSWR, PICT 999-045-0016.)

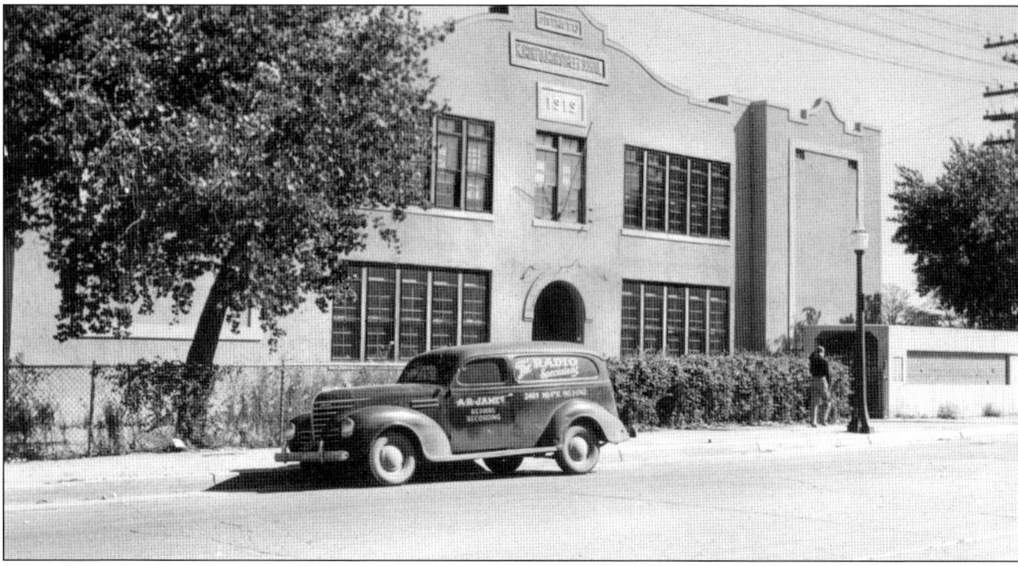


Built in 1919, the North Fourth Street School brought a first understanding to the urban nature of growing Albuquerque. The gentleman on the right in this photograph is entering the pedestrian underpass. The structure allowed the students to safely cross busy North Fourth Street. The school is pictured above in 1944. Later, the building became used as area district offices. (Courtesy ERH.)

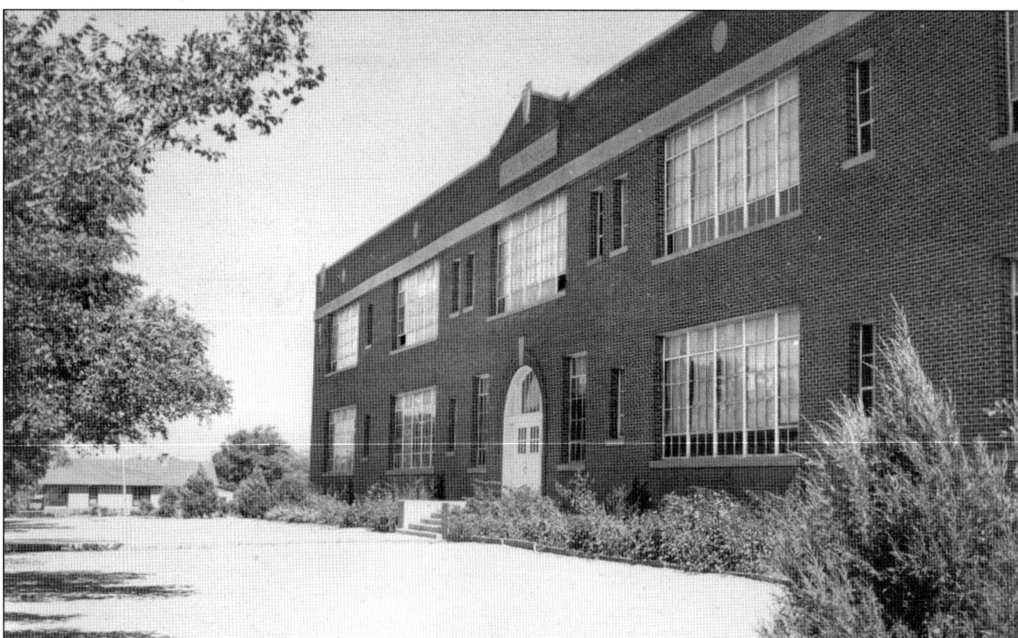

John Marshall Elementary opened in 1922 and was named after a US Supreme Court judge who championed the power of the federal government. Superintendent Milne and his savvy business manager John Varney would come to value, access, and utilize federal funds available to local schools in a masterful way. Marshall was the first city elementary constructed in Albuquerque after the four ward schools. Today, it still serves as a city multipurpose service and recreational center. (Courtesy ERH.)

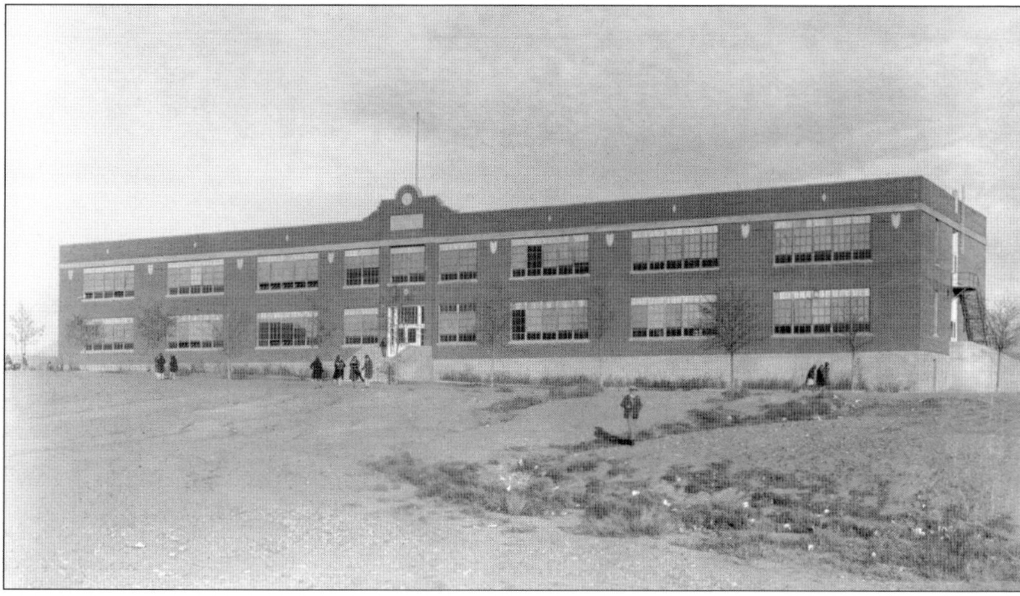

Lincoln Junior High, above, opened in 1922 as Albuquerque's first junior high in the city system. Set in a largely vacant area, the school operated until 1964 when the district moved their maintenance offices to this fine building that stands largely unchanged in appearance today. The vast spaces east of Lincoln School now house the school district's vehicle fleet lots, print services, library hub, cafeteria central services, and the district's first athletic field, Bulldog (now Milne) Stadium, built in 1940. (Courtesy of ERH.)

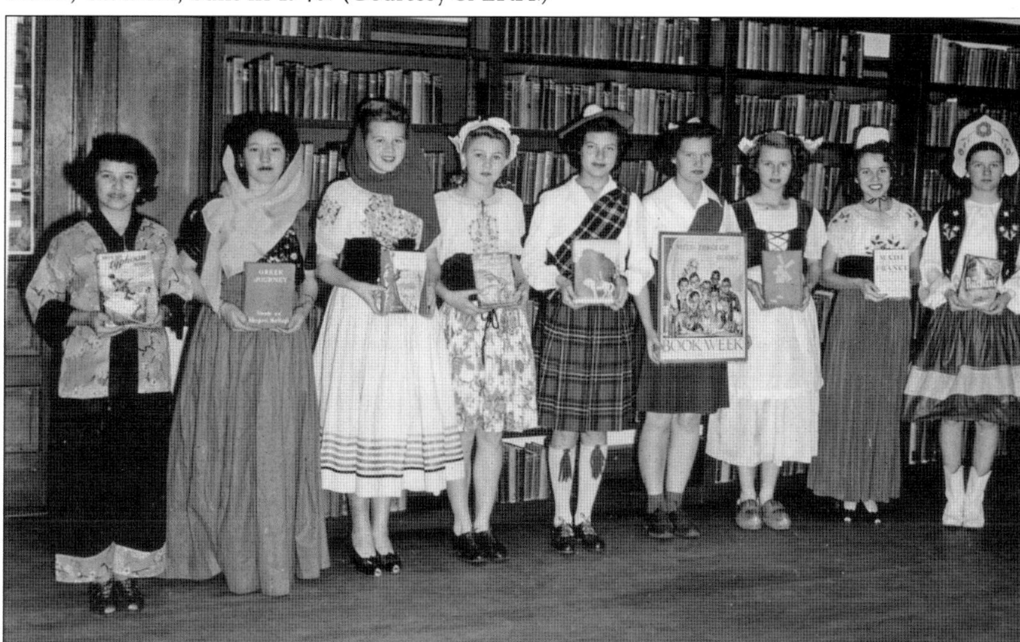


Standing proudly in the library of Lincoln Junior High are young ladies celebrating Book Week, around 1944. Land contiguous to Lincoln houses a host of district services as well as serving, beginning in 1964, as the home for Albuquerque Technical Vocational Institute, now Central New Mexico Community College. (Courtesy ERH.)

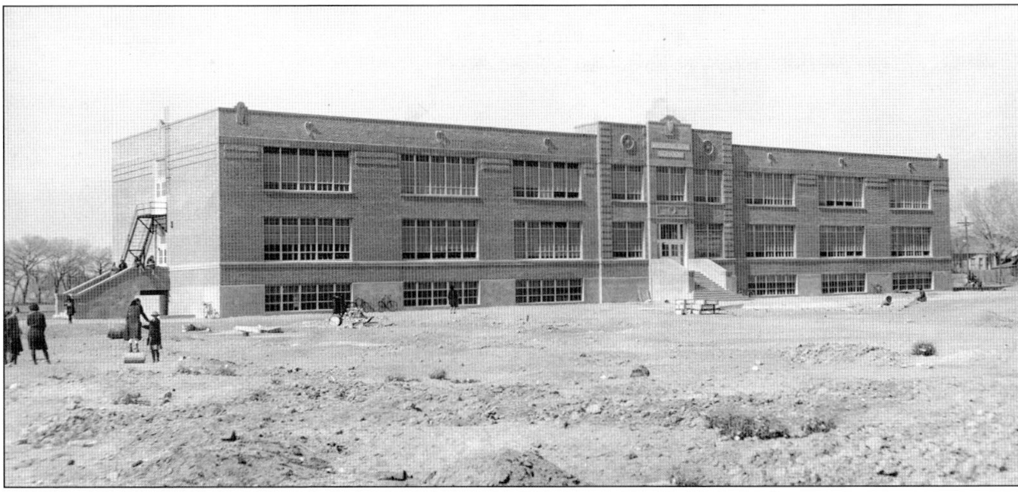

Washington Junior High opened its doors in the sandy flatlands near the Albuquerque Country Club and Huning Highlands Castle neighborhood in 1923. In 1938, the Works Progress Administration and federal funds aided the school in adding a library and other amenities to Washington. Superintendent Milne and his long-term business manager John Varney were wise to access federal funds available to communities in the 1930s through not only WPA, but also through other arms of the National Recovery Act of 1933 such as the Emergency Public Works Administration, the Federal Emergency Relief Administration, and the Civil Works Administration. (Courtesy APS.)

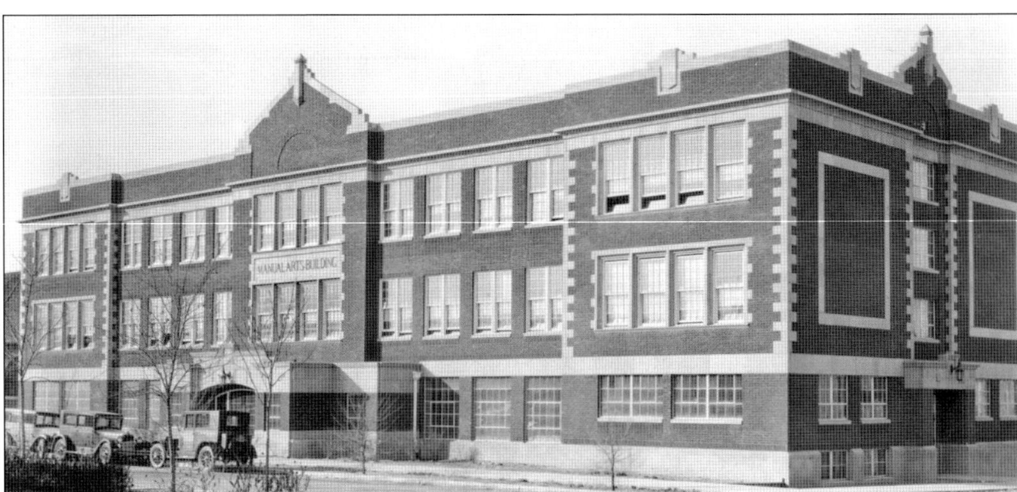

The Manual Arts Building of Albuquerque High was completed in 1927 and is pictured above from around that time. The long-standing belief in educating students for a variety of career choices made Albuquerque at the forefront for implementing job-readiness training when World War II broke out. (Courtesy APS.)

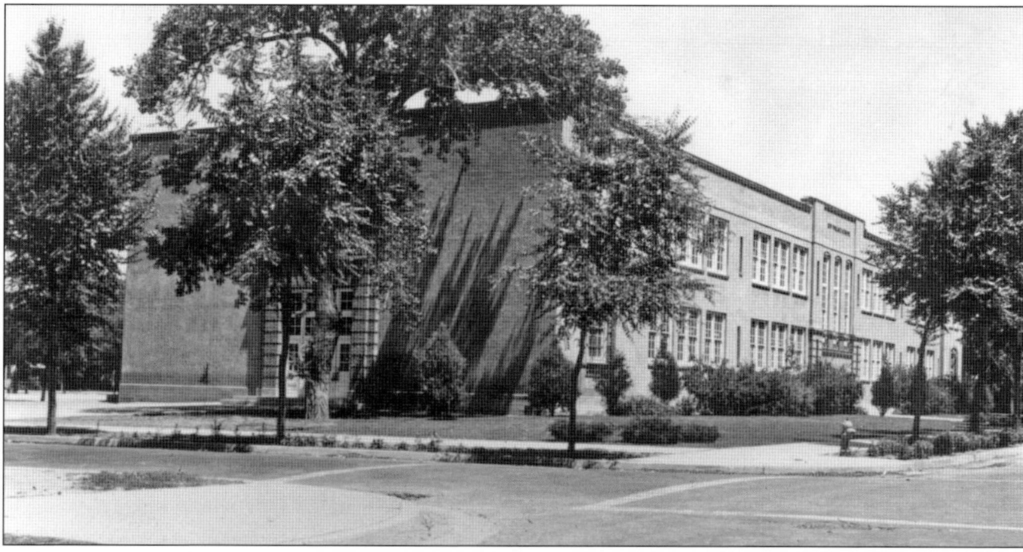

In 1935, Lew Wallace Elementary replaced the Fourth Ward School that burned to the ground on April 25, 1933. Clever John Milne quickly applied for a Pubic Works Administration grant, and combined the awarded sum with the meager insurance and funds saved. A new school was opened and named after New Mexico's literary governor who served in office from 1878 to 1881 and penned the novel *Ben Hur*. Other APS schools that opened around this time include Reginald Chavez, Stronghurst, and River View—the latter stood on the site of what is now the National Hispanic Cultural Center. (Courtesy APS.)

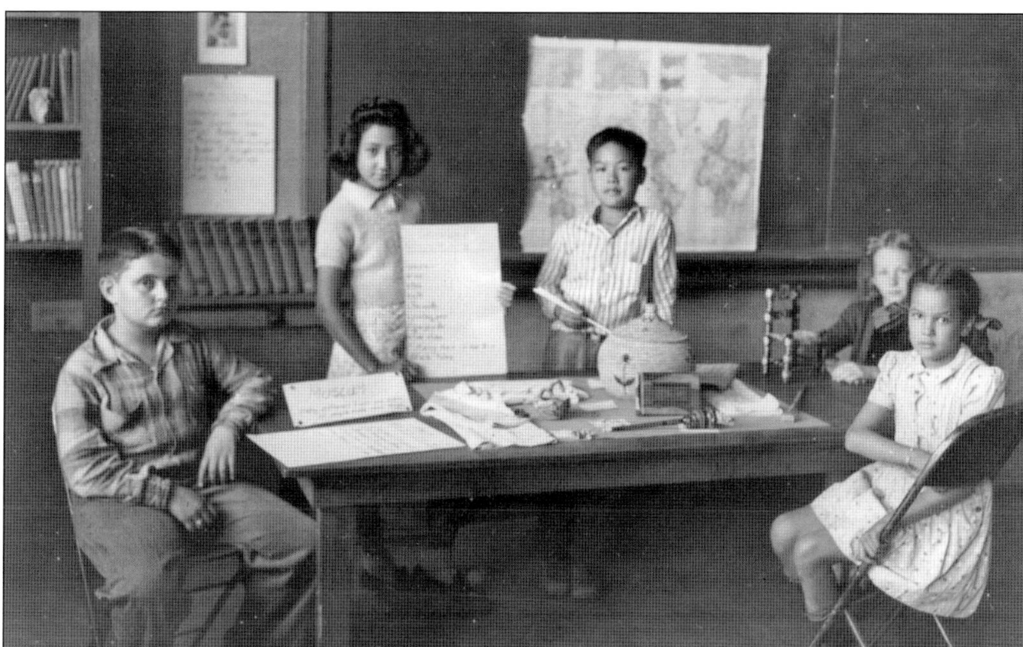

This c. 1944 classroom at Lew Wallace epitomizes the ethnic diversity at work in Albuquerque's schools. Children from many backgrounds and religions mixed, mingled, met, married and coexisted. (Courtesy ERH.)

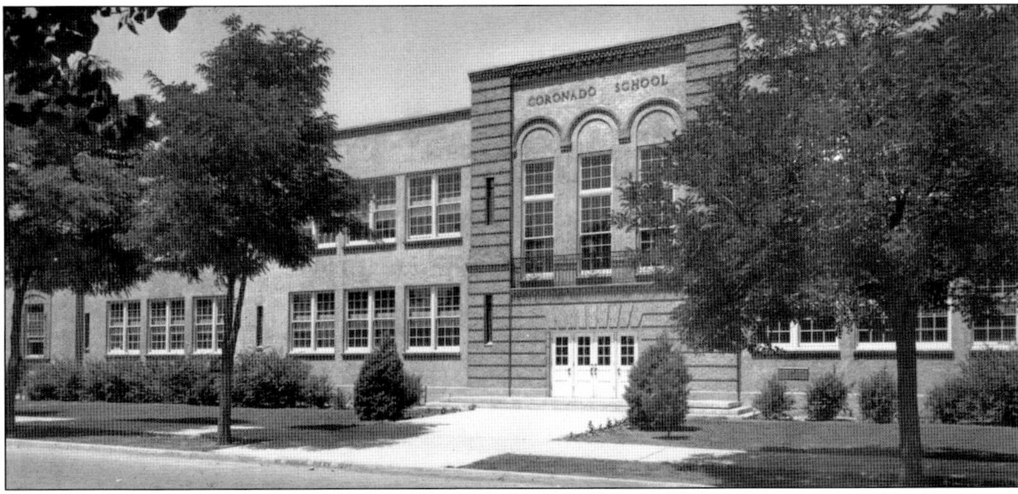


By 1940, when the above photograph was taken, Coronado school (the site of the old Third Ward School that was torn down and rebuilt with Public Works Administration funds in 1937) was being designed by APS staff architect Louis Hesselden. Coronado closed due to low enrollment in the 1980s and housed district services instead. Due to the revitalization of the downtown neighborhoods, Coronado reopened in 2009 after a grand refurbishment. (Courtesy APS.)

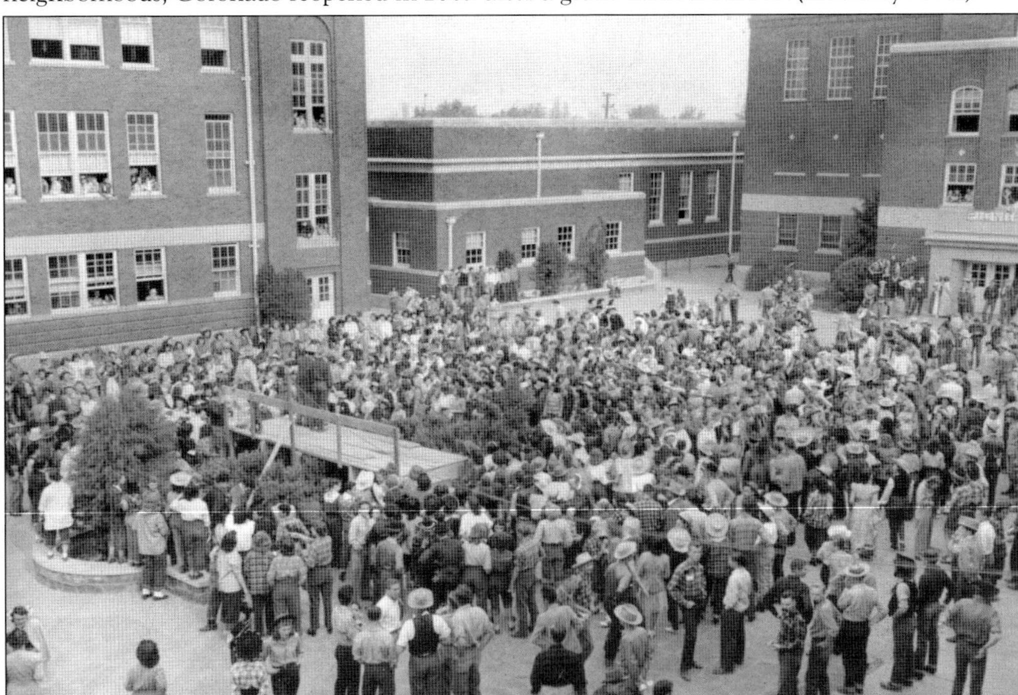

Pioneer Days was an annual spring event at Albuquerque High. Festivities included a beard-growing contest, performances of all kinds, including ethnic and cowboy music and skits, a parade down Central Avenue, and more. Pictured above are Albuquerque High students preparing for Pioneer Day festivities. Note an onlooker from the open windows of the relatively new gym and cafeteria building (upper right) that was built with Works Progress Administration funds. Considering the time period, the number of young ladies wearing pants is impressive. (Courtesy ERH.)

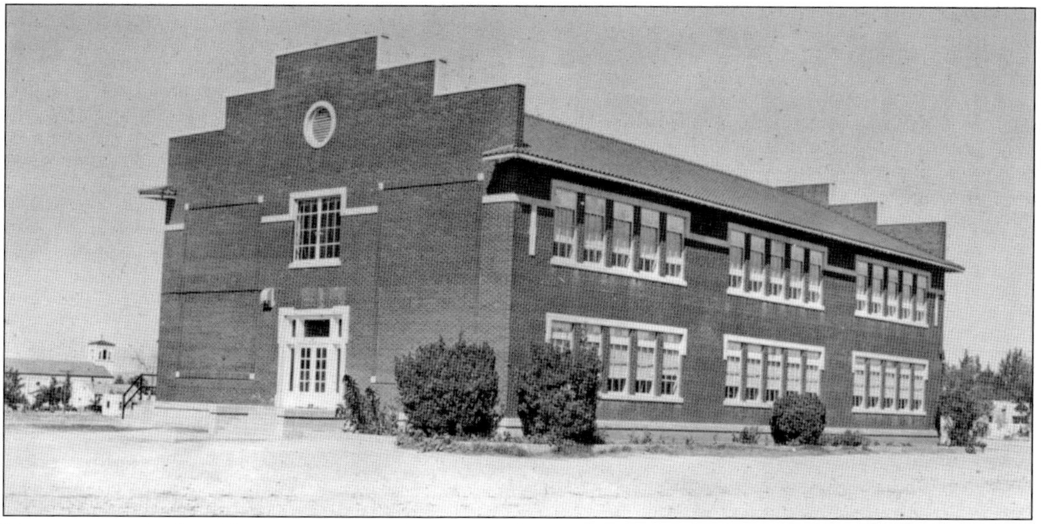

University Heights Elementary rose from the dust in 1923 made from the red bricks that still stand today. This school housed the new families way out on the east mesa of Albuquerque as the University area began expanding. Some remember University Heights as housing the first special education programs in the city, and today the jagged brick roof's facade peers out from the Central New Mexico campus as one drives up Coal Avenue. It is now known as "M Building." Irma Bobo is a well-remembered principal of the school. (Courtesy ERH.)

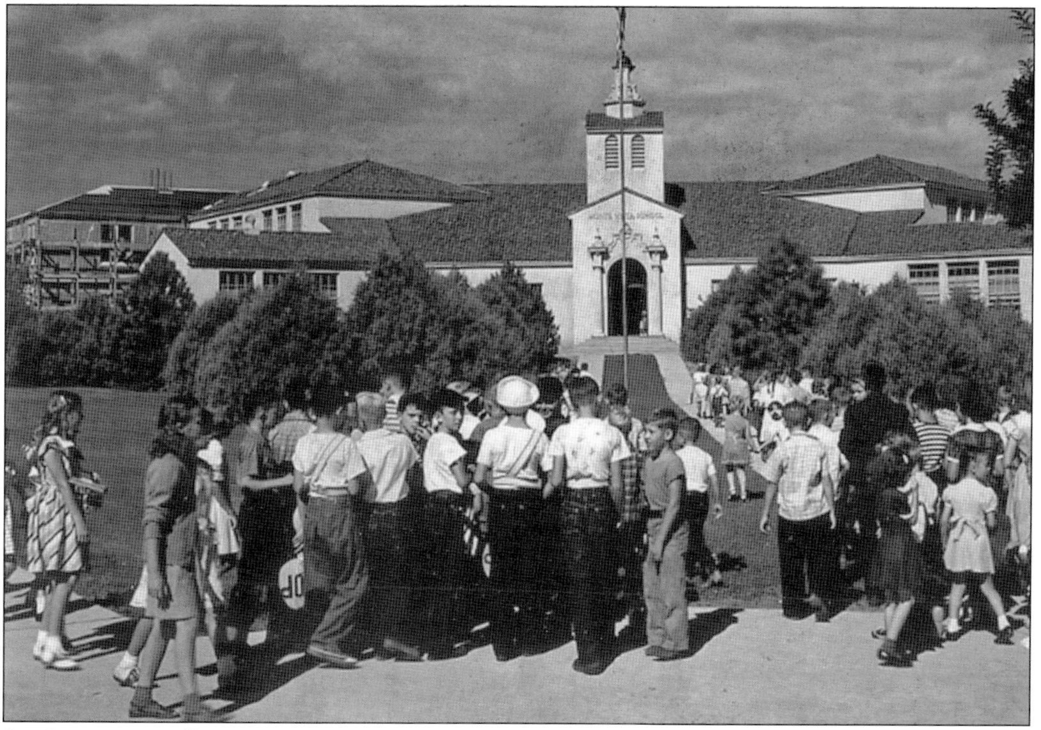

Students excitedly stream into their school on a 1947 morning. Built in 1931, Monte Vista Elementary served the new heights area of Albuquerque near the University of New Mexico. Just blocks from the Nob Hill Business Center, Albuquerque's first shopping center, Monte Vista and its neighborhood exploded in population after World War II. (Courtesy APS.)

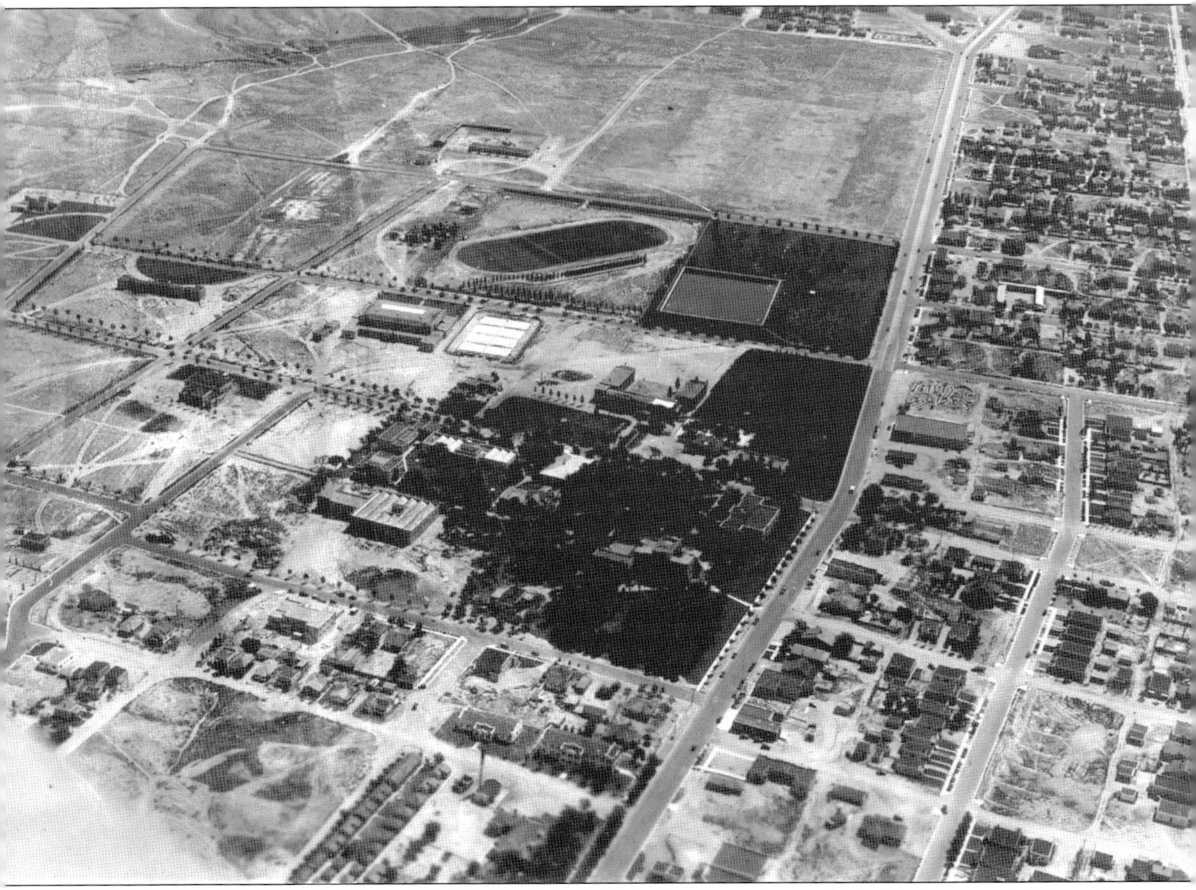

This c. 1931 aerial view of Albuquerque shows the UNM area with Zimmerman Field in the upper center and Carlisle Gym just to the left and below the field. Reservoir Park is to the right of Zimmerman Field, and Hodgin Hall stands in the lower right of the shadowy part of the center portion. Toward the upper right, Monte Vista Boulevard breaks away on the left from Central Avenue. (Courtesy APS.)

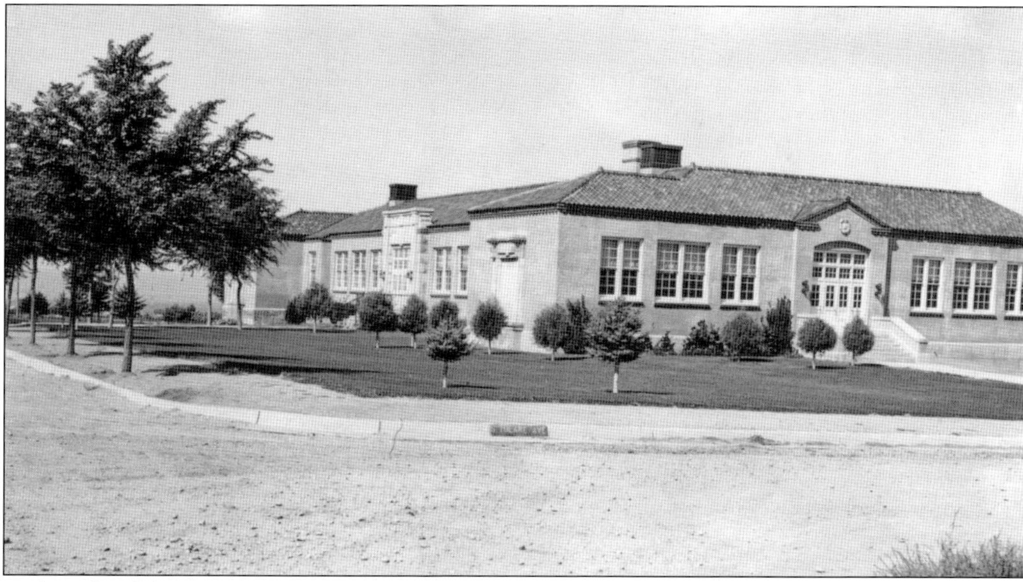

Built on land donated by developers D.K.B. Sellers, the Hyder brothers, and Salam Mama, Bandelier Elementary was named after the famed conservationist. Mimicking Jefferson Junior High's architectural style (both schools were designed by Louis Hesselden), Bandelier still serves a diverse community drawing from the University and Southeast Heights Albuquerque area. Well-known Harold Goff opened the school as principal and remained there many years. (Courtesy ERH.)

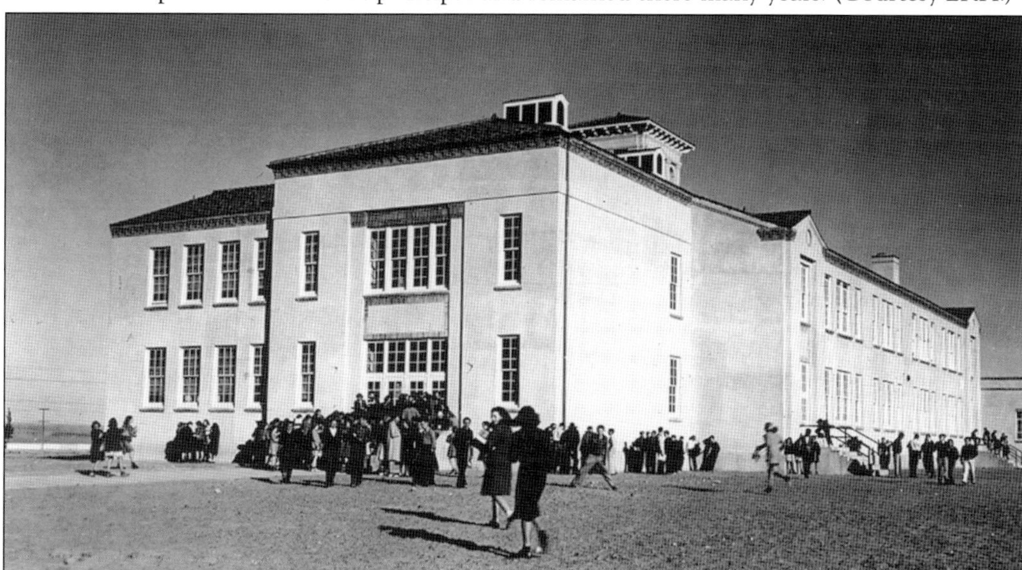

Jefferson Junior High, pictured above, opened in 1938 on the then-deserted northeast corner of Girard and Lomas. For several years, only the Congregational Church (still standing) and Jefferson occupied the area and residents complained about how "far out there" the buildings stood. One of the first of many schools designed for APS by architect Louis Hesselden, Jefferson rises today from a grassy corner with well-established trees. Maynard Bowen served as Jefferson's first principal, and when Highland High (APS's second high school) opened in 1949, Jefferson was so overcrowded that Jefferson's ninth graders moved to the new high school for two years until Wilson Junior High opened its doors in 1953. (Courtesy ERH.)

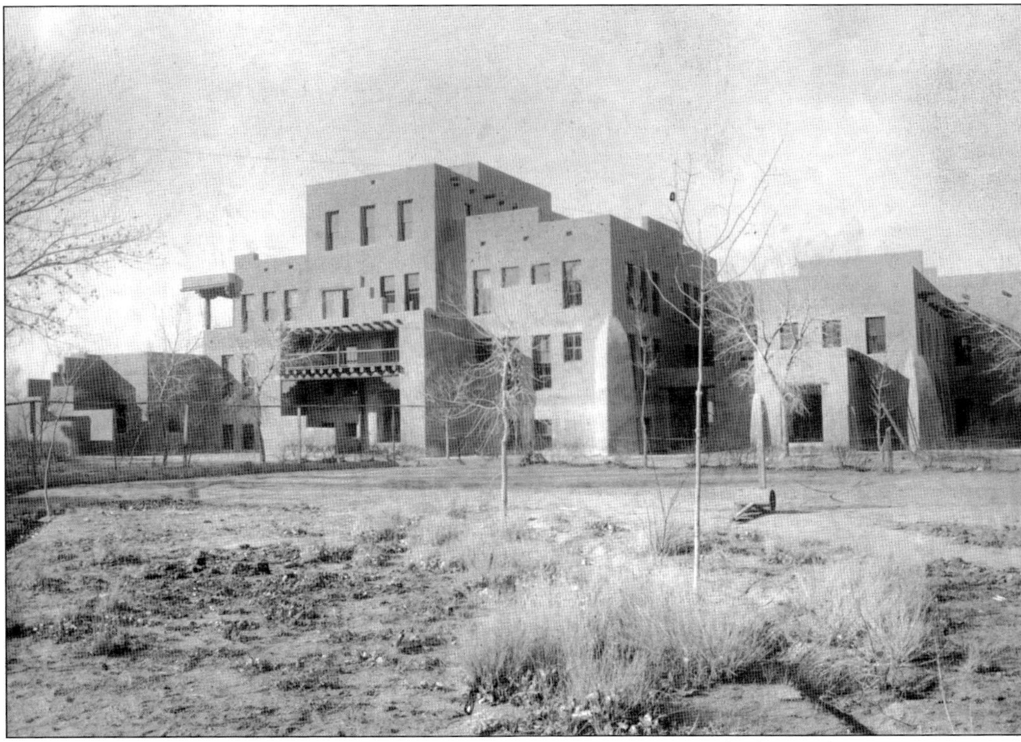

The "first building of the University of New Mexico" was renovated when John Gaw Meem was engaged as the architect for the school. The red bricks were plastered over and enhancements were made to the building to give it a Pueblo-style look. Located on the northeast corner of University and Central, the structure was named Hodgin Hall after Charles Hodgin, first superintendent of the city's pubic schools and longtime head of the university's education department. (Courtesy CSWR, PICT 000-003-0093.)

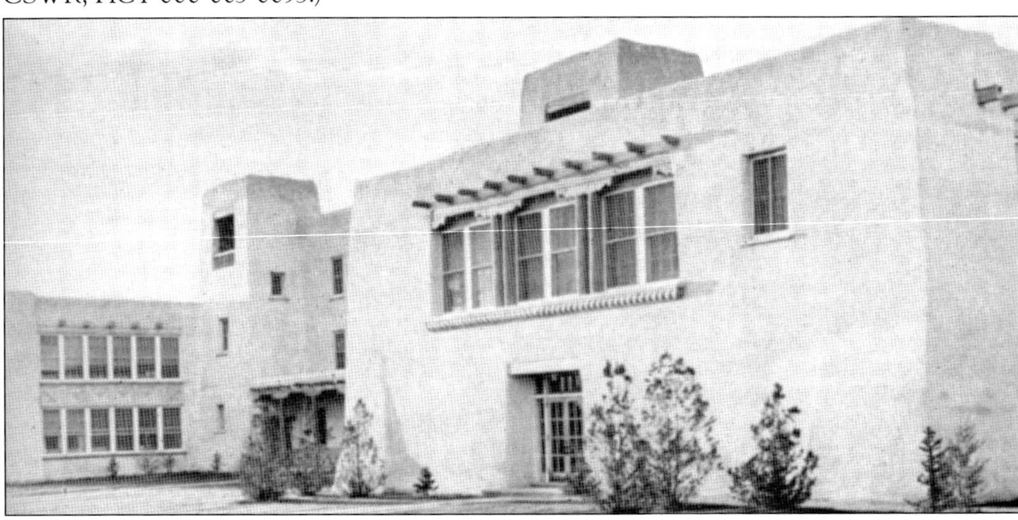

Designed by John Gaw Meem and funded in large part by federal depression relief funds, the University of New Mexico's administration building opened in 1937. Now known as Scholes Hall, this building was one of many that sprang up in the 1930s to help propel UNM into the national education scene. (Courtesy APM.)

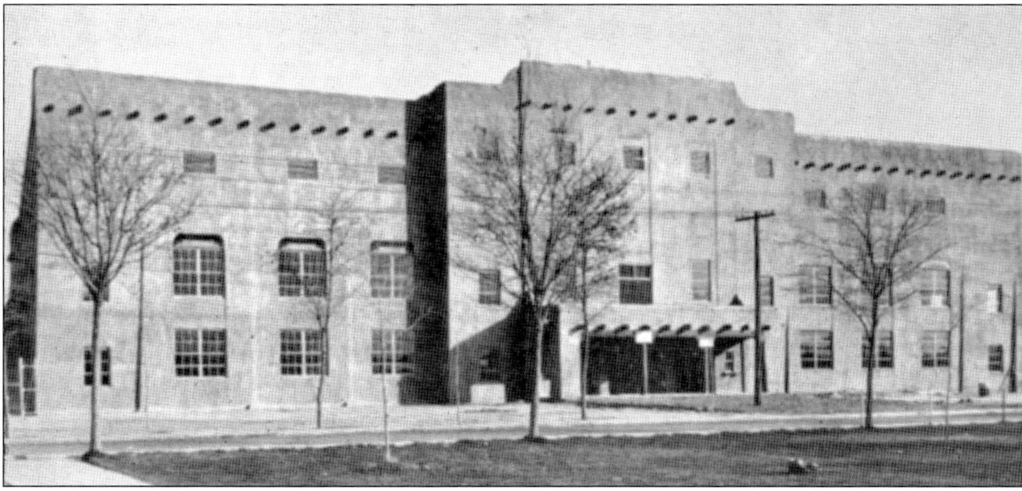

Designed by architects Brittelle and Wilson, bids for the University of New Mexico stadium building opened in June 1934. Lavishly scaled, the stadium would be 285 feet long, and the buildings would house classrooms, coach's rooms, showers, locker rooms, and handball courts. The contract went to Mount and Mead of Denver who were coincidentally building—at the same time—the renovated Fourth Ward School (Lew Wallace). The university took advantage of depression relief funds available from the federal government to fund this project. (Courtesy APM.)

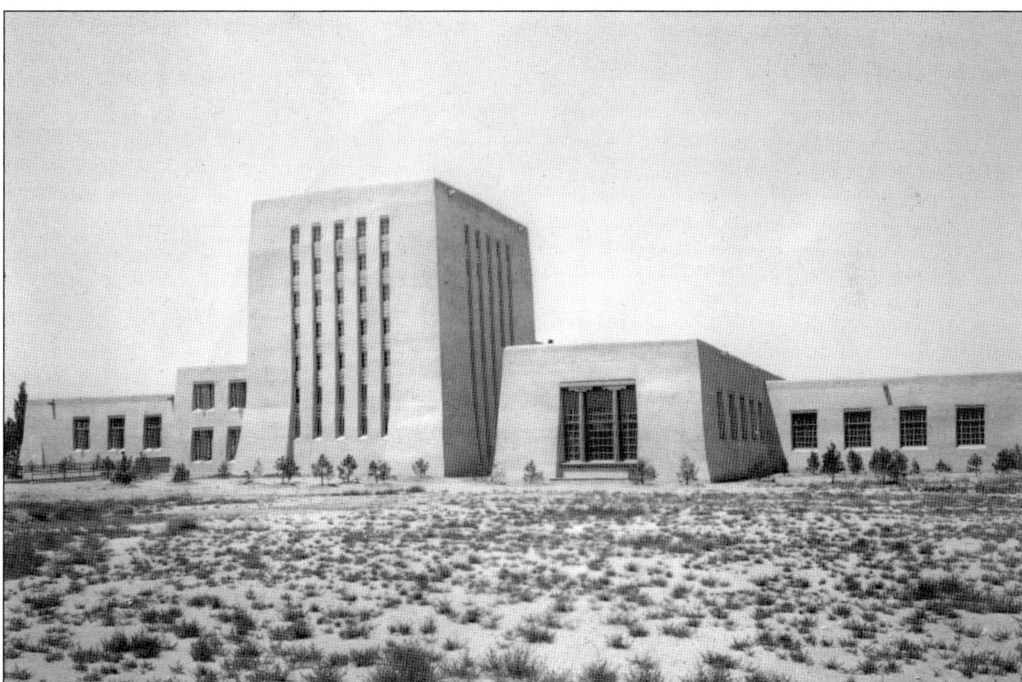

Zimmerman Library is pictured here just after completion in 1937. Many consider it as the crown jewel of the University of New Mexico's architecture. Named for James Zimmerman, president of UNM from 1927 to 1945, and designed by architect John Gaw Meem, this Pueblo Revival–style building was financed in large part with Public Works Administration depression relief funds. (Courtesy CSWR, PICT 000-003-0075.)

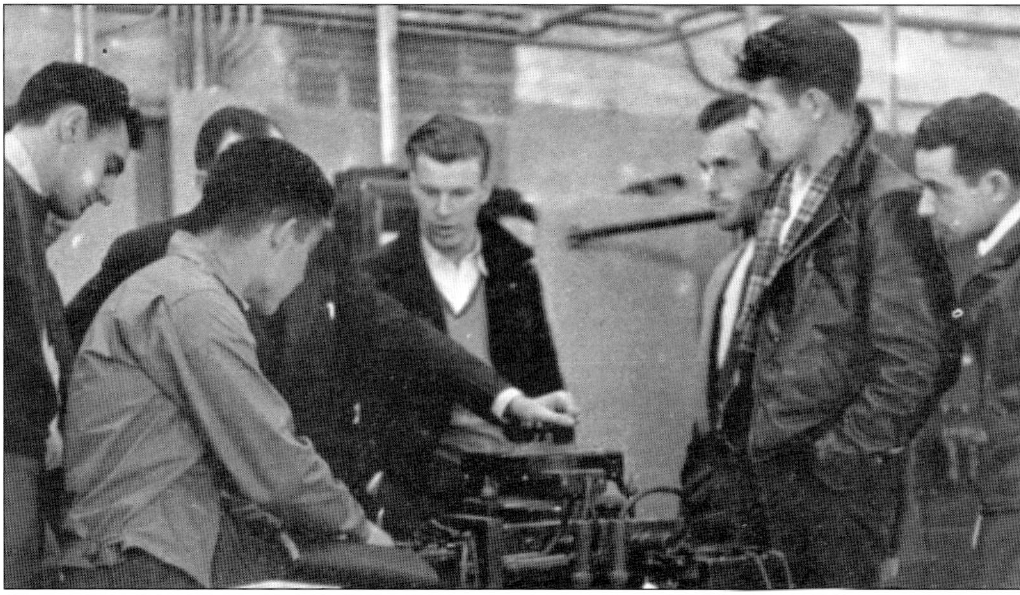

Above, Naval Junior Reserve Officers' Training recruits discuss engineering topics at University of New Mexico. The university's enrollment dropped drastically during World War II, and UNM's President Zimmerman quickly vied with other institutions to house military training programs, bolstering enrollment and hence funding. (Courtesy APM.)

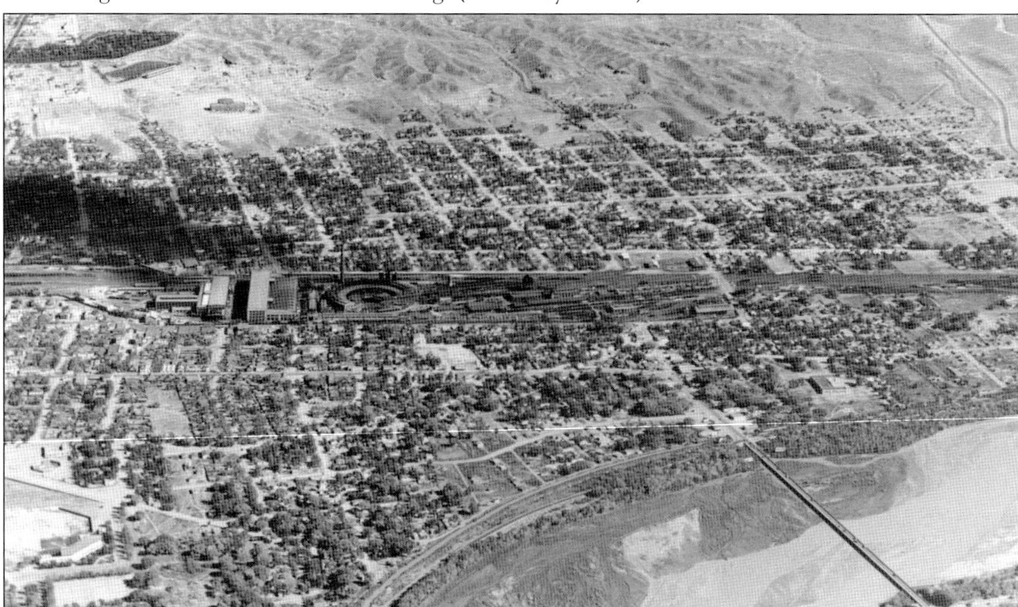

This aerial c. 1931 view of Albuquerque shows the dominance of the rail yards over the city's physical space. By then, the Santa Fe Railroad fueled Albuquerque's economy. The city was situated as a perfect waypoint between the east and Los Angeles, California as concerned freight, flight, and car transport. The railroad was the major employee for African Americans in Albuquerque in the first half of the century, and many African Americans settled in the South Broadway and Kirtland Addition neighborhoods of Albuquerque, becoming part of the vibrant growing community and contributing to the cultural diversity and acceptance of the city. (Courtesy APS.)

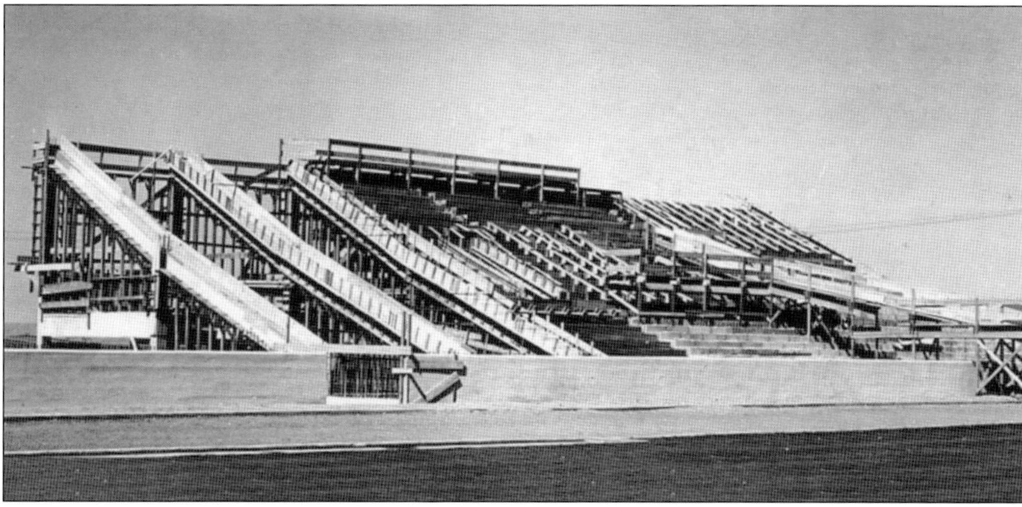

Above is Bulldog Field under construction in 1940 for use by the only APS high school at the time, Albuquerque High. Later renamed Milne Stadium and used by Albuquerque's growing bouquet of high schools through the 1950s and 1960s, the stadium became a dramatic scene for football, track and field, and other events. The university used Zimmerman Field at Yale and Central more and more for its own events, and it was time for the city school to grow its own venue. Today, Milne Stadium partners with its sister across town, Wilson Stadium opened in 1963, to host all high school football matches. A third state-of-the-art stadium opened in fall 2013 on the west side. (Courtesy APS.)

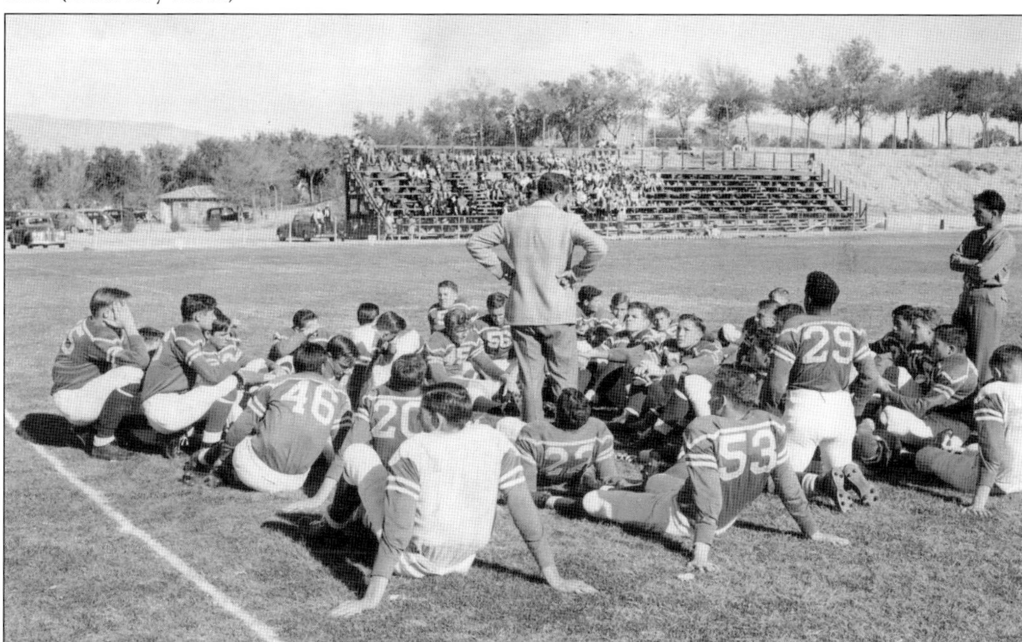

F.M. Wilson converses with his Albuquerque High Bulldog team at a practice around 1944. Wilson coached several sports for years at AHS and eventually became the city schools' athletic director. Visible in the background are the visitors' stands at Bulldog Stadium. Bulldog Stadium later was renamed Milne Stadium, and when the city schools had resources to open a second public schools' stadium it was named for F.M. Wilson. (Courtesy ERH.)

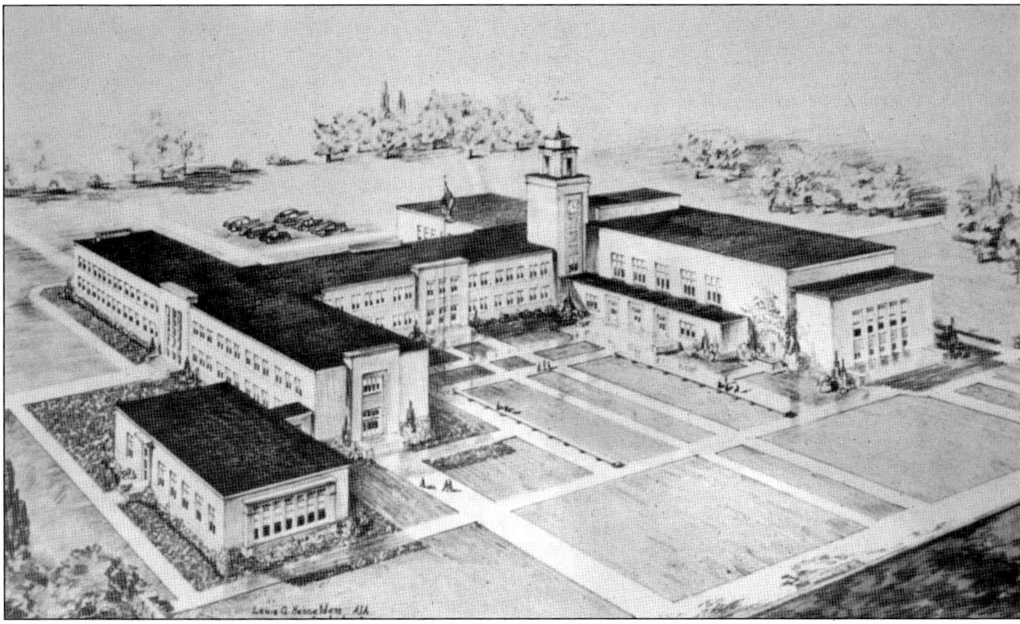

Louis G. Hesselden enjoyed a long tenure as the chief architect contracted by APS beginning in the 1940s and designed most APS schools built through the early 1960s. Above is his sketch envisioning the Highland High campus that opened in 1949. The buildings form an "H," and the building pictured on the far left was set farther away from the classrooms and became the gym. Due to finances, the bell tower never materialized, and the building on the far right became the cafeteria, not a theater as originally intended. (Courtesy CSWR, Louis G. Hesselden Architectural Drawings Collection, Drawer 10 & 11.)

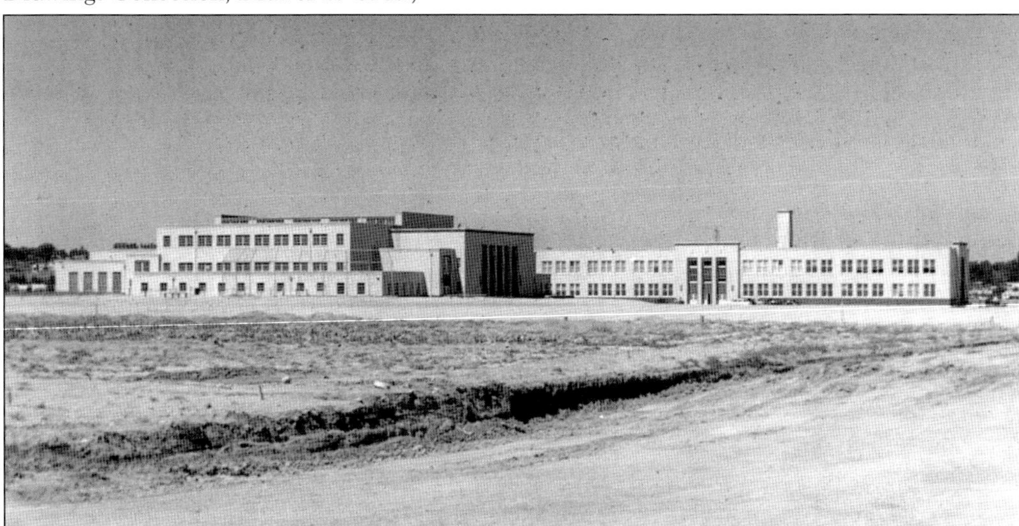

Highland High, pictured above, flung open its doors against the east mesa dust in the fall of 1949. The opening of Highland forever changed the educational landscape of the city, as Albuquerque High had for over 60 years been "the" high school. Epitomizing the carefree and economically euphoric era of the 1950s that swept across post–World War II America, Highland—along with many other United States high schools—experienced a period of glory days even though the tumultuous Korean War period, 1950–1952, sapped confidence and resources. (Courtesy APS.)

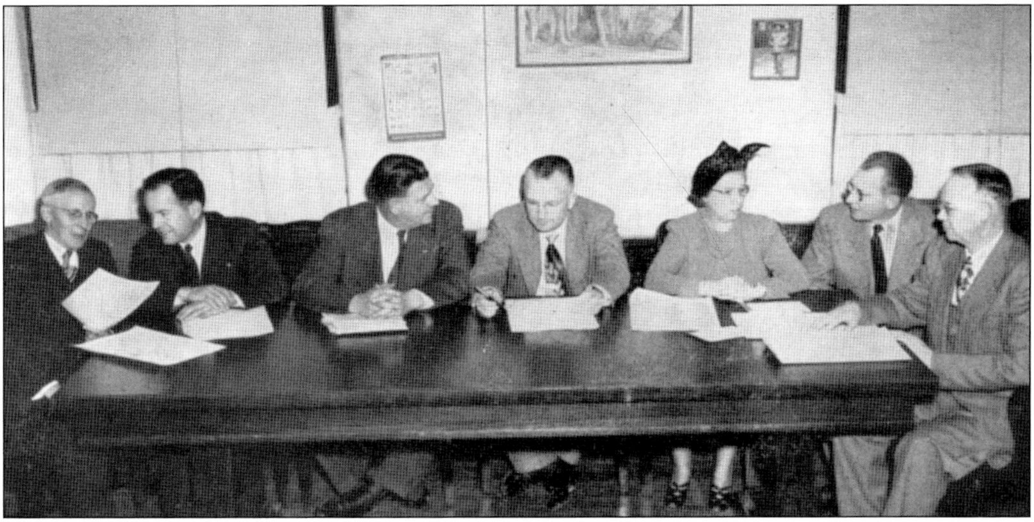

The inaugural (1950) edition of the Highland High yearbook included this photograph. From left to right are superintendent John Milne, school board members Danny McPherson (board vice-president), Sticker Thorne, S.Y. Jackson (board president), Mrs. A.H. Nicolai, Bob Elder, and school business manager John Varney. All well-connected business people, these board members rarely voted against each other on issues, were elected at large, and served with rare harmony and foresight. During Milne's 1911–1955 reign, the trio of Milne, Varney, and Louis Hesselden spearheaded the school district's purchase of thousands of acres of land at low prices. The trio designed and opened 38 schools.

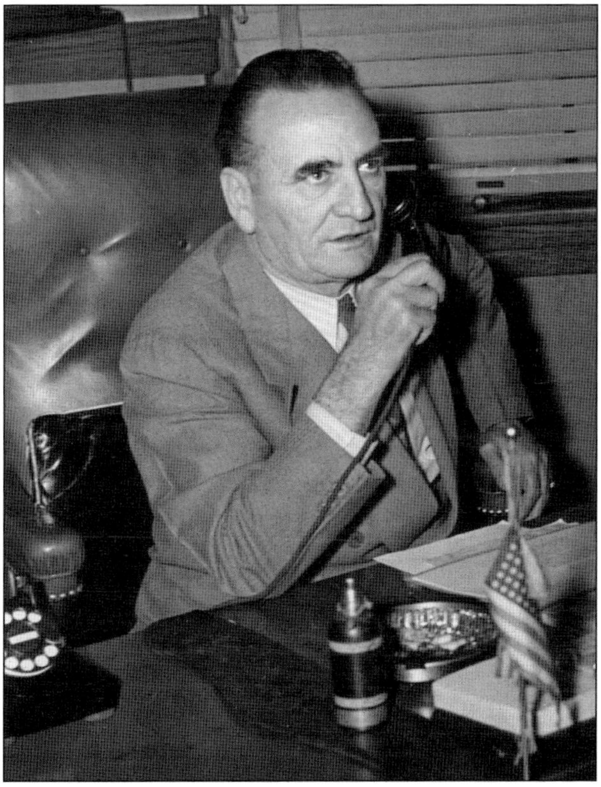

Clyde Tingley was a powerful and colorful player in New Mexico and Albuquerque politics between 1912 and 1955. He was the first person to serve two consecutive terms as governor of New Mexico, and he was bitter not to serve a third term—reportedly taking the keys to the governor's mansion when he left. He championed Albuquerque's growth as a unified, annexed area city, thus benefitting the public schools. His wife, Carrie Tingley, came to Albuquerque to recover from tuberculosis. She brought her family fortune with her and married Clyde. After World War II's increased charitable efforts took place across America, Carrie was instrumental in founding Carrie Tingley Hospital for disabled children, which is still serving children today. (Courtesy CSWR, PICT 000-742-0146.)

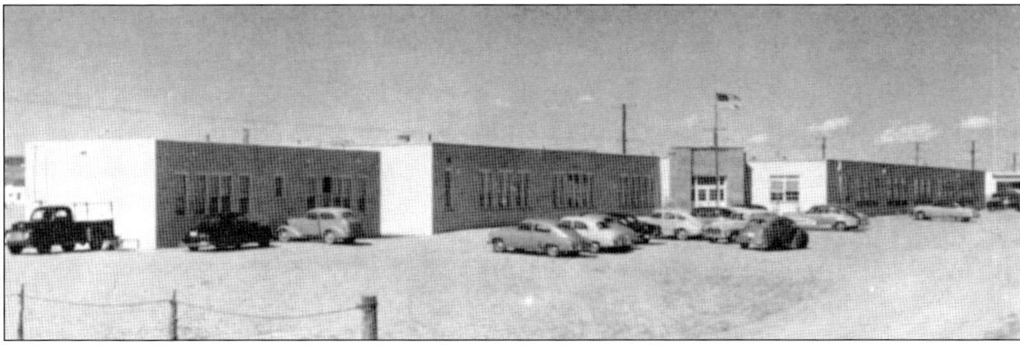

La Mesa Elementary (above), opened in 1939 and served a population of Albuquerque that hopped the university area and sprang up near what would become the state fairgrounds built in the 1930s. Anticipating heavy business activity, the area grew rapidly. Douglas MacArthur School (below) welcomed students in the near north valley of Albuquerque in 1946 and garnered its name from the World War II general. Other APS elementary schools that opened during this time include La Luz, Pajarito, Duranes, MacArthur, and Montezuma. (Both, courtesy APM.)

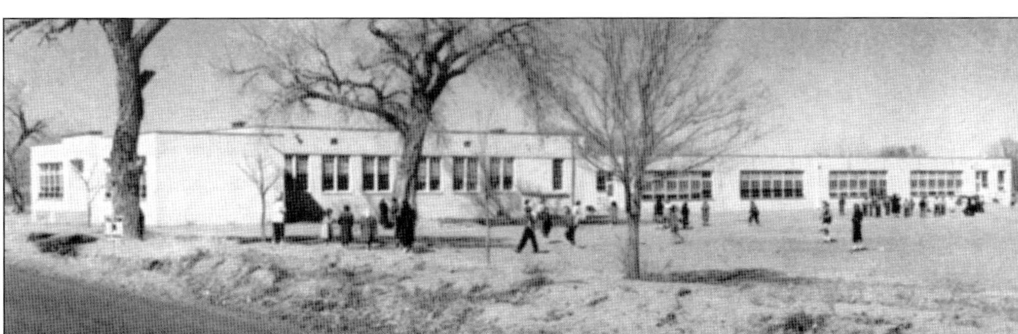

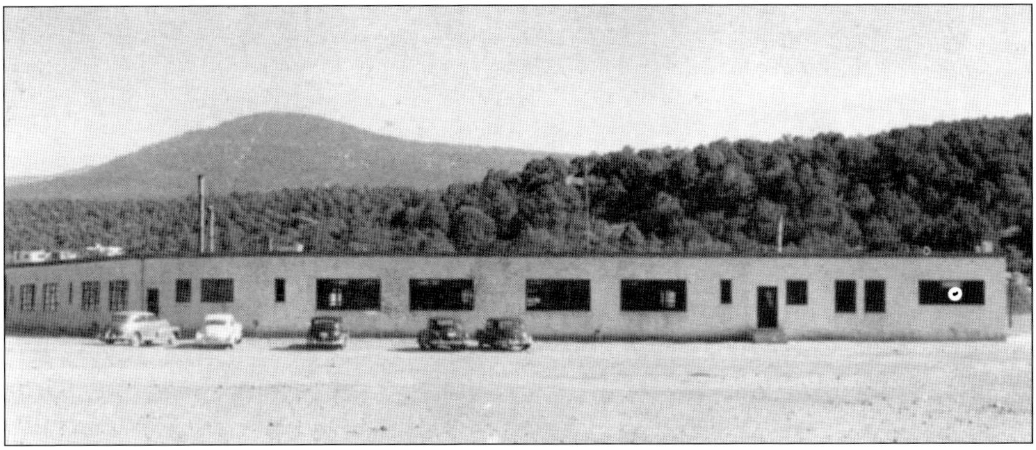

Superintendent Milne achieved a political win-win in 1945 by beginning to move his loyal school board and county superintendent Adolfo "Tiny" Chavez's board into a merger. In 1949, Bernalillo County (happily) relinquished its obligations for education to the Albuquerque city schools, and the two entities merged. Pictured above, A. Montoya School opened in 1949 in the high mountains east of Albuquerque as a need was seen for students throughout the far-sweeping mountain area to go to school. (Courtesy APM.)

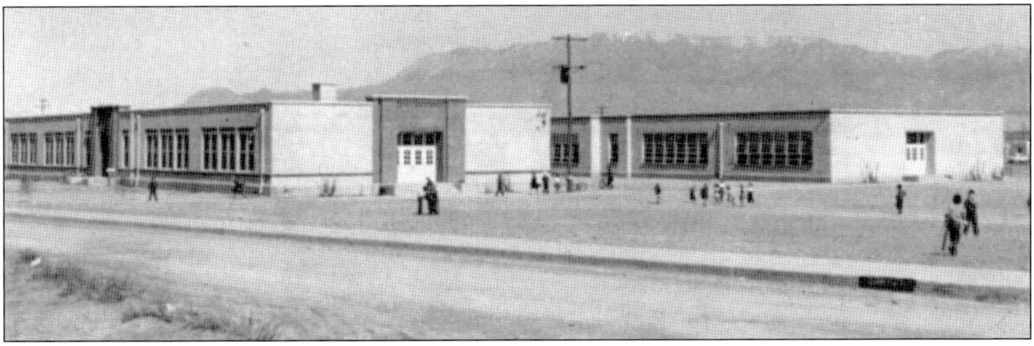

Meanwhile, Whittier (above) near the Sandia Base area opened the same year as Zia Elementary (below), near Lomas and Washington. (Both, courtesy APM.)

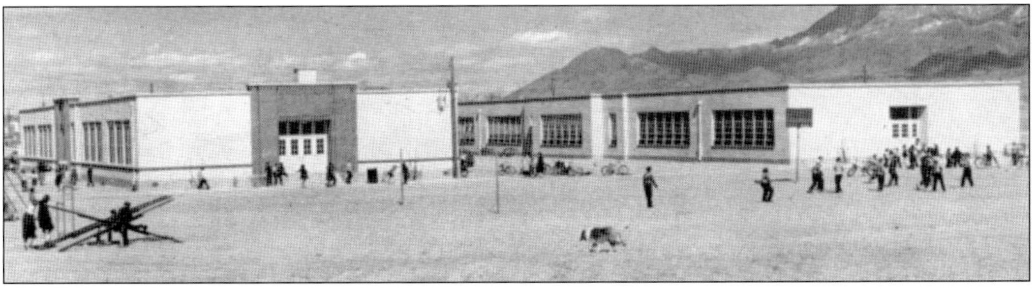

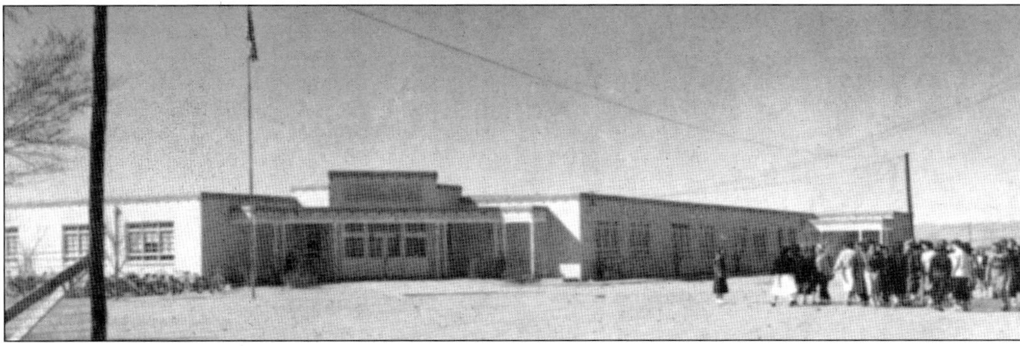

Following a national trend, Albuquerque took on a junior high model that included grades seven through nine after World War II, and opened three schools to add to the needs Lincoln and Washington Junior Highs were already serving. Above, Ernie Pyle, named after Albuquerque's relocated native World War II media correspondent who perished in the final years of the conflict, opened in 1948. (Courtesy APM.)

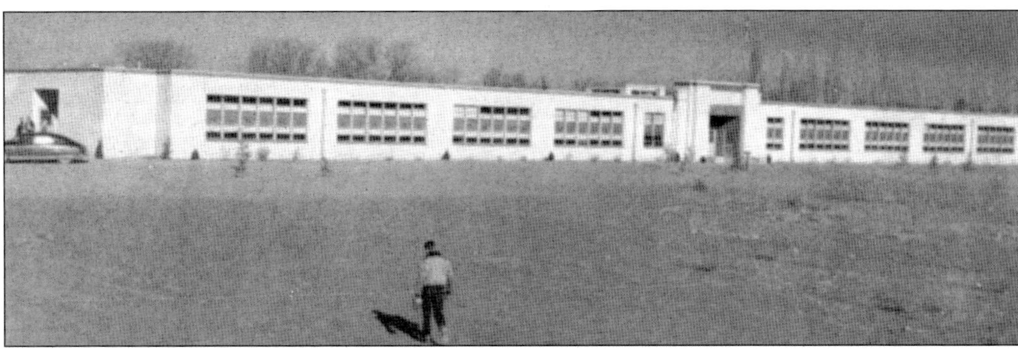

Garfield Junior High (above) returned to the tradition of naming junior schools after presidents and stood its doors open in 1950. Soon after, Wilson Junior High (below) relieved overcrowding at Jefferson Junior High and started breeding a new batch of Hornet students for the blossoming Highland High. (Both, courtesy APM.)

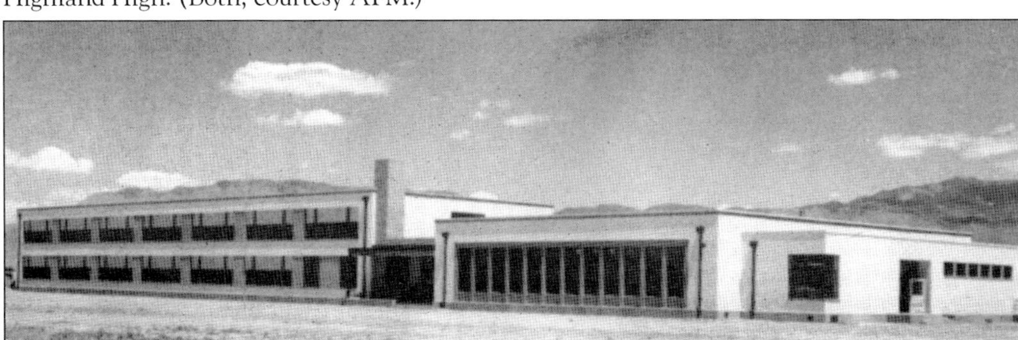

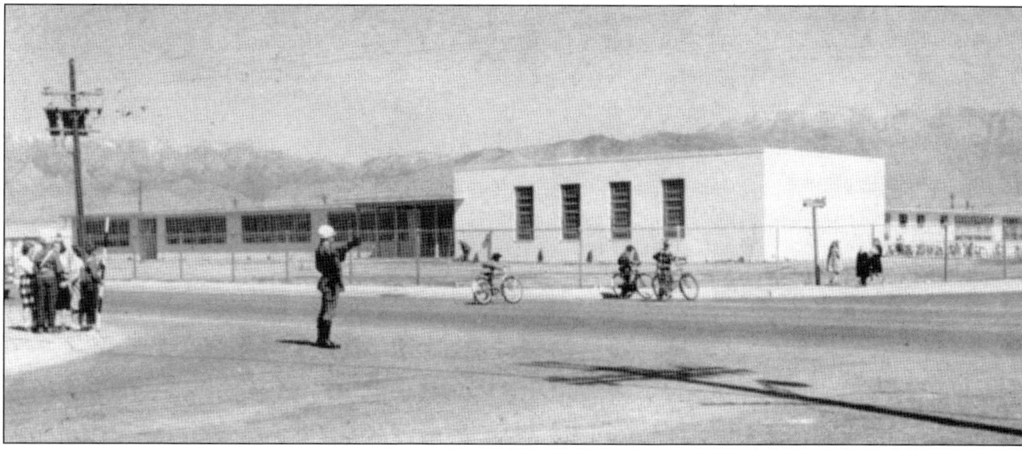

John Milne, superintendent of Albuquerque Public Schools, set up an arrangement with Kirtland Air Force Base for the students of base personnel to be serviced by APS. Visible here (above) is Sandia Base Elementary. Clear in the photograph is the fabled dust that blew across the east mesa as construction exploded in Albuquerque in the late 1940s and early 1950s. The base's and lab's histories became ever entwined, mingling with Lovelace Hospital opening in the same era. An influx of Easterners, sometimes dubbed "technocrats," arrived in Albuquerque after World War II. With the opening of Sandia Labs, the expansion of Kirtland Air Field with its ensuing Kirtland Elementary (below), the opening of Lovelace Hospital, and the general growing of the southwest, Albuquerque's population increased from 30,000 in 1944 to 96,000 in 1953. (Both, courtesy APM.)

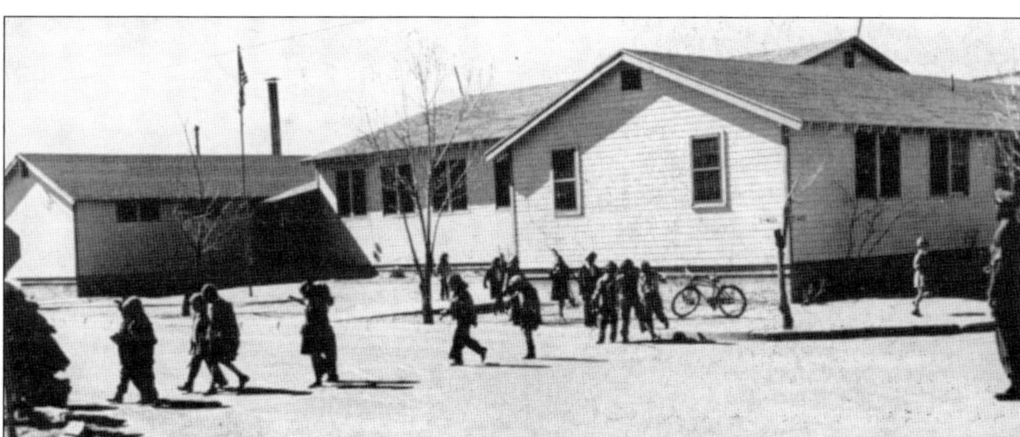

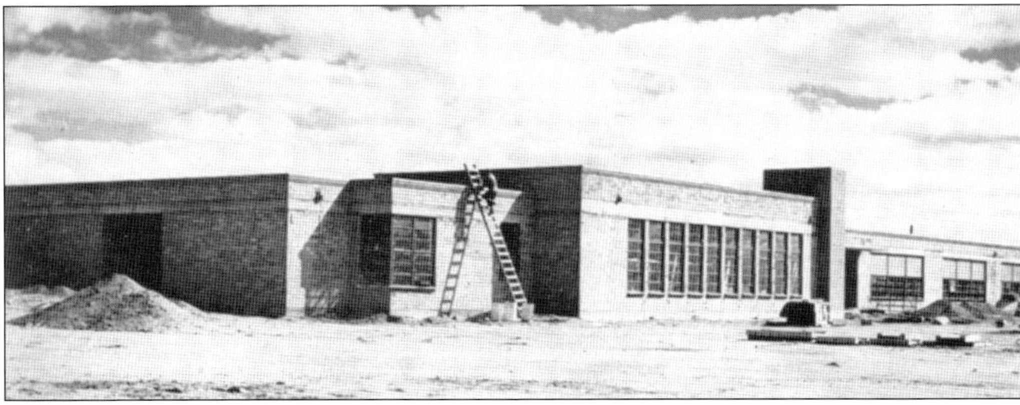

The Bel Air Addition caused the City Commission some heartburn as it contentiously resisted annexation into the city. By 1952, the area conceded and north Bel Air Elementary opened under the city schools' system. A south Bel Air welcomed students in the same year, but seems to have morphed into what is known as Cortez Elementary, which later changed missions to operate as Freedom High at today's I-40 and Cutler Northeast. Other APS schools that had opened by this time include Atrisco, Roosevelt, Lowell, and Hawthorne. (Both, courtesy APM.)

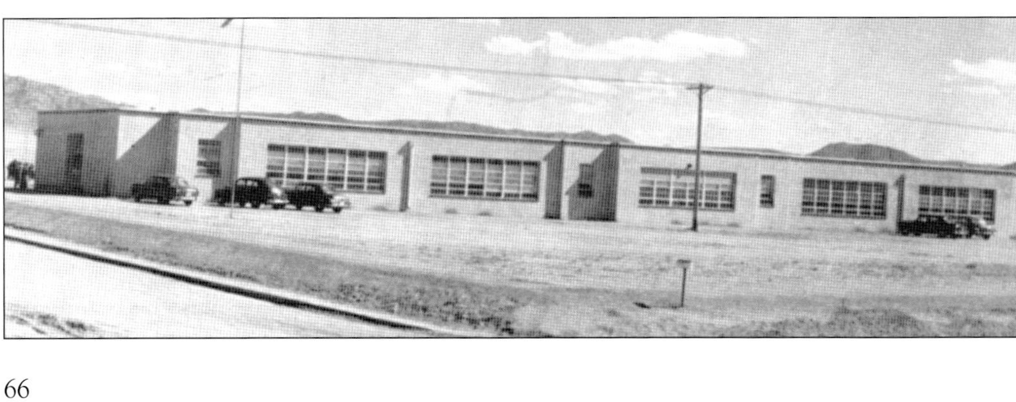

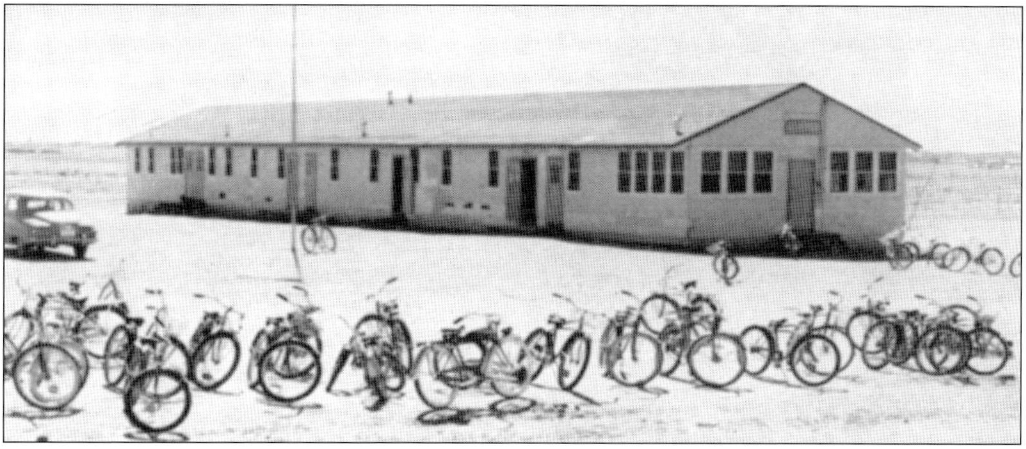

The early 1950s continued a relentless march of school openings across northeast Albuquerque. Mirroring the scattered spread of needs in the city, Inez Elementary (above) opened in 1959 near what became the large shopping malls of Coronado and Winrock. Below, Valle Vista on the south end of the city in 1952 opened to serve south valley families. (Both, courtesy APM.)

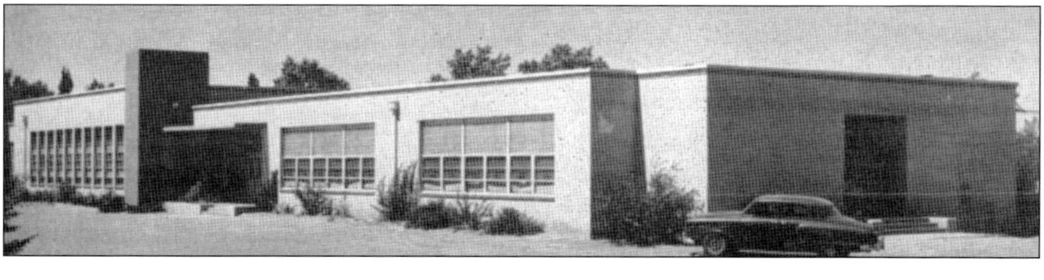

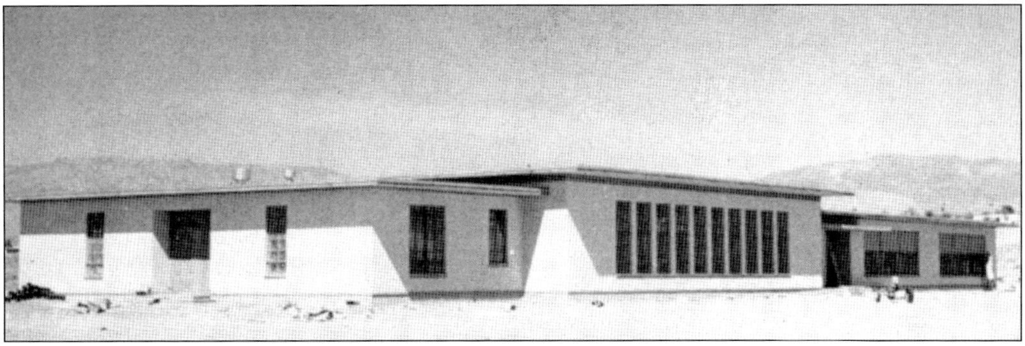

When Milne, Varney, and Hesselden (city schools' superintendent, business manager, and architect, respectively) could even sleep during the 1950s is puzzling. Wherry (above) embraced students from the southeast heights whose families of modest means were filling job niches in the expanding economy, particularly on base or with Lovelace Hospital. Mark Twain Elementary (below) scooped up students whose families settled in the open east mesa of the city between Nob Hill and Bel Air. Both schools opened in 1954. (Both, courtesy APM.)

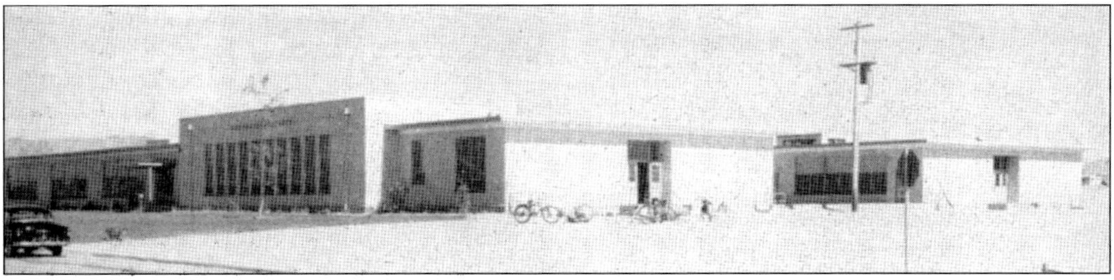

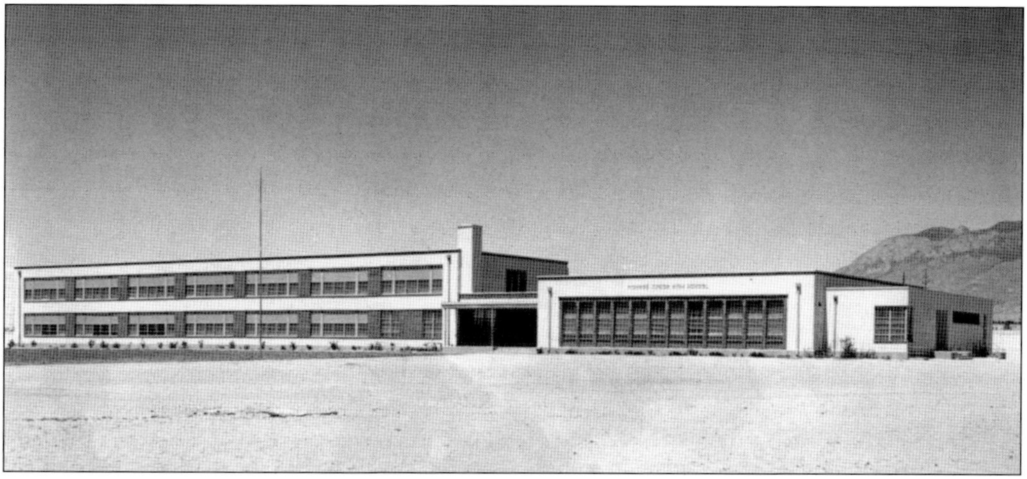

James Monroe Junior High ushered in its first batch of students in 1953, garnering families from the near heights areas. Louis Hesselden designed the building that looks similar to Wilson Junior High that opened southwest of this sight in the same year. When the Monroe area became saturated with businesses, Monroe's old building was used for district services, leveled to make way for a shopping mall, and finally in 2001 a new Monroe was opened on the city's far west side under the leadership of principal Vernon Martinez. (Courtesy APS.)

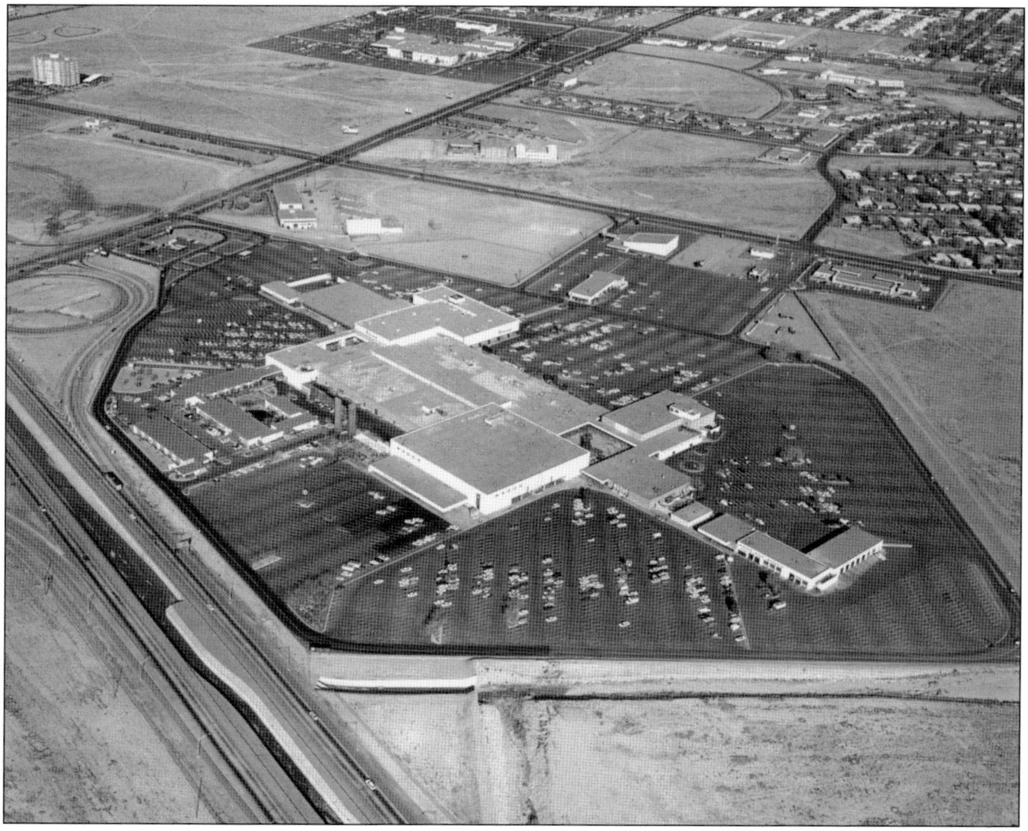

Winrock Mall, the first of the area's premier shopping mall areas, is visible in the above 1957 photograph. Monroe Middle School's complex is in the near upper left. (Courtesy APS.)

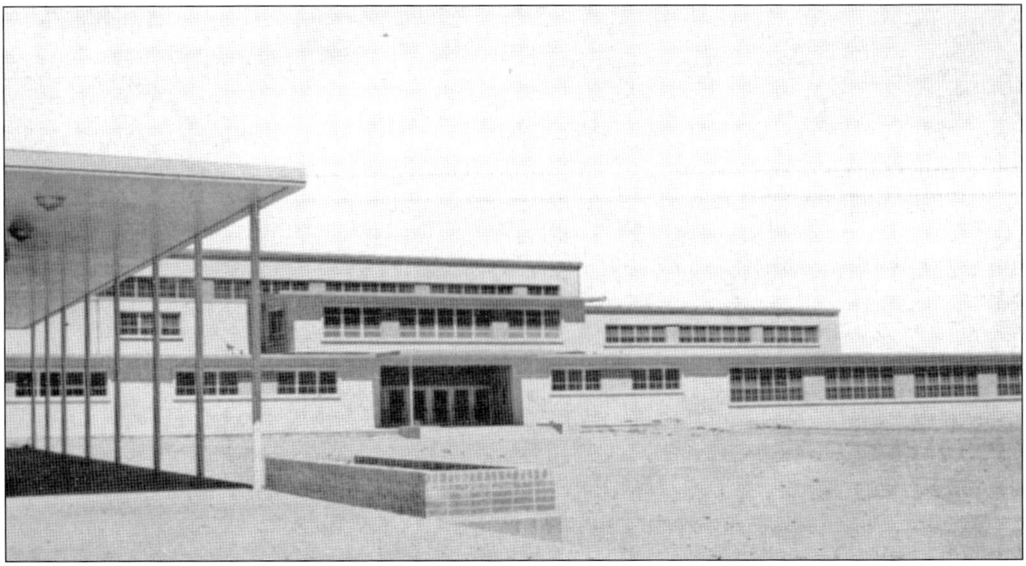

Much planning went into Albuquerque city schools' third comprehensive high school, Valley High (pictured above and below), which opened in 1954 under first principal Warren Smart. Louis Hesselden, staff architect, designed the plant. The steady school board approved Superintendent Milne's plan for the much-needed north valley school, adding to the two other comprehensive high schools already in operation in the city system, Albuquerque High and Highland High. (Courtesy APM.)

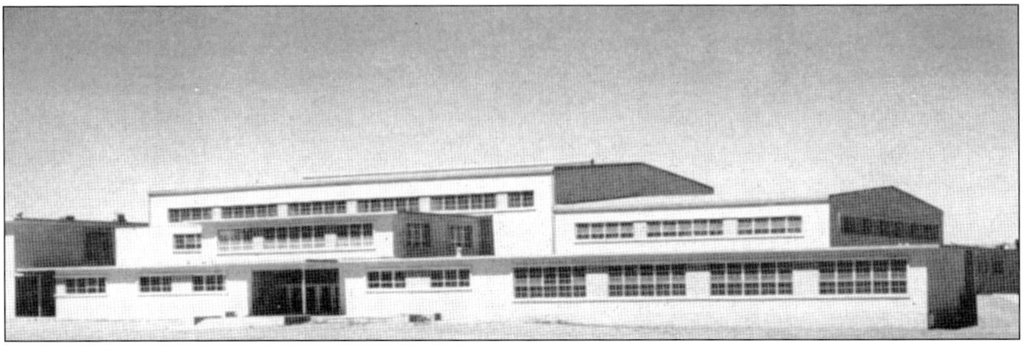

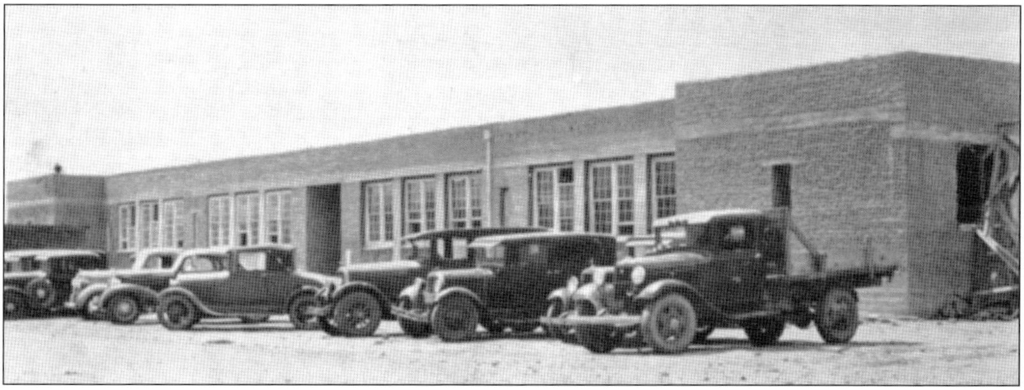

By 1938, old Five Points Elementary (above) was constructed by the county system with the aid of depression relief funds. Old Town Elementary (below) was sold to San Felipe de Neri Church Catholic parish mid-century and thrives today as a parochial school. (Both, courtesy APM.)

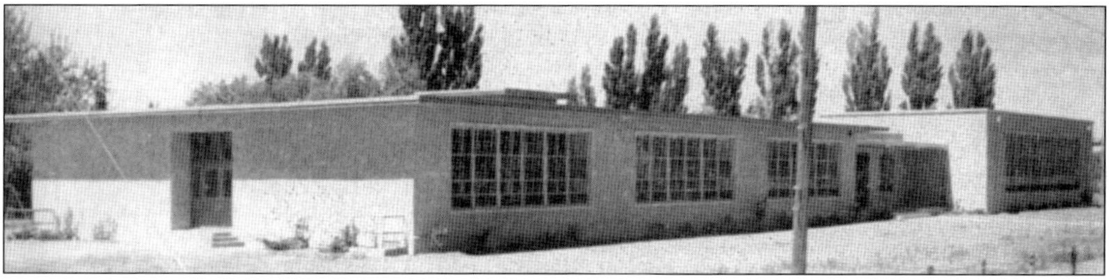

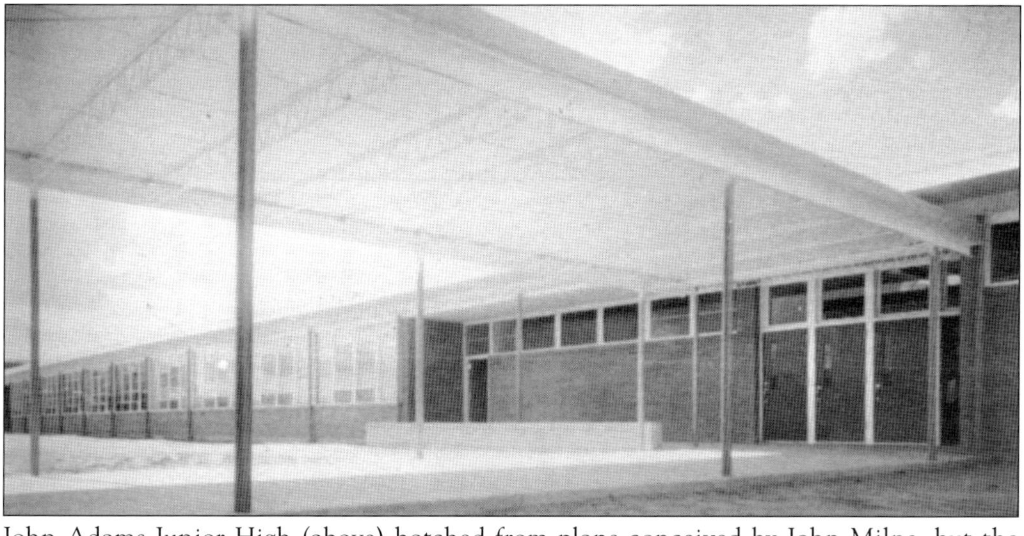

John Adams Junior High (above) hatched from plans conceived by John Milne, but the superintendent's retirement in 1955 and sudden death never allowed Milne to see how far his dreams and schemes would reach in Albuquerque. (Courtesy APM.)

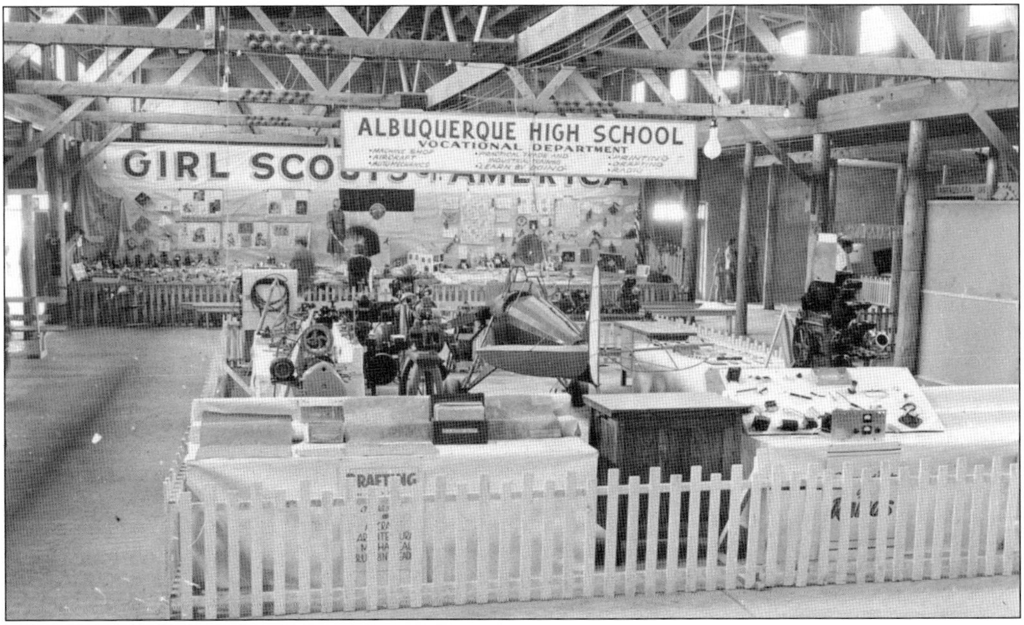


A belief—be it progressive or realistic—existed in the 1950s that public schools should offer a range of educational options for students. This c. 1944 vocational education display at the New Mexico State Fair hosted by Albuquerque High showcased the myriads of employment paths a student might choose while attending the city's high school. (Courtesy ERH.)

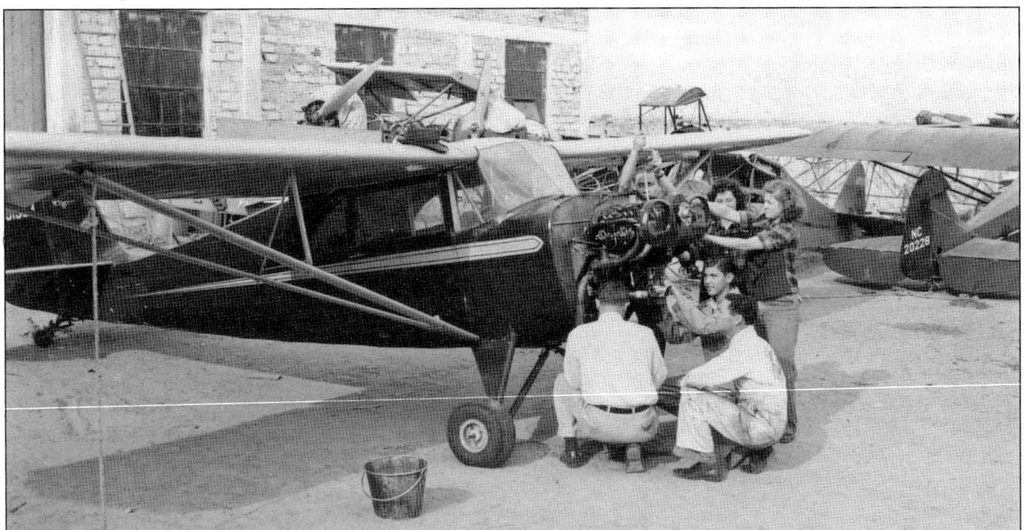

As one of the lone larger cities positioned in the southwest along Route 66 and the railroad lines between Kansas City, Denver, and Los Angeles, Albuquerque stood poised to respond to the material and labor needs of World War II. Albuquerque High prepared young and old alike during World War II to fill job demands. A print shop, machine shop, wood shop, and more opened up 12 hours per day to respond to training needs not only of the high schoolers, but of older "students" at night and on weekends. Visible above, a small group of Albuquerque High students work on an airplane under the supervision of Mr. Sullins, who was, per E.R. Herrington, "an expert welder and certified pilot" at "West Airport." (Courtesy of ERH.)

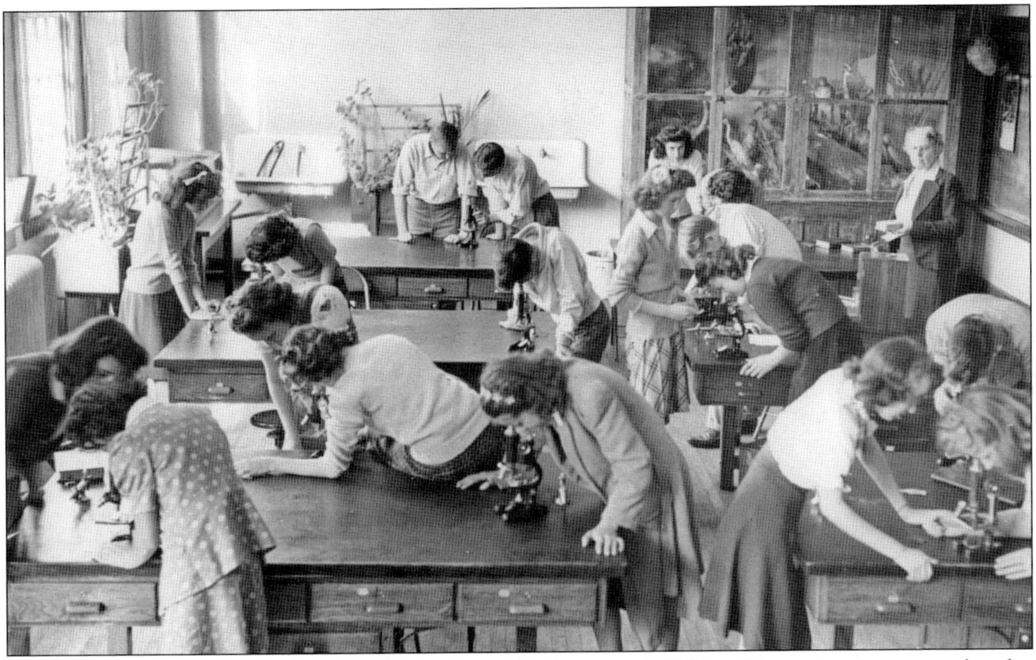

Above, girls in a science class at Albuquerque High around 1944 utilize microscopes under the tutelage of teacher Anna Reiter. We continue to close the gap on educational expectations of boys and girls in public schools concerning math, sciences, and technologies, but powerfully embedded cultural ideas from the 1950s continue. (Courtesy of ERH.)

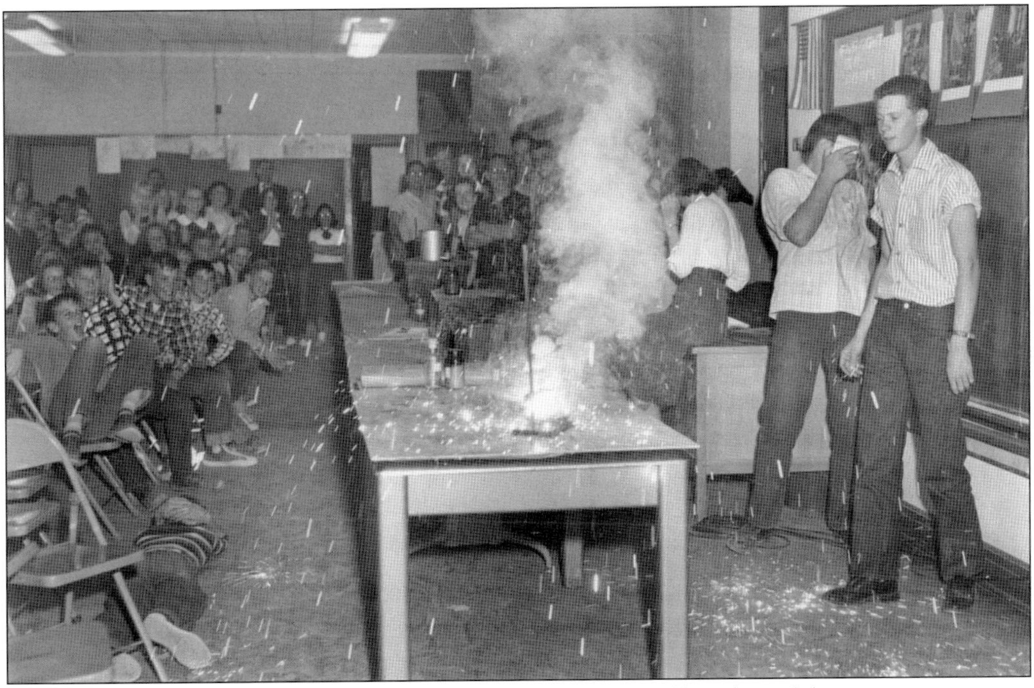

This photograph speaks to many as the fun and excitement of hands-on laboratory experiences learned in schools evoke memories. The c. 1944 photograph above, taken at Albuquerque High, tells a story to which many can relate. (Courtesy of ERH.)

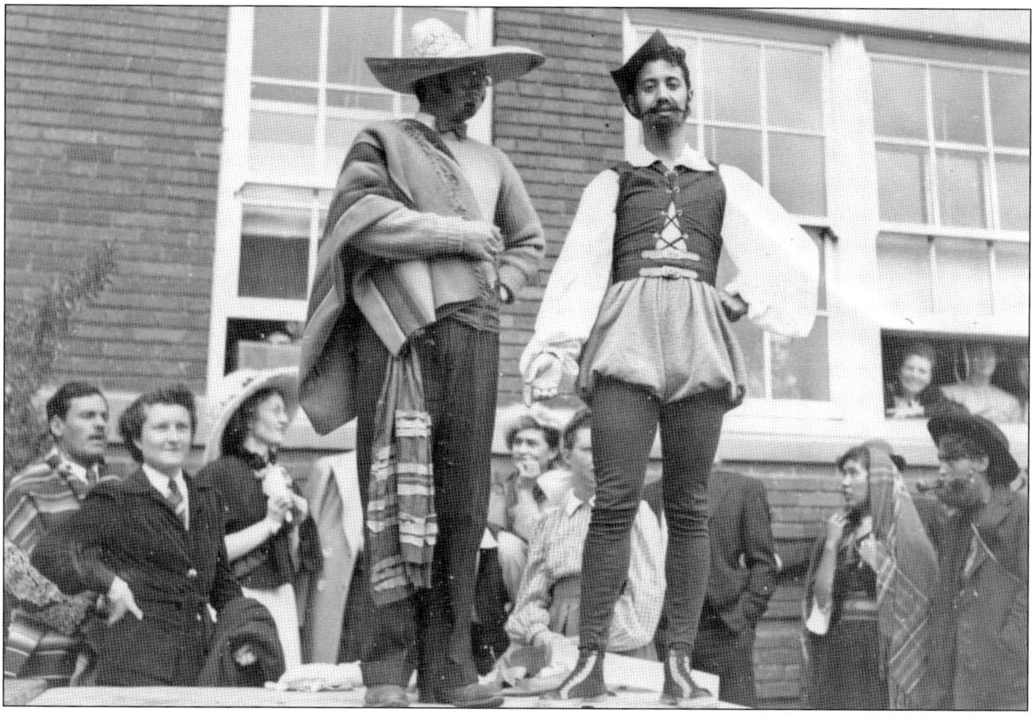

While no community is a utopia, Albuquerque (in studies and retrospectives) continues to reflect a historical better-than-average acceptance of ethnic, religious, economic, and social diversity as the town grew and took wings. Above, students of Albuquerque High represent the range of diversity present in Albuquerque in a c. 1944 Pioneer Day demonstration. (Courtesy of ERH.)

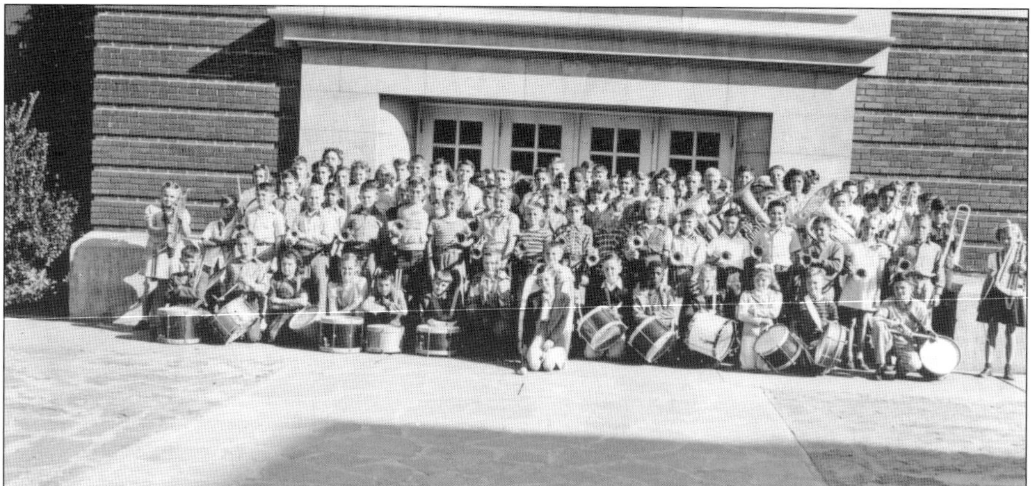

The Higgins family's commitment to music education is legendary in the Albuquerque area. The family founded Hummingbird Music Camp in the Jemez Mountains, which still hosts thousands of area students each year as they participate in clinics and hone their skills. Visible above is the legendary City Elementary Band that rehearsed each Saturday morning at Albuquerque High during the 1940s and beyond under the direction of renowned area music director Mr. Higgins. The band, at times reaching nearly 100 members, marched and played at numerous community events. (Courtesy ERH.)

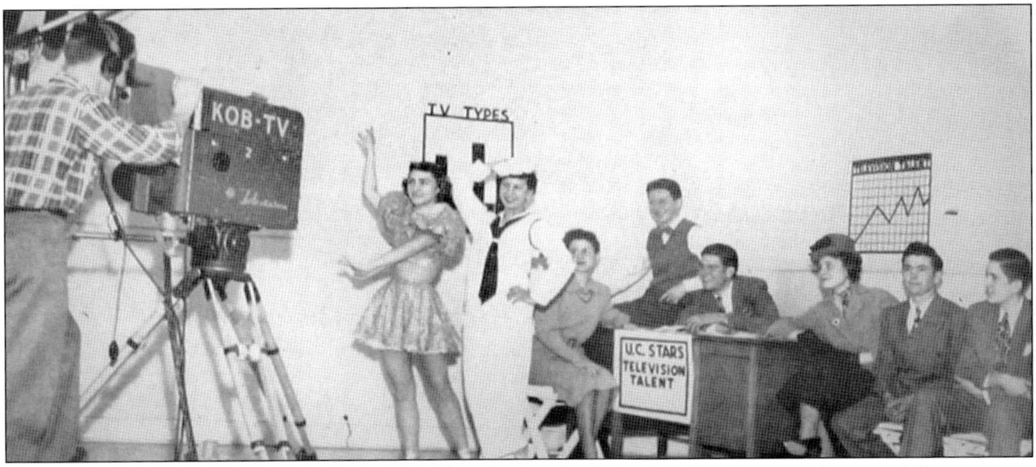


Technology was exploding in 1950—telephones, mail service, and radio transformed Albuquerque and America. The phenomenon of television reached the city, and Albuquerque High students report they were the first high school group in America to broadcast a television performance. Above, Albuquerque High students perform for a television camera. (Courtesy *La Reata*.)

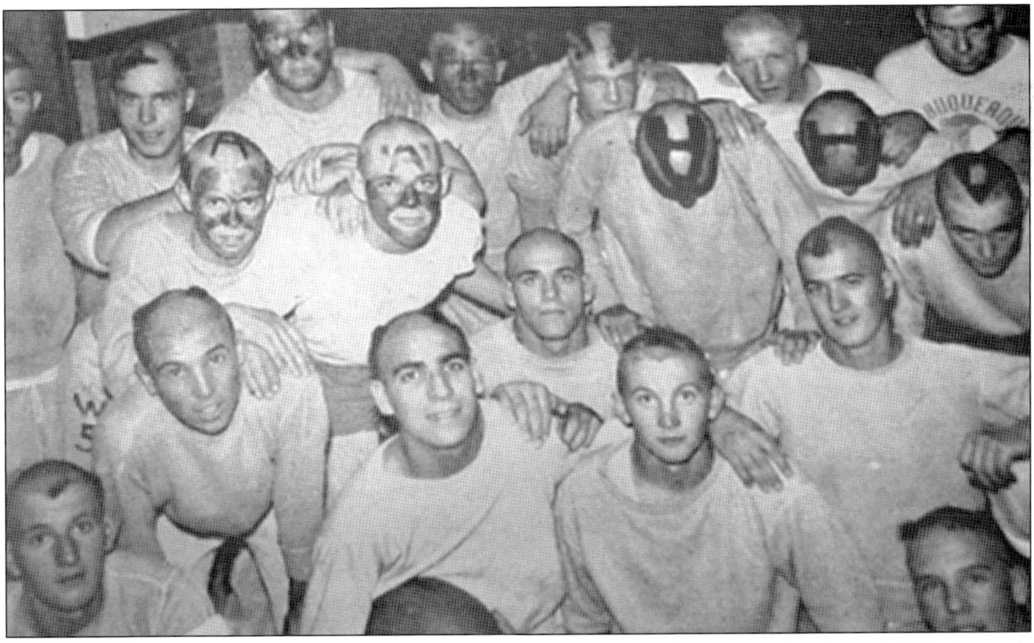

These proud boys of Albuquerque High sport their hazing hair cuts in the fall of 1950. Rituals and celebrations were commonplace in schools during this time as were, unfortunately, exclusion and discrimination. Superintendent John Milne actively worked to create a sense of openness and acceptance in Albuquerque, both concerning ethnicity and religion. (Courtesy *La Reata*.)

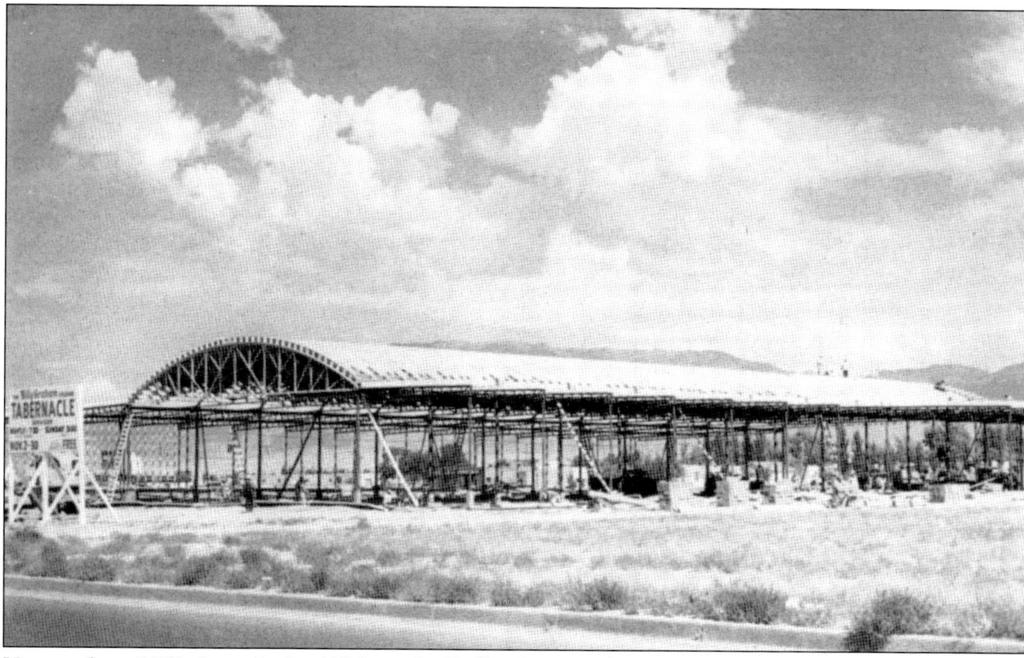


Known from 1953 through the 1990s as the Roller Drome Skating Rink, this structure's construction was put on hold by the building materials shortage of the Korean War, only to receive a go-ahead for the Sanderson family to quickly construct the building when evangelist Billy Graham announced his coming to Albuquerque in late 1952 for a multiple-day engagement. Located on San Mateo just south of Central Avenue, the curved roof is still recognizable. Many seasoned residents recall the excitement of this tabernacle event. (Courtesy APM.)

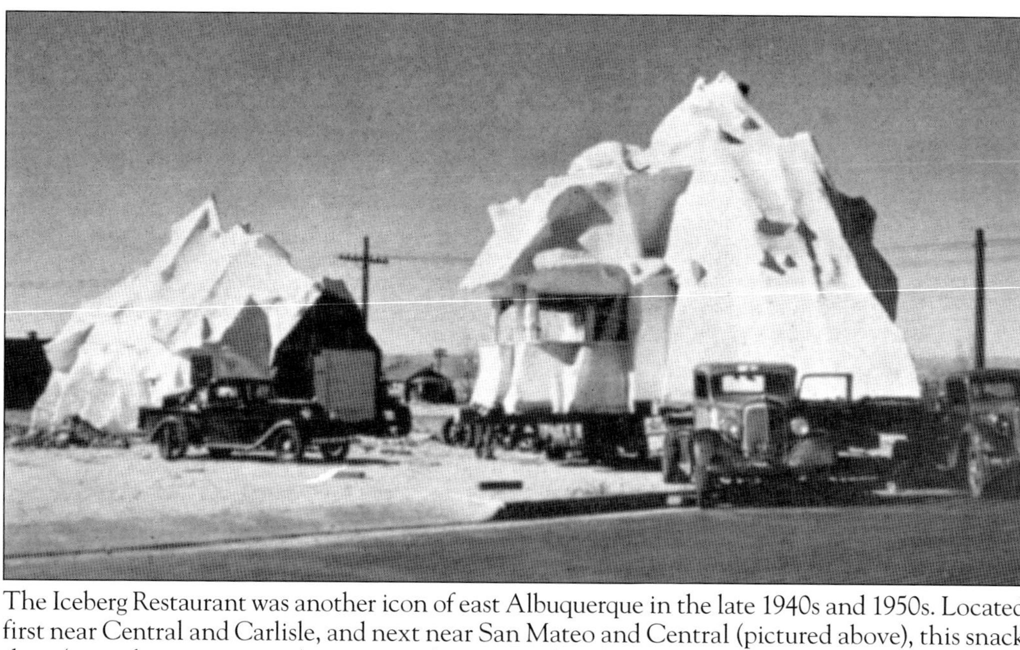

The Iceberg Restaurant was another icon of east Albuquerque in the late 1940s and 1950s. Located first near Central and Carlisle, and next near San Mateo and Central (pictured above), this snack shop (turned service station) was a city favorite. Urban legend indicates that the structure was dismantled in the 1950s and moved north to Bernalillo until its demise. (Courtesy APM.)

# *Six*

# Schools in Albuquerque 1955–1989

The United States entered the Korean War in June 1950, and a wave of intense fear concerning the spread of Communism swept across America, culminating in 1957 when the Russians successfully launched the first artificial Earth-orbiting satellite, *Sputnik*, designed to gather scientific data. These events combined to set the educational community of the United States into a scramble to ramp up science and math curriculum. The post–World War II GIs' children were in upper elementary grades, and in Albuquerque the need for junior highs and high schools created a strain on the city's public school systems.

At the same time, scientists and teachers were flooding into the Albuquerque area to staff Sandia Labs, Kirtland Air Force Base, Lovelace Hospital, APS, and a myriad of other needs throughout the city, bringing their families with them. Between 1955 and 1990, APS constructed or significantly refurbished nearly 100 schools. Largely due to a philosophy begun by longtime Albuquerque leader Clyde Tingley, the city—and therefore APS—followed a tradition of annexing land and schools into the current system, maintaining singular city-based control rather than leave smaller new cities or districts to govern themselves.

Beginning in 1950, Albuquerque's multicultural community spearheaded an organized effort to legally ban racial discrimination, and by 1952 the City Commission proudly passed legislation on Lincoln's birthday creating penalties for discrimination in public places. The ordinance was put to the test shortly thereafter by a caravan of people bound from Phoenix to the National Association for the Advancement of Colored People convention in the Midwest. Purposefully, their cars stopped at different cafes and restaurants all along Route 66 through Albuquerque, and nowhere were the African Americans refused service or treated poorly, per their reports.

By the 1960s, the national zeitgeist turned to advocating for peace, and as the United States involvement in Vietnam dragged on into the 1970s, Albuquerque—with its ear to the pulse of the nation—reflected some student rebellion that fomented in June 1971 with overt rioting triggered out of the university area. However, Dr. Ernie Stapleton, as superintendent of APS from 1971 to 1977, moved Albuquerque through a peak growth era, and the community began to turn its eyes solely from its center toward the city's north and east.

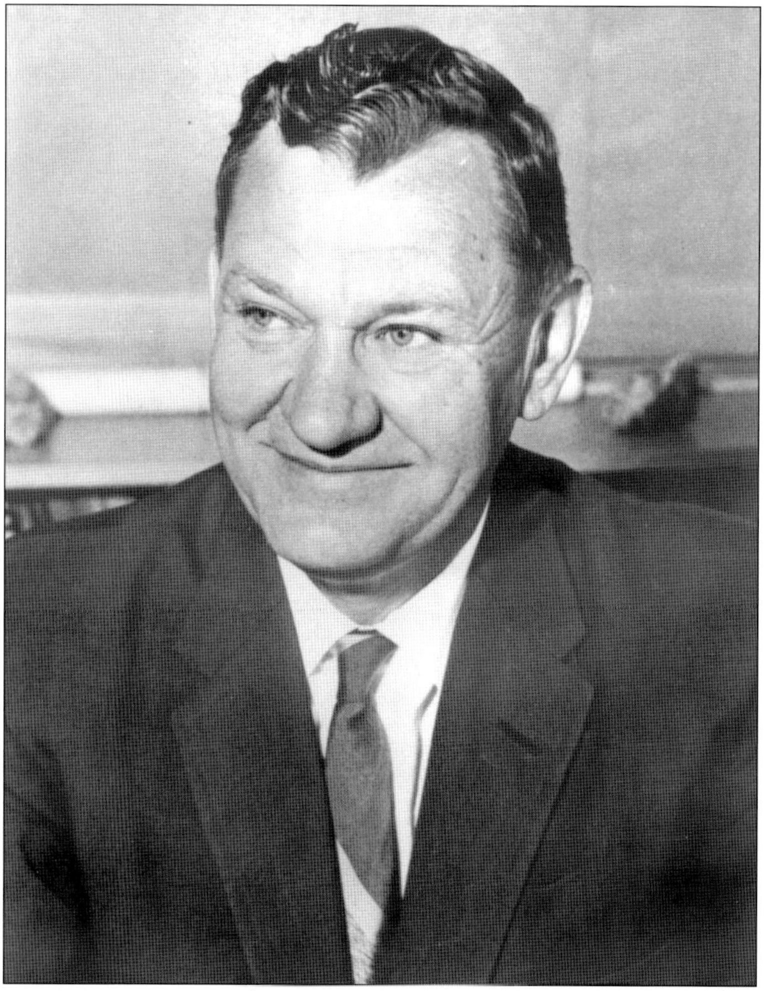

Charles Spain, left, took over as the APS superintendent after John Milne's retirement in 1955. He shepherded the city's school system as explosive growth continued, supported post-*Sputnik* era scientific curriculum, and assisted in opening over 40 city schools. Coincidentally, Spain succumbed to a sudden fatal heart attack in 1965, as did Milne in 1957. (Courtesy APS.)

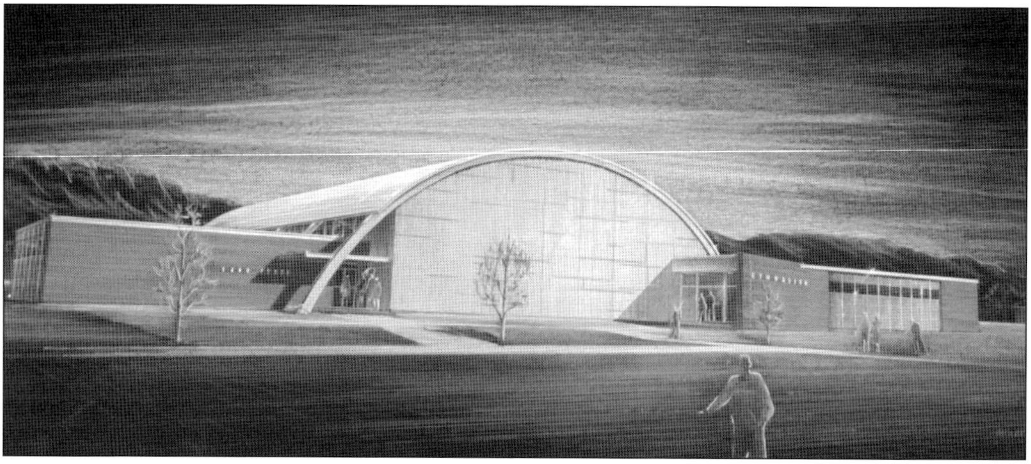

Above is architect Louis Hesselden's sketch for a proposed McKinley Middle School gym. McKinley opened in 1955 to serve the students near San Mateo Boulevard and Comanche. The gym did not develop as presented here but emerged as a square brick building. (Courtesy CSWR.)

Right, in March 1947, a page of *Albuquerque Progress Magazine* depicts children at The New Mexico Boys' Ranch. The Boys' Ranch sprang up in 1944 as an initiative funded by a cooperative of service and business groups to place young men transitioning from the state corrective Industrial School to productive lives. Philanthropic models of social education grew exponentially after World War II. The Boys' Ranch is still functioning today. (Courtesy APM.)

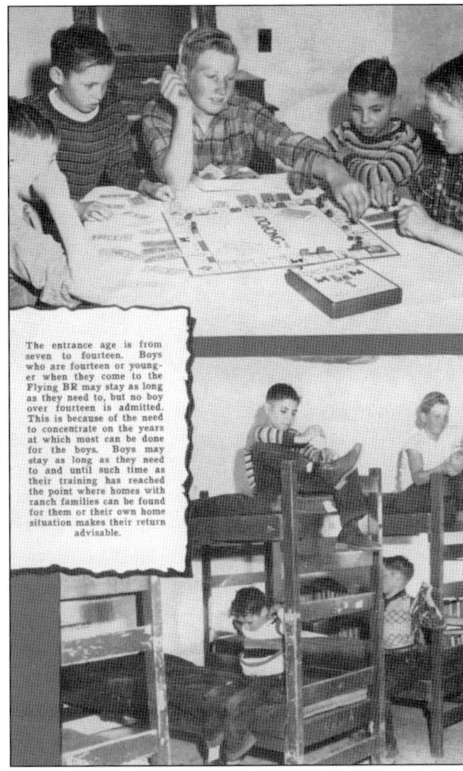

The entrance age is from seven to fourteen. Boys who are fourteen or younger when they come to the Flying BR may stay as long as they need to, but no boy over fourteen is admitted. This is because of the need to concentrate on the years at which most can be done for the boys. Boys may stay as long as they need to and until such time as their training has reached the point where homes with ranch families can be found for them or their own home situation makes their return advisable.

As World War II ended, America turned its prosperity toward helping its citizens who were less fortunate. Civic involvement, charity work, and social engagement prospered. Many schools and organizations emerged to assist those with special needs. Below, the Albuquerque cerebral palsy school is pictured in April 1949. (Courtesy APM.)

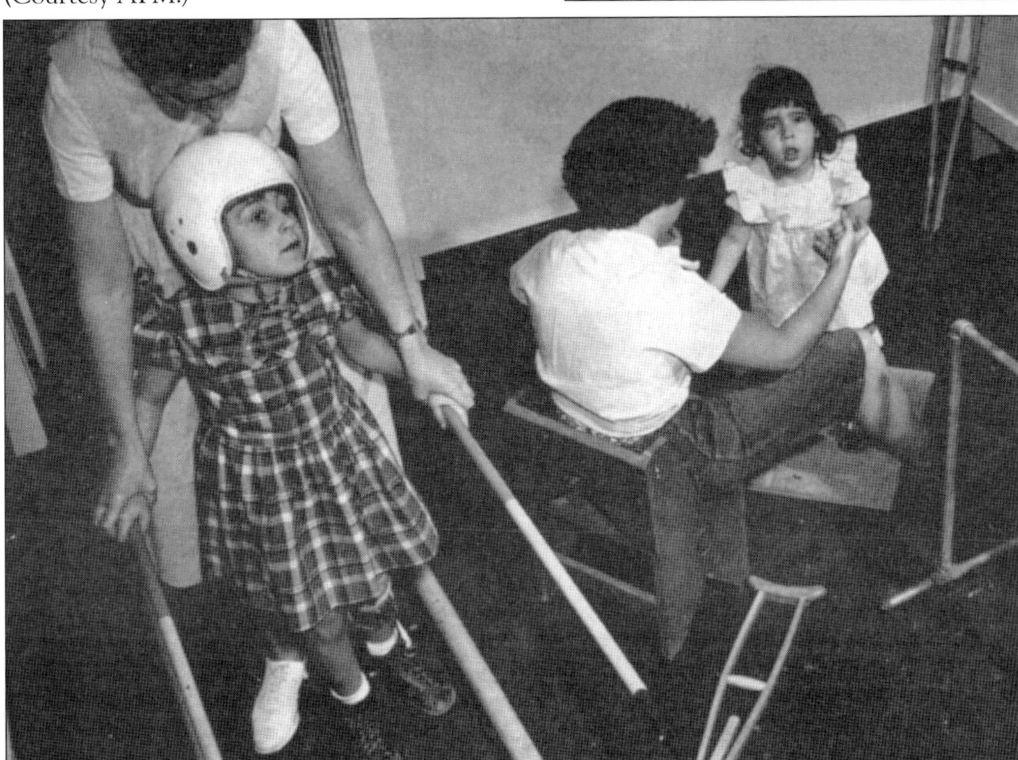

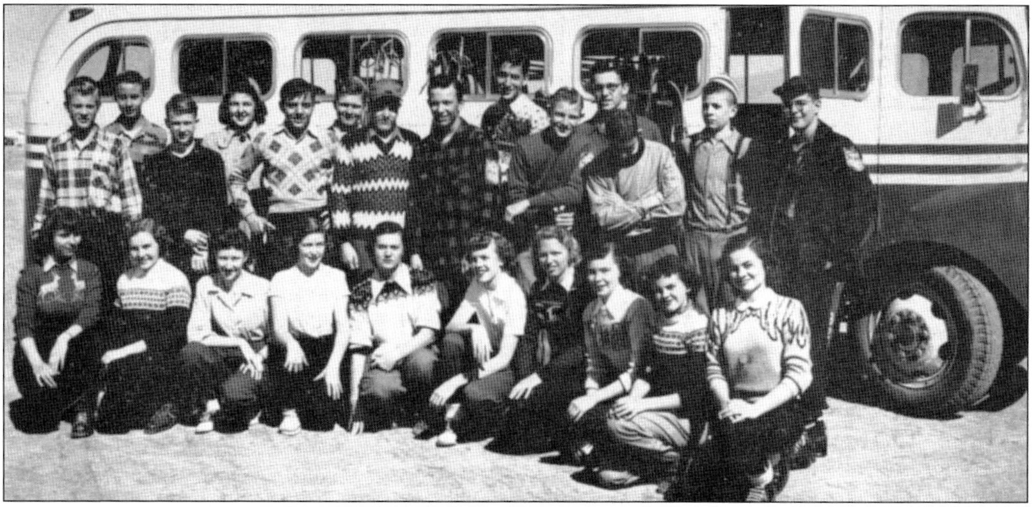

Pictured above is the 1949–1950 Highland High Ski Club, whose members ventured up the winding road to the east of the school into the mountains several times a year to ski at La Madera. At least one member recalls the group piling out of the bus in the midst of falling snow to collectively push the bus out of a drift. This image was included in the 1950 Highland High yearbook.

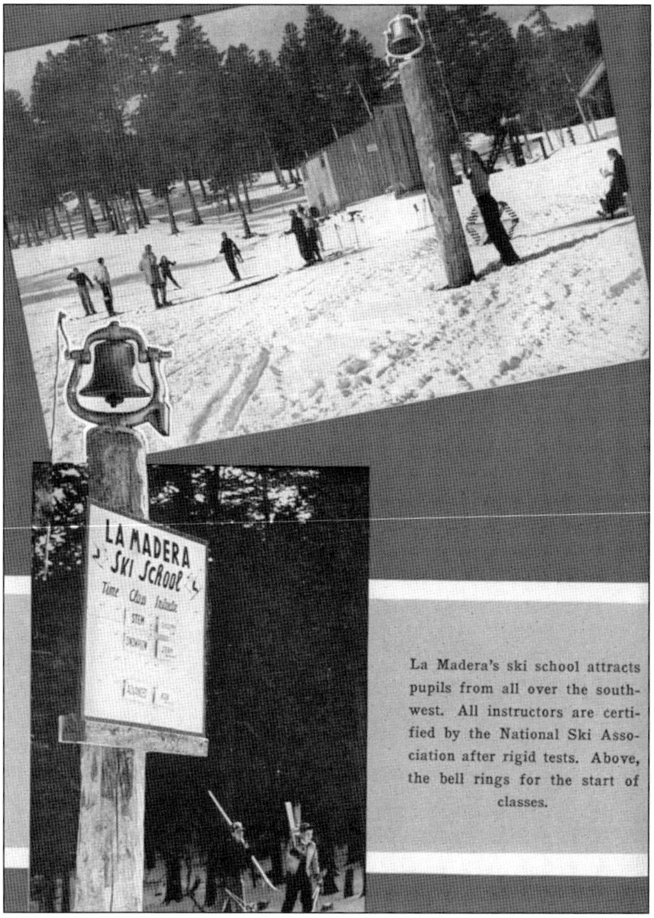


Despite the depressed economy, Robert Nordhaus, first president of the Albuquerque Ski Patrol, opened La Madera Ski Area with other ski fanatics in the Sandia Mountains in 1937. The area's scope and mission continued to grow. In 1957, Nordhaus and Ben Abruzzo shared operations, and by 1963 the area became Sandia Peak. Abruzzo, who was aboard the *Double Eagle V*'s 1981 successful balloon crossing of the Pacific, tragically died in an airplane crash is 1985. This image was taken in April 1948. (Courtesy APM.)

After World War II, Albuquerque's schools committed heavily to pledging resources to vocational training. Shown here is Albuquerque High's Mr. Perea in a 1944 photograph, helping a student to manage an adding machine to assist with the "Pereaville Store." (Courtesy ERH.)

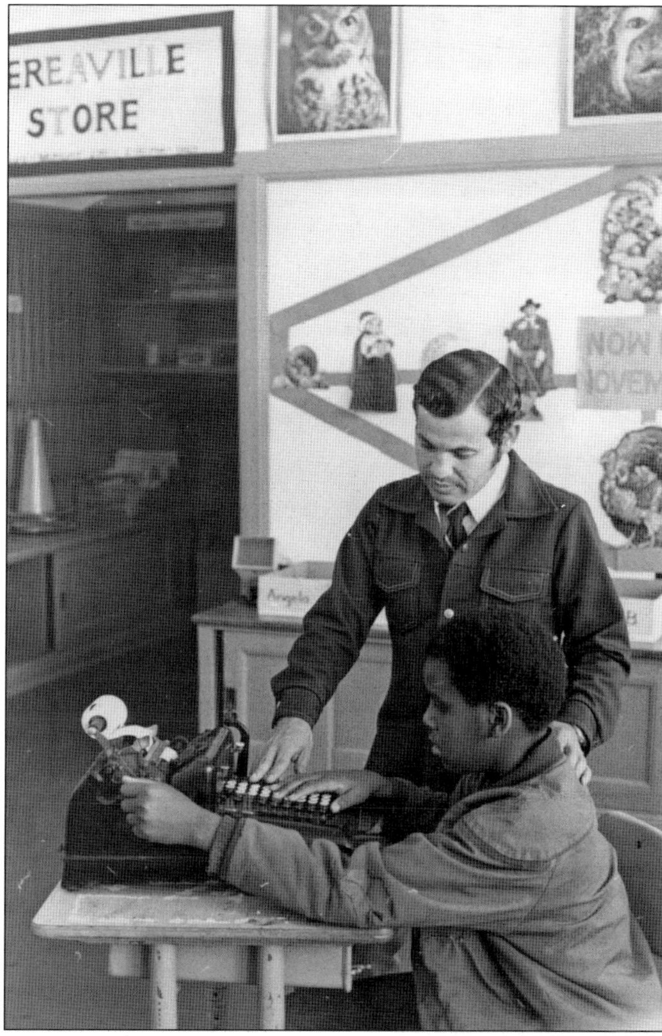


Below is Sombra del Monte Elementary School, which opened in 1955 and was termed Hoffmantown Elementary as it was being designed. The school was one of many that kicked off a new style of building design with large window panels, colorful tile, and beveled breezeway covers. Sam Hoffman, along with contemporary Albuquerque builders Latif Hyder, Ed Snow, and Dale Bellamah, peppered northeast Albuquerque with thousands of residences between 1955 and 1965. Success cannot always be measured in dollars, however, and Hoffman's life ended tragically in 1959 when he killed his wife and then himself. (Courtesy APM.)

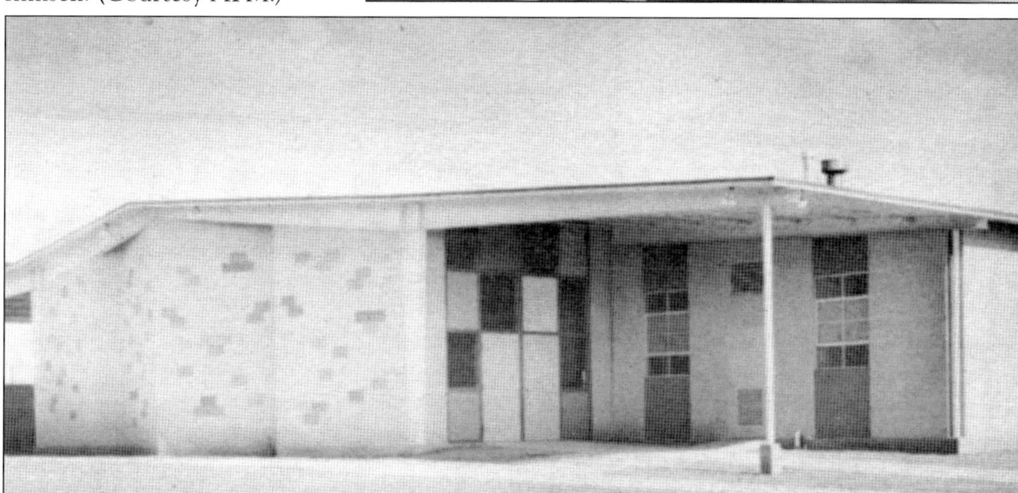

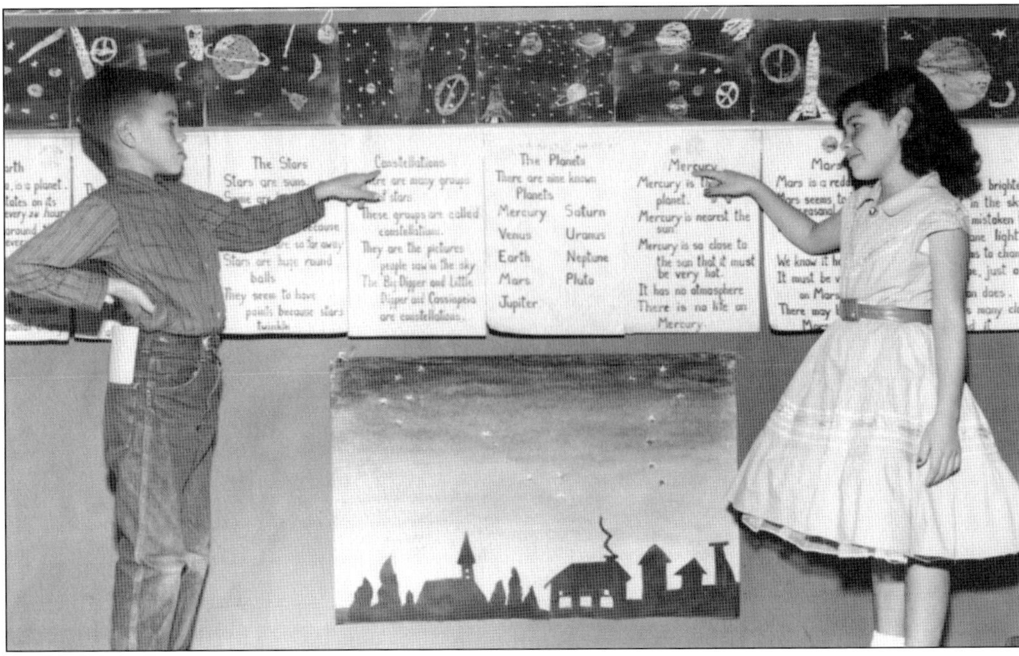


The United States received a wake-up call in October 1957 when the Russians launched *Sputnik*. A sudden interest in science and math swept across America's schools, and Albuquerque—home to Sandia Labs—was no exception. Pictured above and below are APS students demonstrating their skills. (Courtesy CSWR, ERH PICT 000-299-0506 and PICT 000-299-0490.)

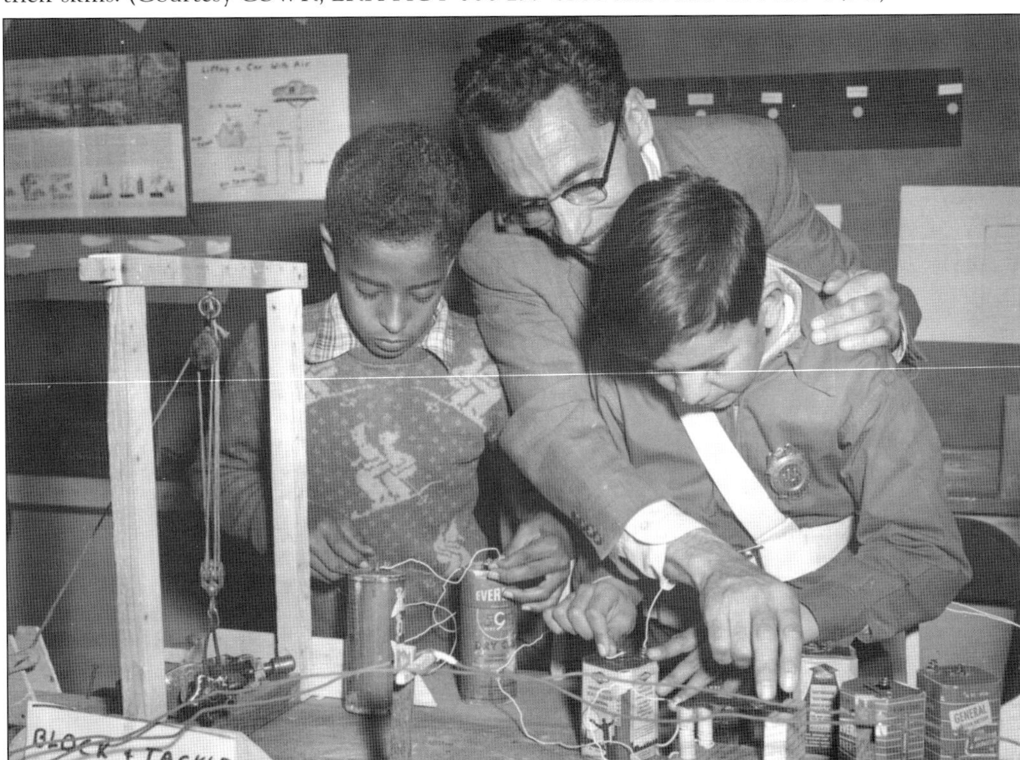

At right is a sketch by architect Louis Hesselden for an addition to Zia Elementary. APS has a continued commitment to keep all facilities updated and equal in provisions of building types, materials, and equipment. Other APS schools that opened in the later half of the 1950s include Armijo, Aztec, Eubank, Acoma, Alameda, Hodgin, San Antonito, Taft, Alamosa, and Zuni. (Courtesy CSWR.)

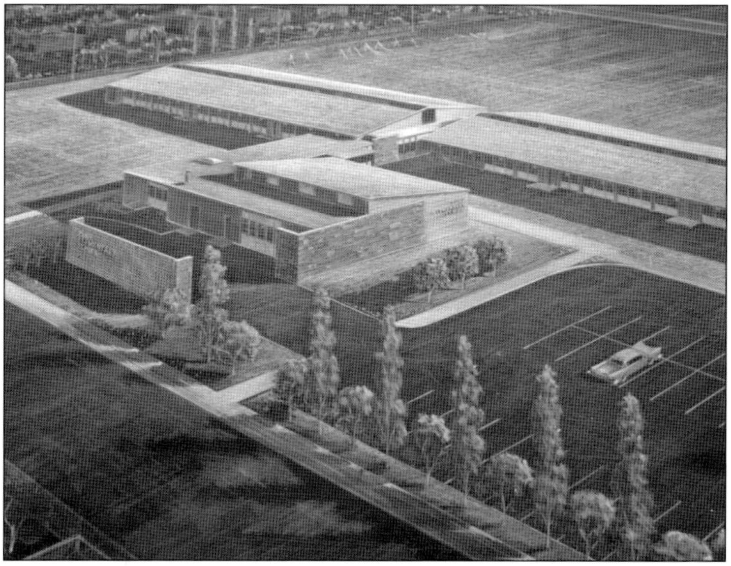

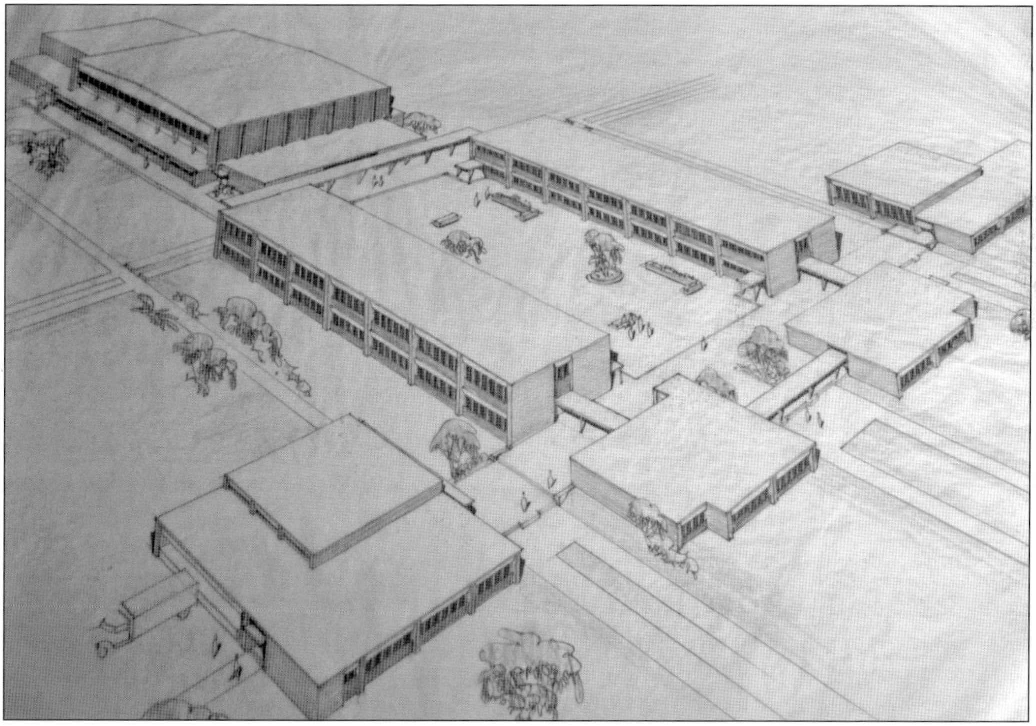

This Louis Hesselden architectural sketch projects the layout for Madison Middle School, opened in 1958. APS had established a precedent by this time of naming middle (then junior high) schools for United States presidents, high schools for geographical features near the school, and elementary schools either for famous New Mexicans or streets near which the school was located. (Courtesy CSWR.)

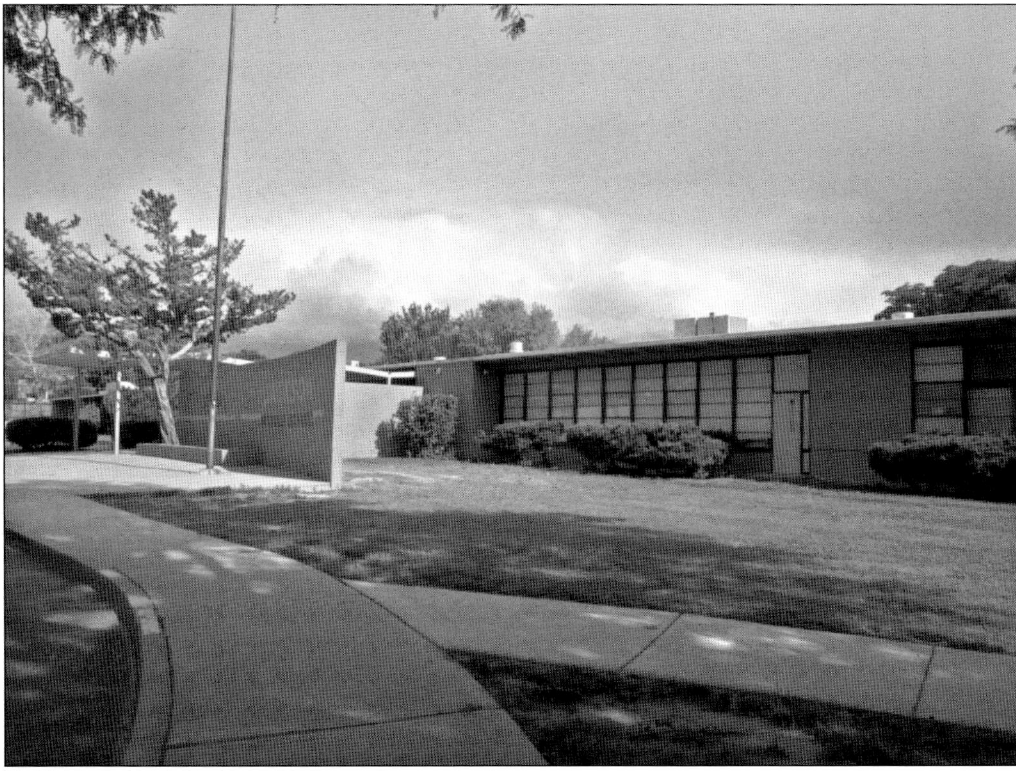

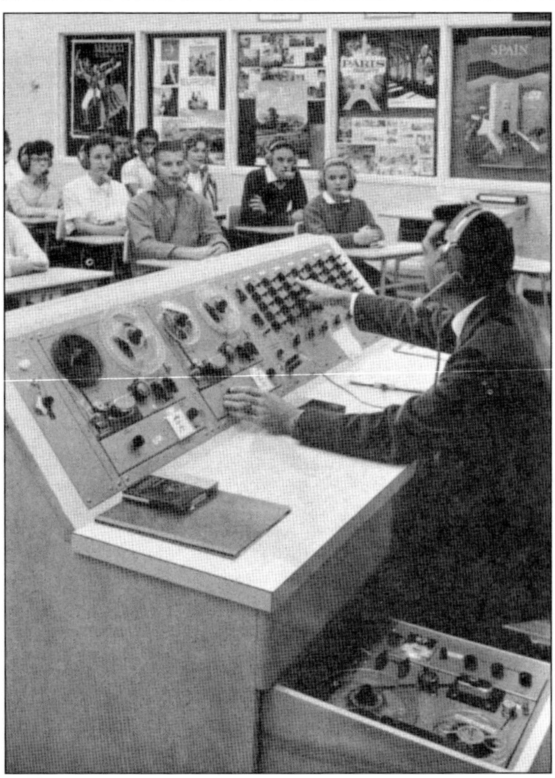


Above is Jackson Middle School, which housed as many as 1,300 students in the 1970s just before nearby Eisenhower school opened. Veteran staff remember many late 1960s to early 1970s schools operating on split shifts out of pods as APS rose to the challenge of serving the by then school-aged baby boomers. Left is a 1960s language lab with state-of-the-art equipment delivering audio instruction at Albuquerque High. (Courtesy APM.)

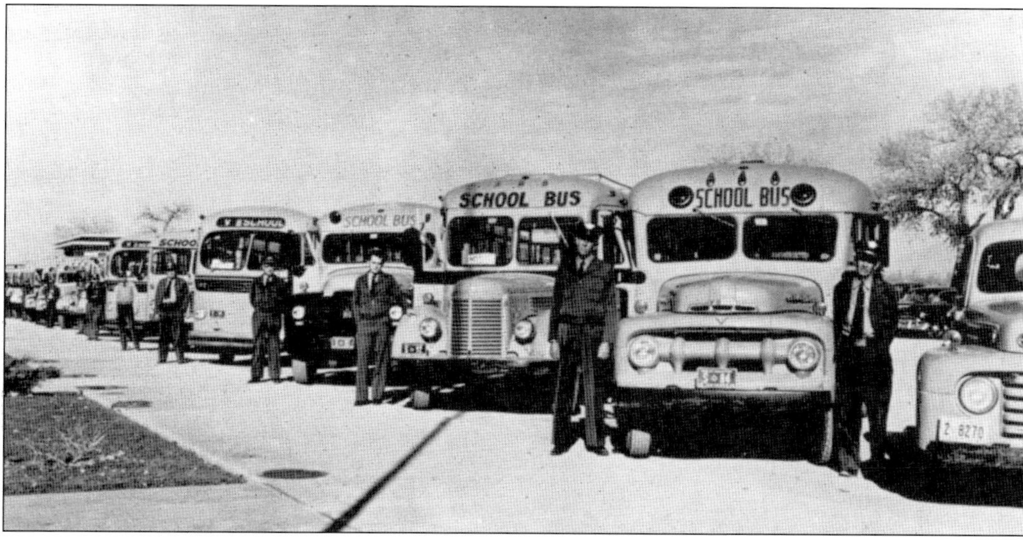


Lined up sharp and ready, above, are the Valley High School buses in 1956. Below are the drivers in snappy ties, caps, and jackets. Both images appeared in the 1956 Valley High yearbook.

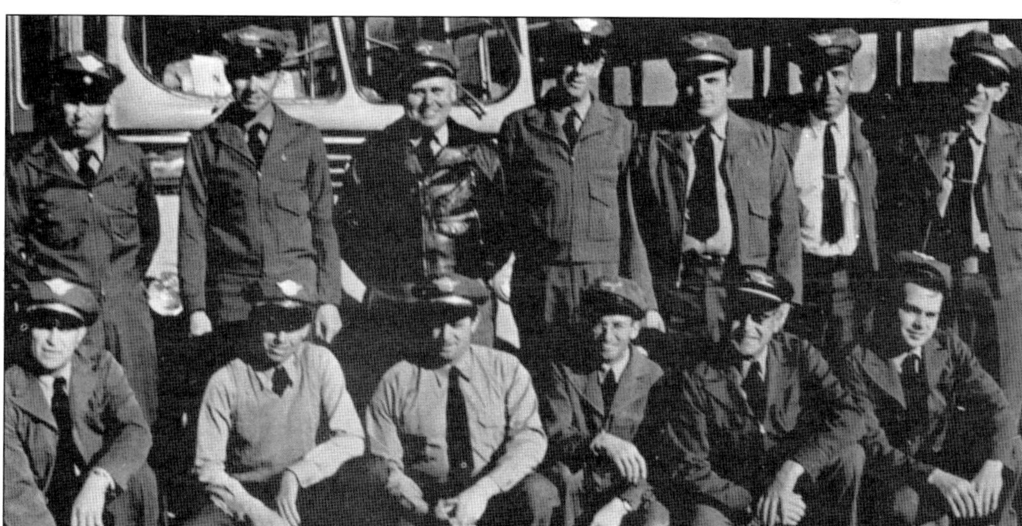

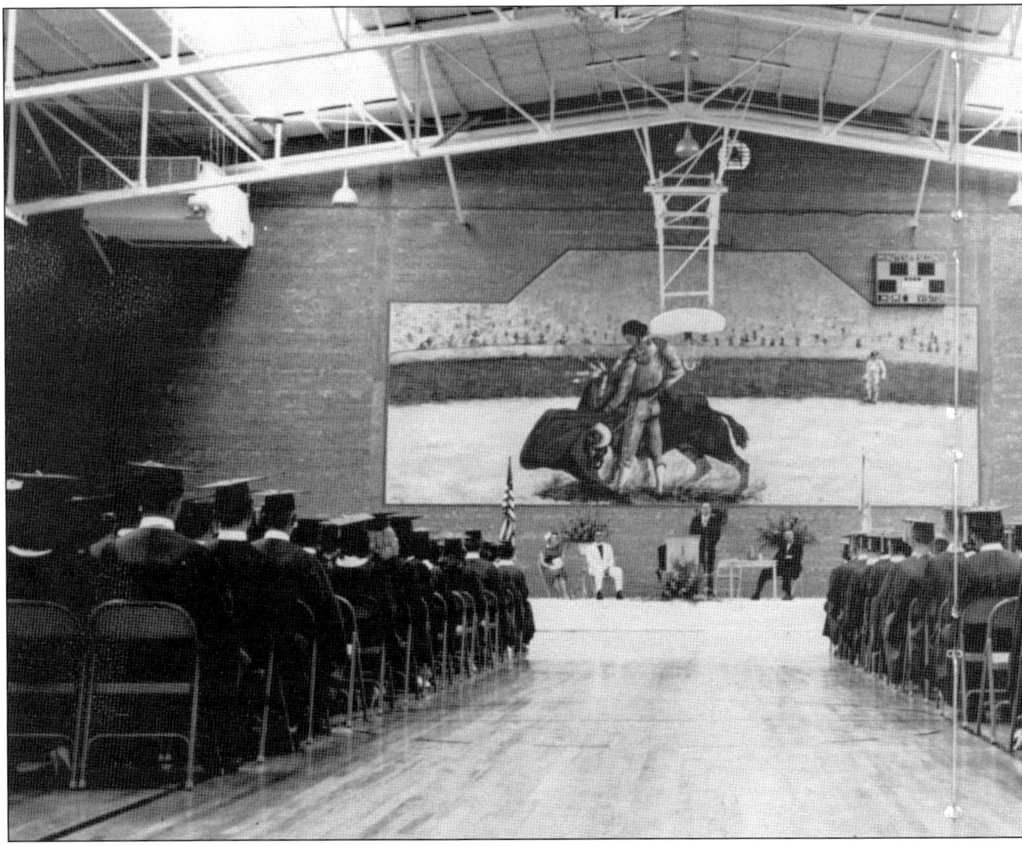

Sandia High opened in 1958 under the first principal LeRoy Brannon. The first graduation was held in the school's new gym with a prominent mural of the mascot, the Matador. This image appeared in the 1959 Sandia High yearbook.

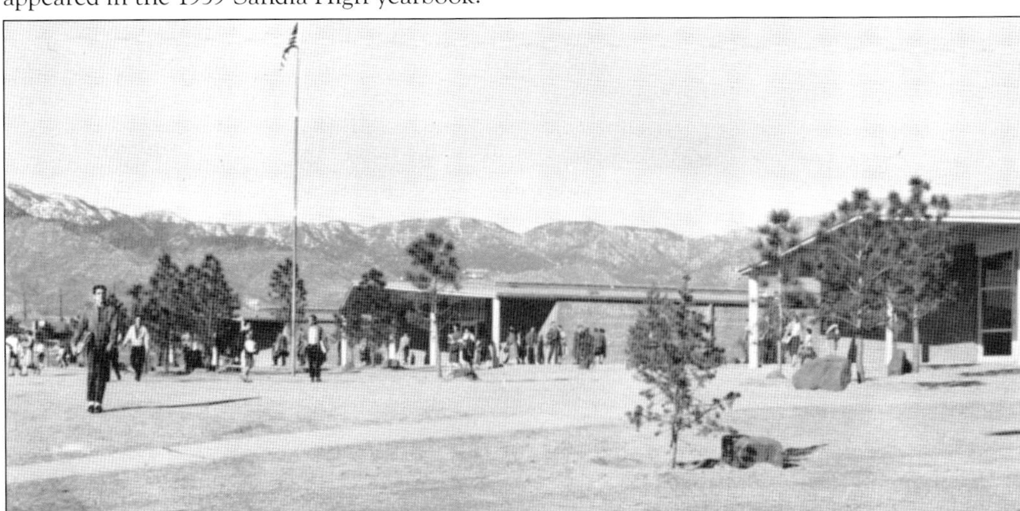

This 1961 Sandia High yearbook photograph shows the campus with the Sandia Mountains as its backdrop. Sandia and Manzano Highs shared campuses and split off slowly to form their own separate entities.

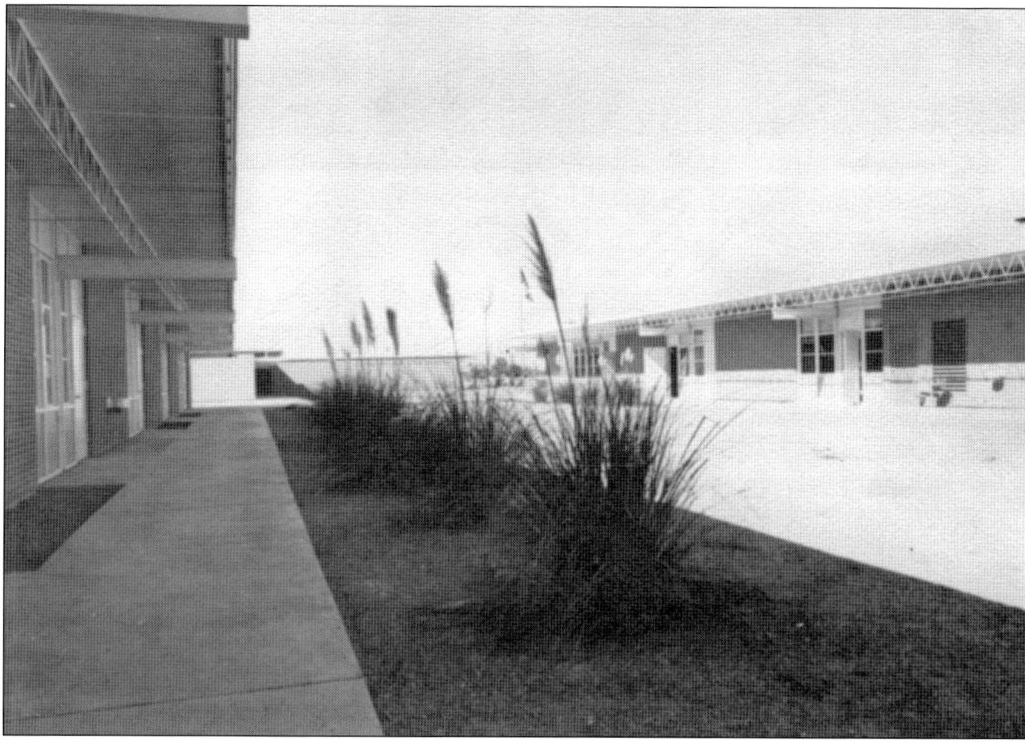

Rio Grande High opened in the fall of 1959, choosing the raven as its mascot and under the direction of principal A.B. Chavez. The first football coach was Al Wright, and the inaugural basketball coach was Larry Tuttle. Pictured above is a slice of desert campus. Students are pictured below around 1963 in front of the newly constructed gym. Both images appeared in the 1963 Rio Grande yearbook.

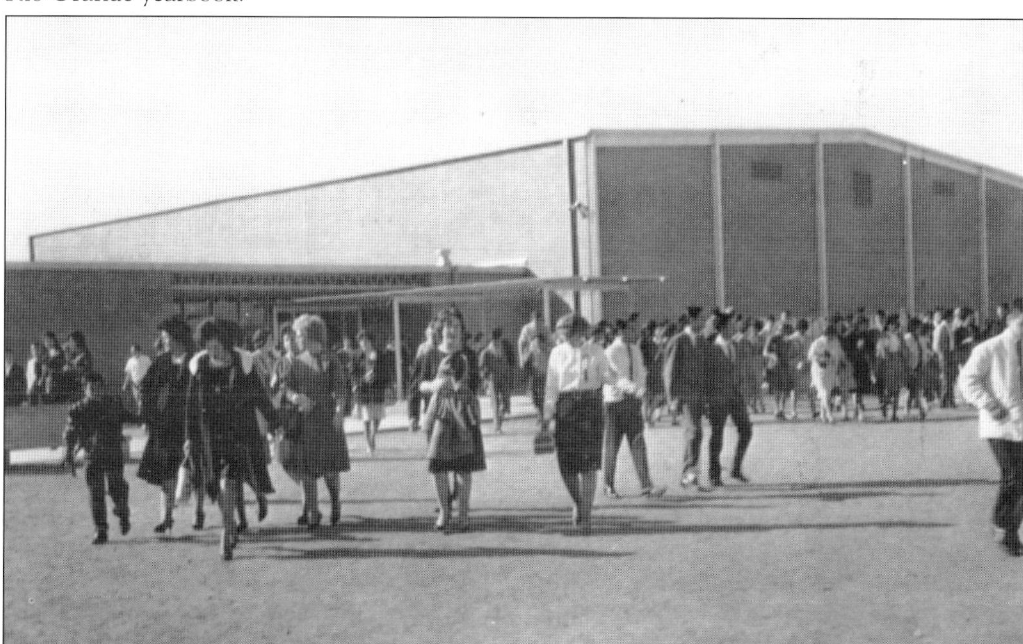

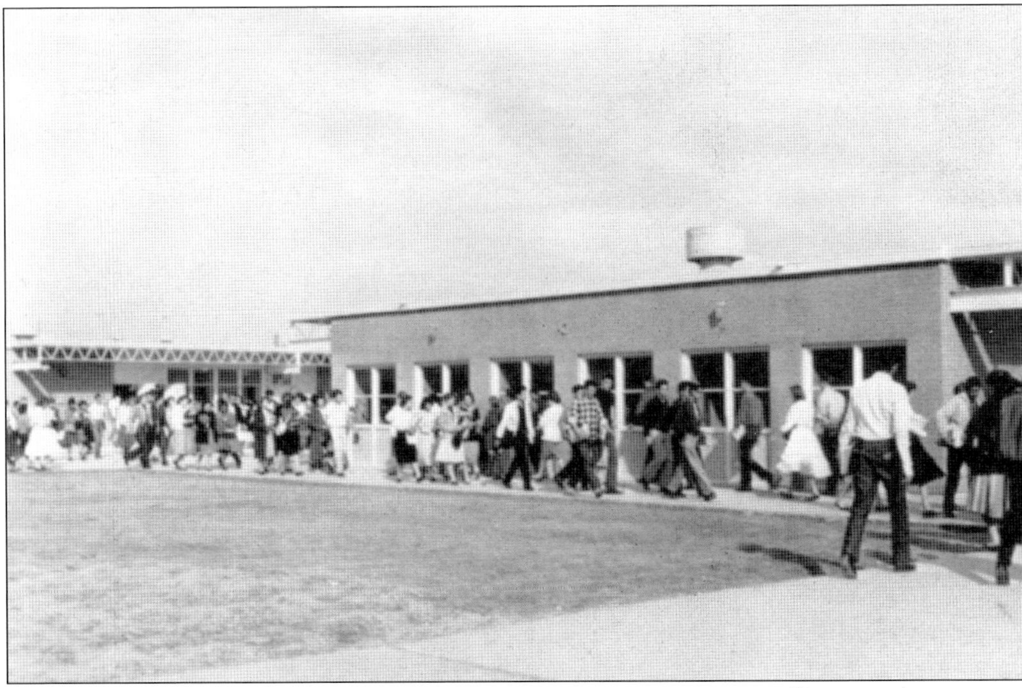

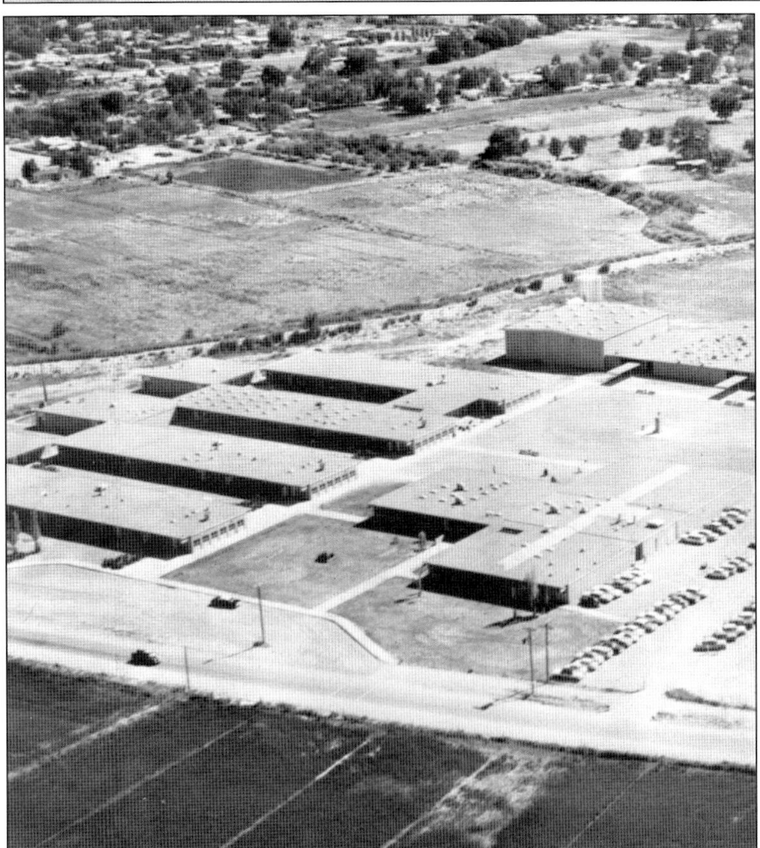

Construction continued at Rio Grande High, pictured above in a c. 1963 Rio Grande yearbook image. At left is a c. 1964 aerial view of the Rio Grande campus that also appeared in the yearbook. Those who know "Rio" find this photograph fascinating—including the infamous "ditch bank" clearly pictured east of the campus.

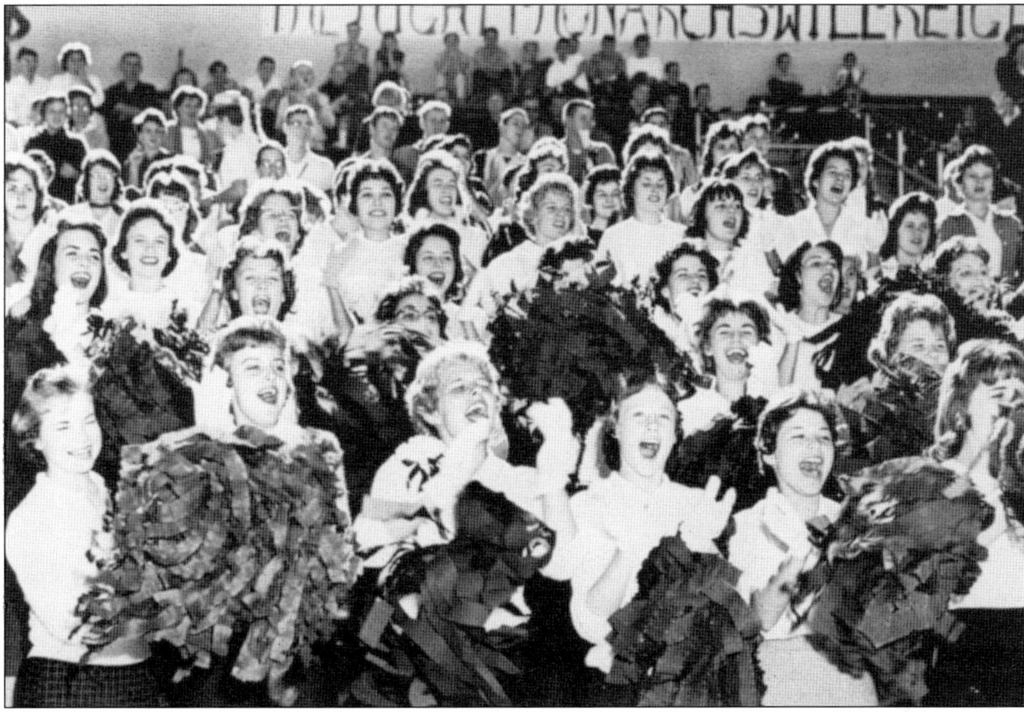

Manzano High's pep squad celebrates in the Manzano High gym during the fall of 1961. The gym was the first building constructed for the new city east side high school, which partially opened in fall of 1960 in order for the sports season to begin even while the Manzano Monarchs continued to attend classes at overcrowded Sandia High. Then a lonely outpost, today the gym and campus form a full urban school setting and students from the East Mountains of Albuquerque are bused in to attend the Monarch Palace. This image appeared in the 1961 Manzano yearbook.

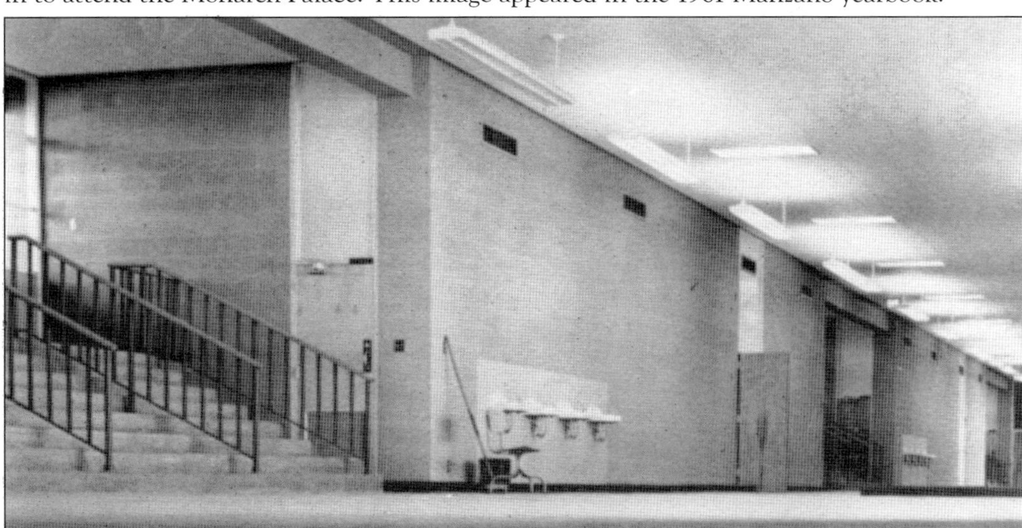

The Manzano High halls opened to students for a preview on December 18, 1960, under the watch of first principal Jewell Brown. There was no senior class in 1961—they all remained at Sandia. Manzano's first senior class crossed the stage in spring of 1962. This image appeared in the 1961 Manzano yearbook.

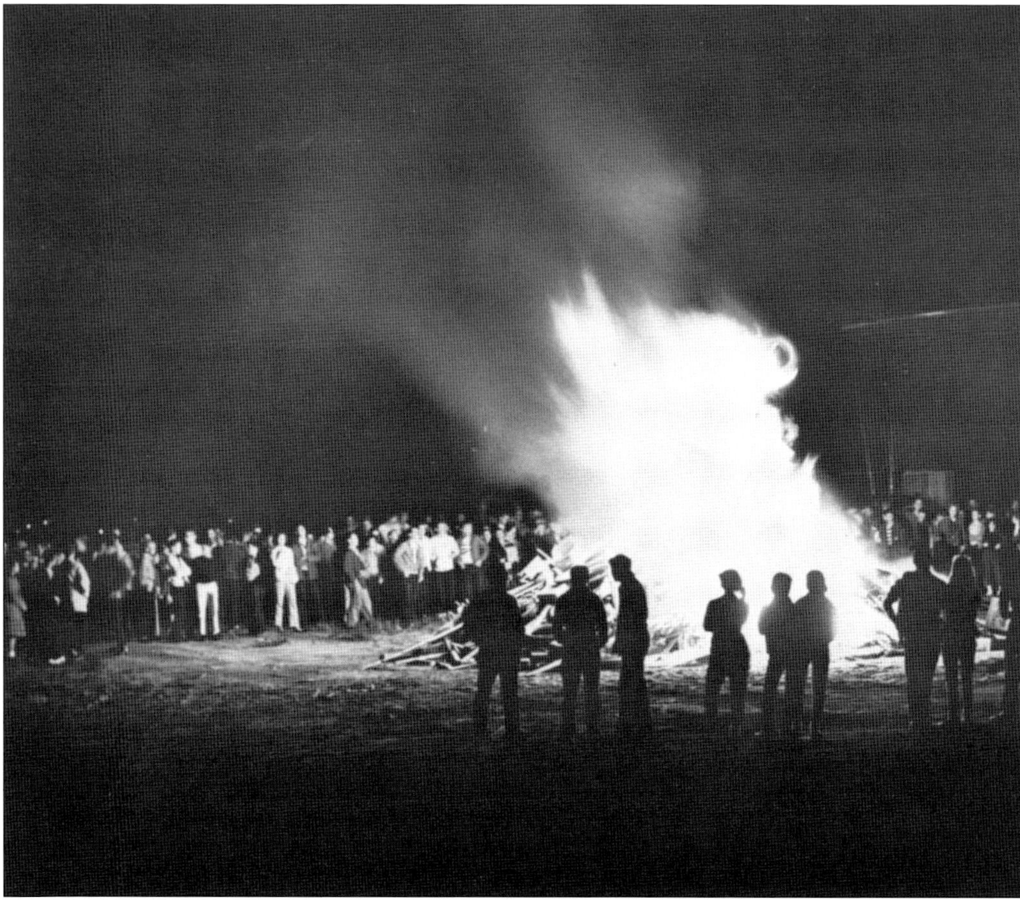

Homecoming bonfires were a long-held tradition in Albuquerque but were phased out by the early 1970s as litigation and supervision issues came to the fore. This image of the fall 1960 Manzano homecoming bonfire was featured in the 1961 Manzano yearbook.

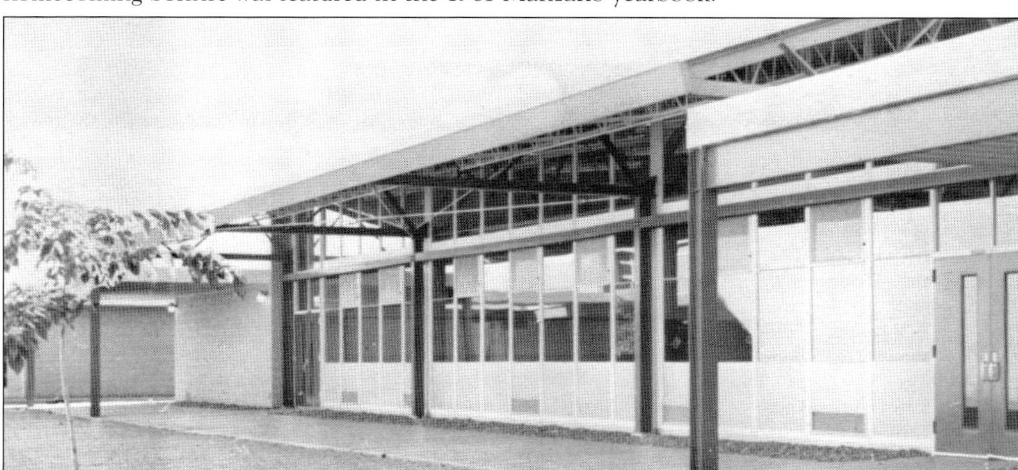

Construction continued at a rapid clip at all APS schools in the 1960s. This image of a nearly completed building at Manzano High appeared in the 1963 Manzano yearbook.

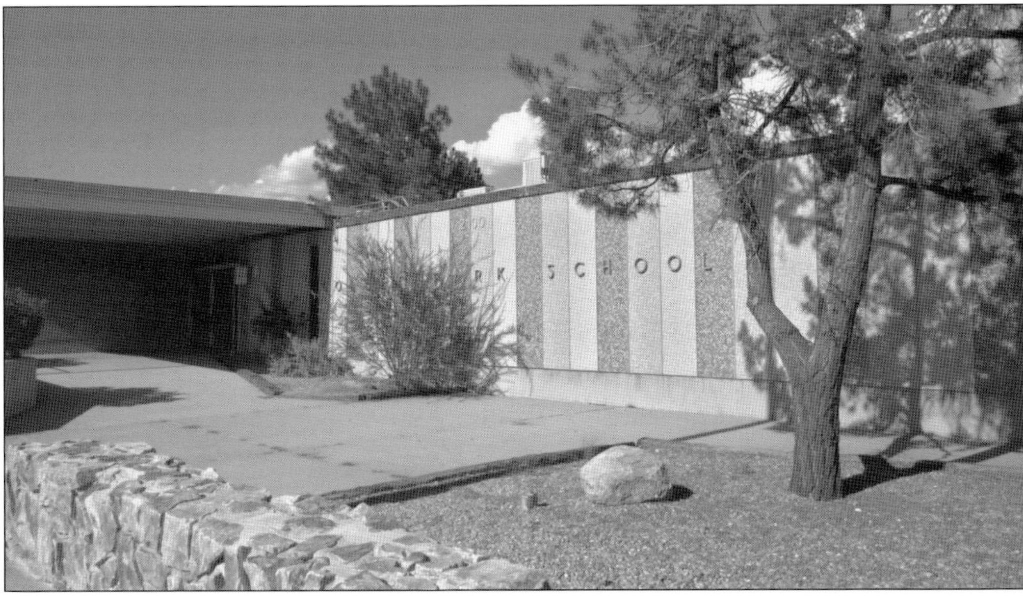

Collet Park Elementary is located in Albuquerque's northeast heights and opened its doors in 1960. It was constructed in a patio-style with heavy use of colorful tile. A recent renovation maintained this unique architectural style. Other APS schools not pictured that opened 1960–1965 include Corrales, Harrison, Cochiti, McCollum, Van Buren, Kit Carson, Mitchell, Bellehaven, Chaparral, Comanche, Governor Bent, Sierra Vista, Adobe Acres, Carlos Rey, Tomasita and Hoover. (Author's collection.)

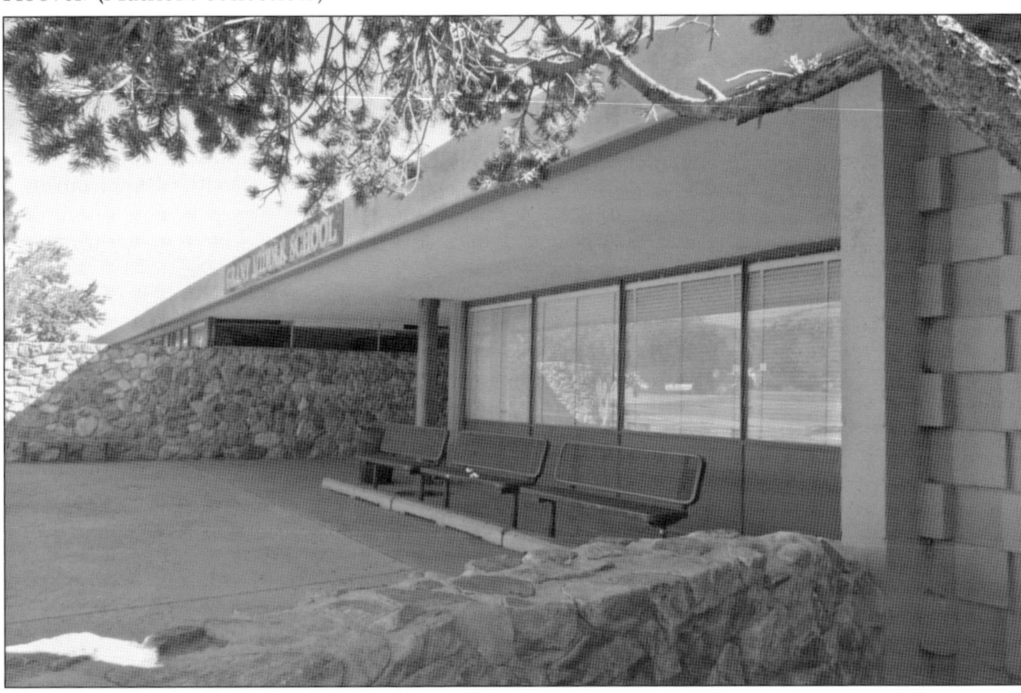

Grant Middle School, opened in 1961, is located near a city golf course and park/swimming pool complex. Grant has a rich tradition as a long-standing community-centered school. (Author's collection.)

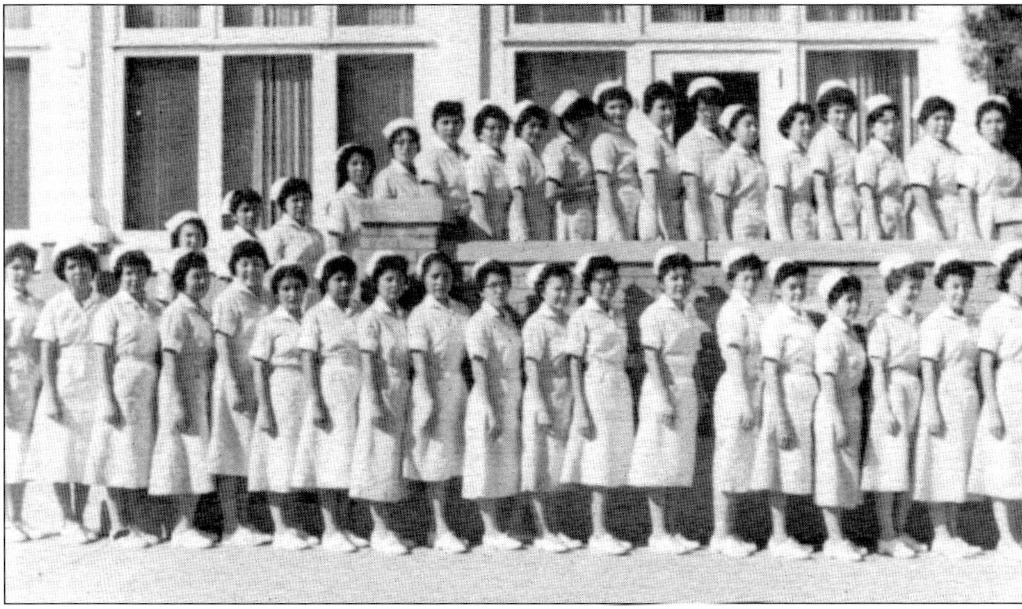

The Albuquerque Indian School was established to provide vocational training to area Native Americans in 1881. By 1925, enrollment was nearly 800. Still a source of controversy and debate concerning mission and intent, the school closed in 1982. The Native American Community School opened on shared property with APS's Wilson Middle School, and formally relocated on AIS land near Twelfth Street and Menaul Boulevard in the fall of 2013 under the direction of founding principal Kara Bobroff. The 1960 class of AIS nursing graduates is featured in the school's 1960 yearbook.

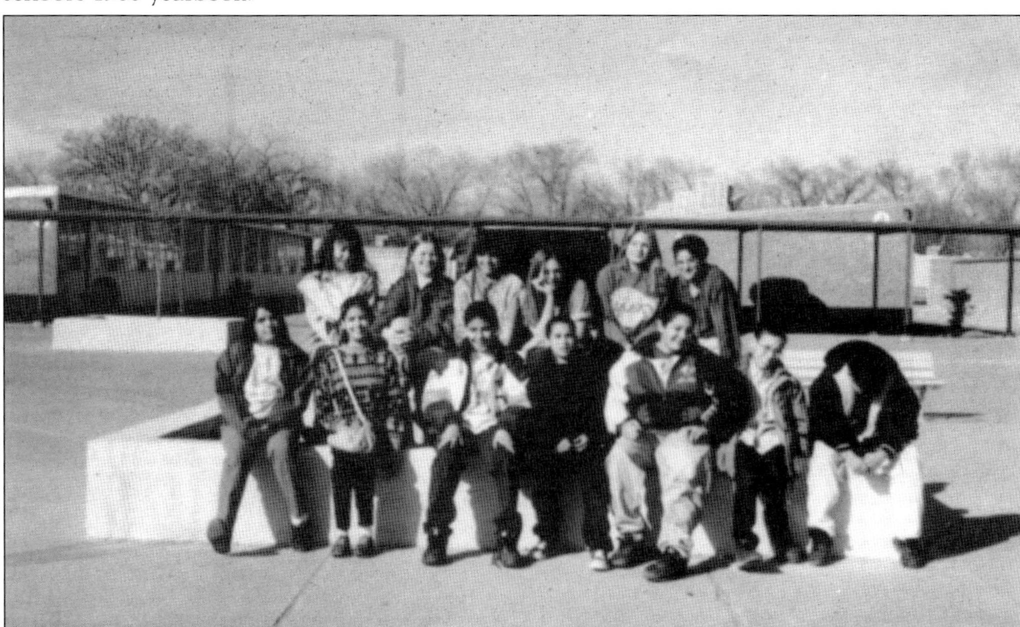

Taylor Middle School opened in the city's north valley in 1962. Rural in nature for many years, the neighborhood continues to retain that character. Students gathered in the center of campus for this 1994 Taylor yearbook shot.

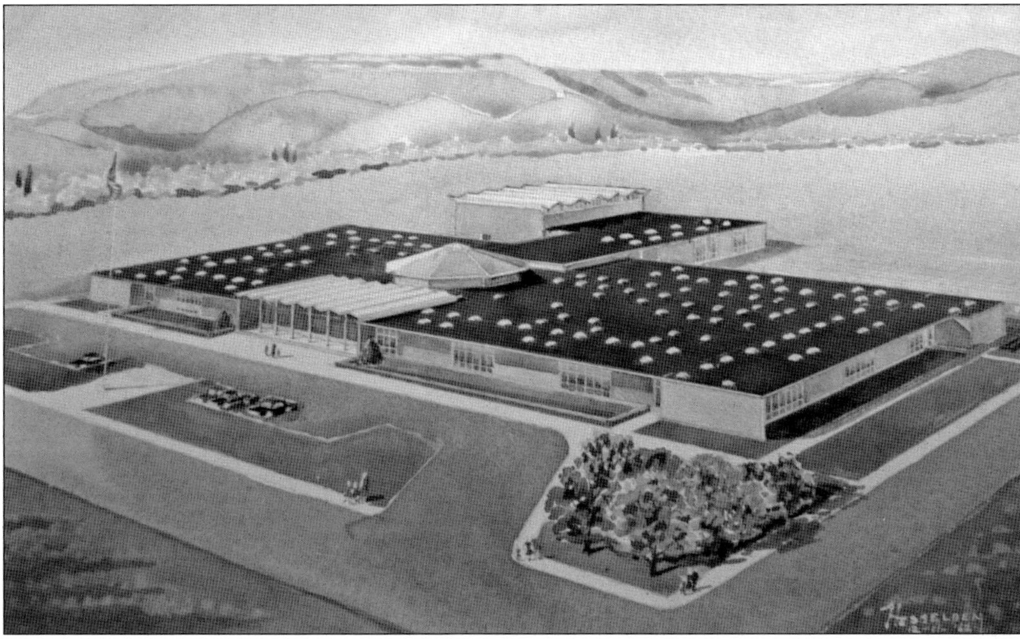

This 1962 sketch by longtime APS architect Louis Hesseden's firm shows a vision for Hayes Middle School, opened as a junior high in 1962. Still sporting the same basic layout, Hayes now operates out of a urban setting near Interstate 40 and Wyoming Boulevard. (Courtesy CSWR.)

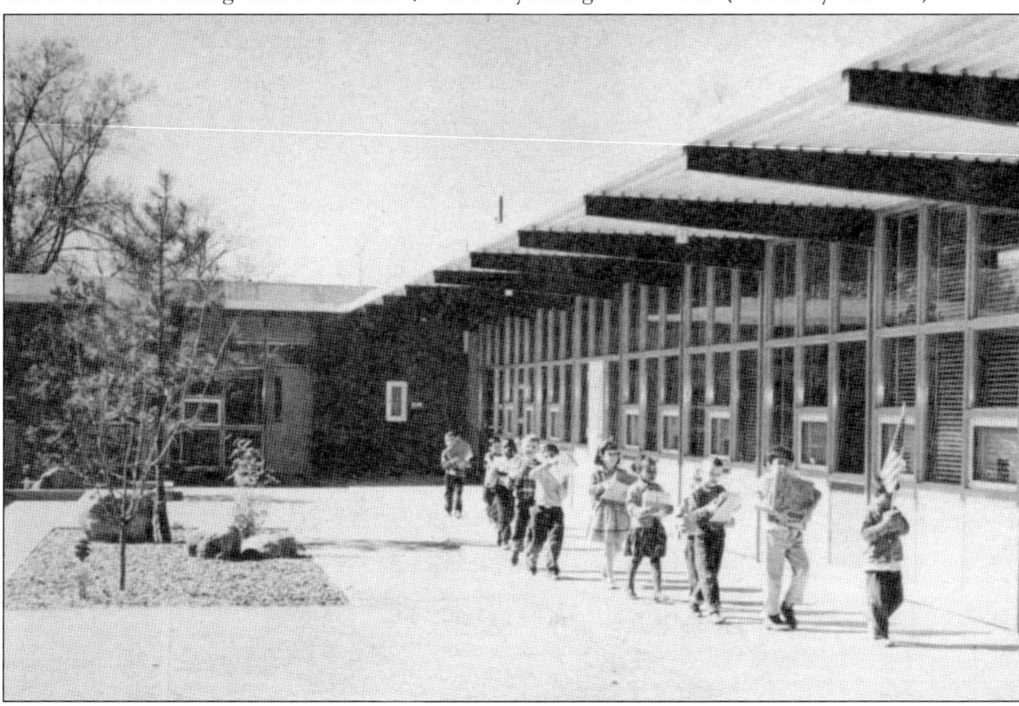

These elementary students are bustling to class. This wide-window style of architecture based on concrete block walls and open concrete pads was the norm in the 1960s construction for APS. Now that energy efficiency has come into play, the district will retrofit these older schools one by one. (Courtesy APM.)

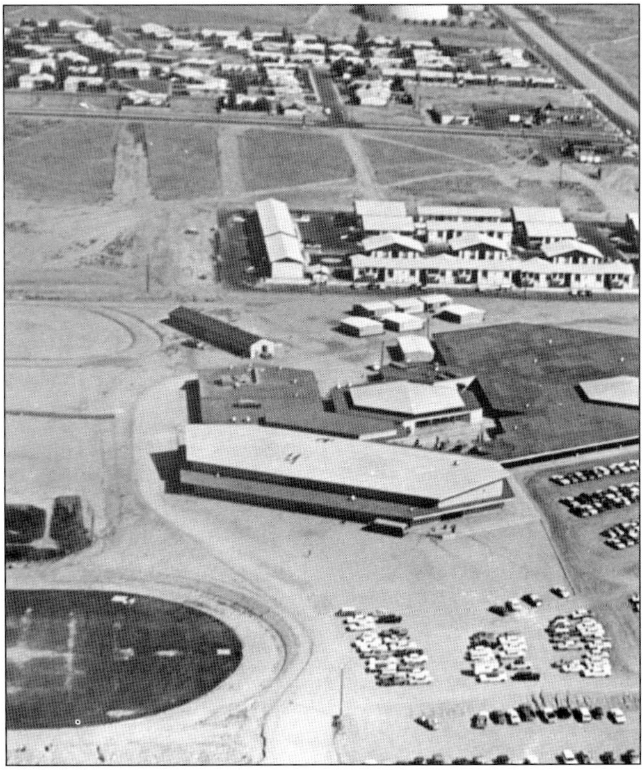

This c. 1970 early aerial view of Del Norte High highlights (to today's Albuquerque residents) the phenomenal changes in our landscape. The school's first principal was John Hoback, with football coach Wyett McGinnis and basketball coach Frank Love. Their first two basketball games were purposefully played away because the gym was not completed. A total reconstruction of the facility is underway, going building by building as of 2013. This image appeared in the 1970 Del Norte yearbook.

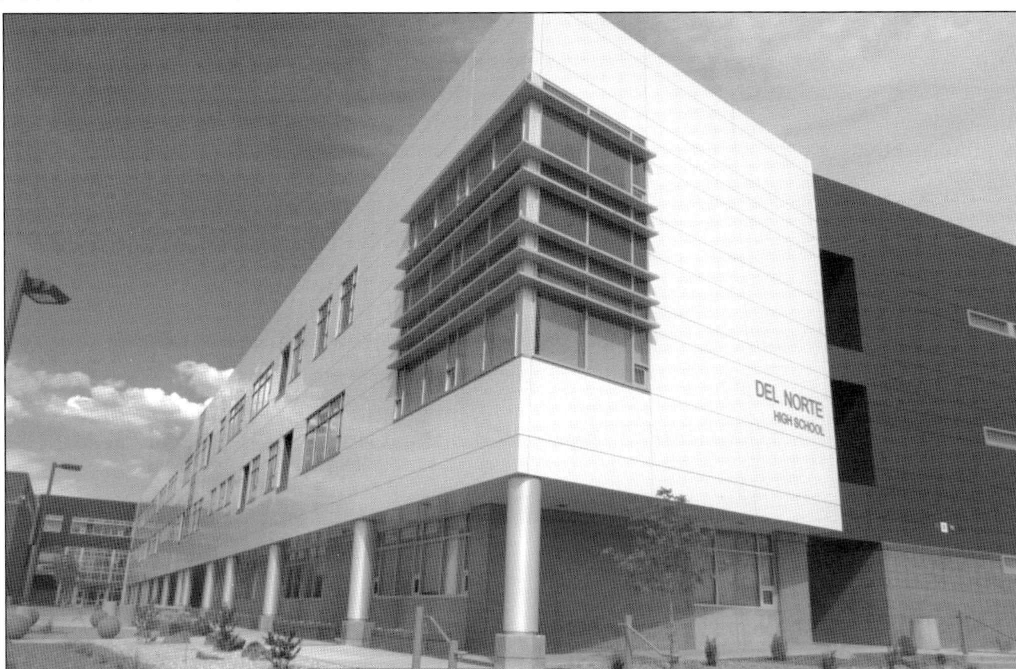


Below, the new main building of Del Norte High rises three stories. This view faces west. (Author's collection.)

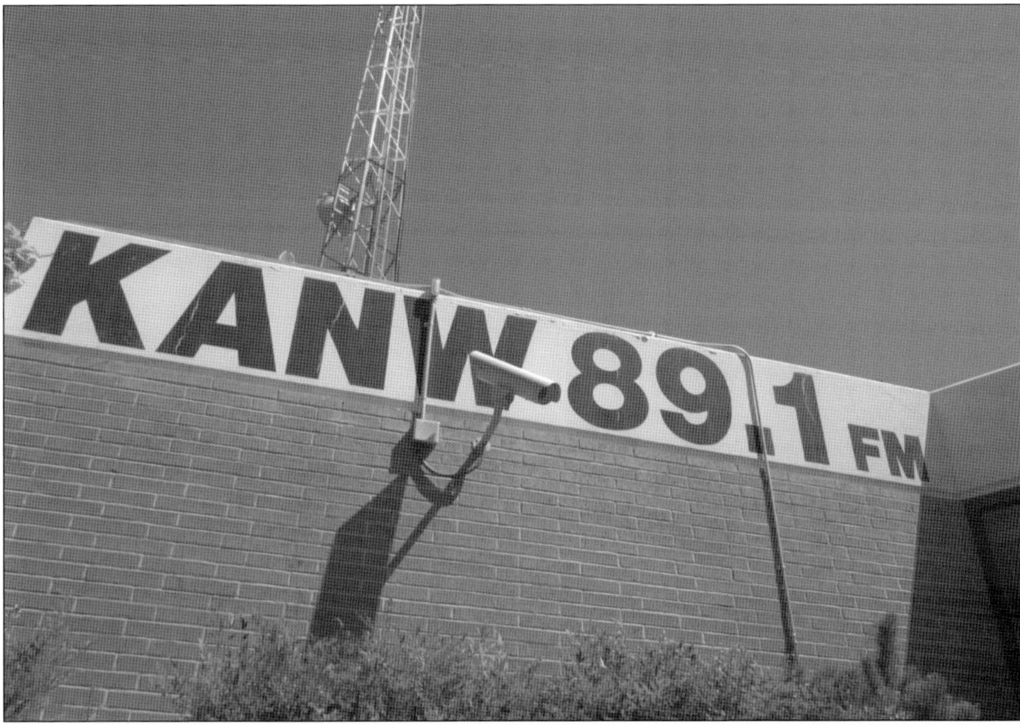


Albuquerque's progressive nature as concerns media surfaced as early as 1949 when John Milne, superintendent of APS, gained approval for a radio station, KANW, to begin operating in 1951. While not on the air during summer recess, the station provided classroom instructional programming during school hours. Still operating in cooperation with APS, KANW has been a National Public Broadcasting affiliate since 1995. Television station KNME (also Public Broadcasting) also has an affiliation with APS, and has a proud tradition of supporting educational programming in the city and the area. (Both, author's collection.)

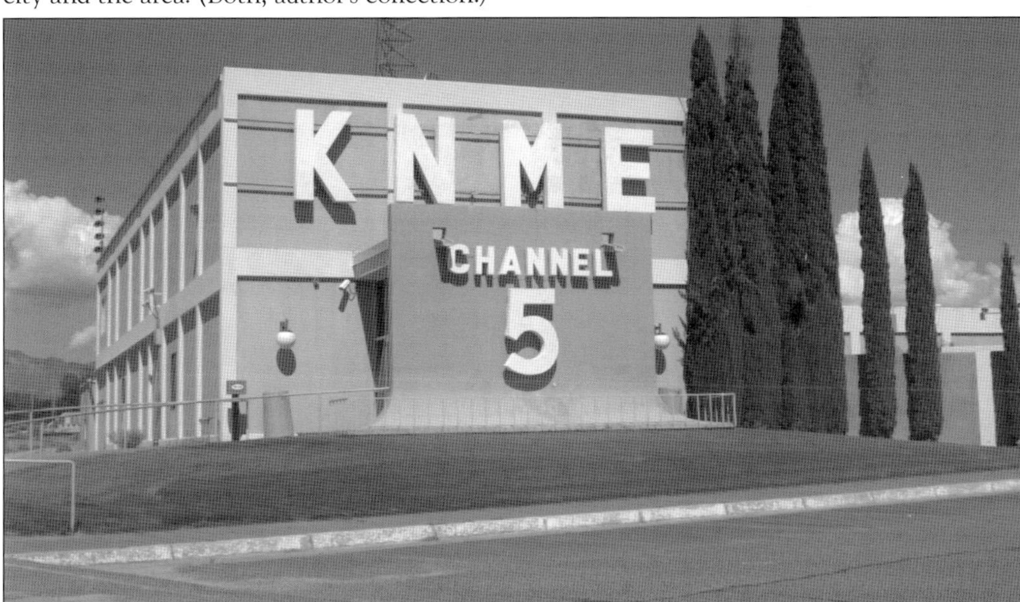

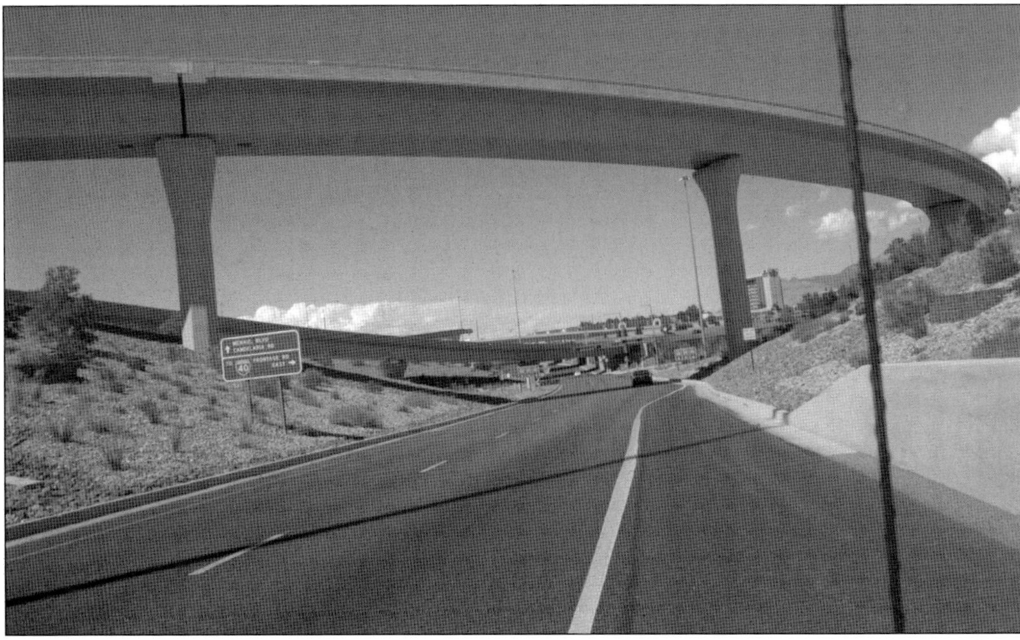

Until 1937, the famed Route 66 cut through Albuquerque through a convoluted route—a driver had to cut north at Santa Rosa, New Mexico (120 miles east of Albuquerque), then north through Santa Fe, then down through what is now Fourth Street, and on south. Due to a flurry of unleashed federal funds, Route 66 was cut through the Sandia Mountains, reducing the drive from Oklahoma City to Albuquerque by hundreds of miles. Then in the 1960s when the interstate highway system unfurled, Interstate 25 and Interstate 40 intersected in Albuquerque, cutting a swath through the neighborhoods and businesses adjoining the concrete and changing Albuquerque's inner city face forever yet contributing mightily to the city's growth and vibrancy. (Author's collection.)

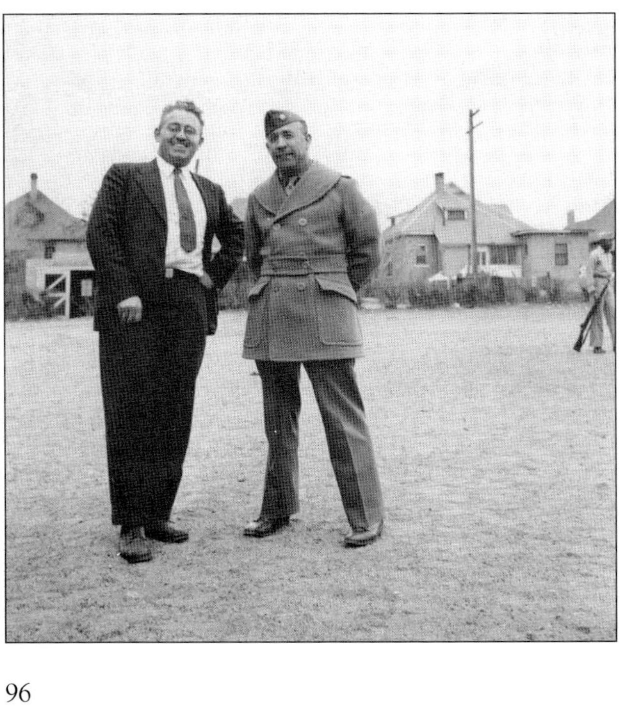

Shown left around 1944, E.R. Harrington stands proudly with Albuquerque High's military science instructor Colonel Gose. Harrington, a science teacher at Albuquerque High for many years and later a member of the central office team, was a local historian and self-proclaimed rebel, often seen gliding around town on his motorcycle. He published the only extant history of APS in 1963, and also compiled a rare document, "A Pictorial History of the Albuquerque Public Schools," given to John Milne around 1945. Many of APS's archival photos were shot by Harrington, and reside with APS and CSWR. (Courtesy CSWR PICT 000-299-0570.)

These unidentified students look at *Time* magazine to review events that occurred during the 1963 school year, a momentous time in American education, politics, and society. These students experienced the death of a pope, the death of a president, the sinking of the *Thresher*, the Panama Crisis, the Cuban Missile Crisis, the Berlin Wall opening in December, Cassius Clay defeating Sonny Liston, the passage of the Civil Rights Act, and more. This photograph appeared in the 1964 Rio Grande yearbook.

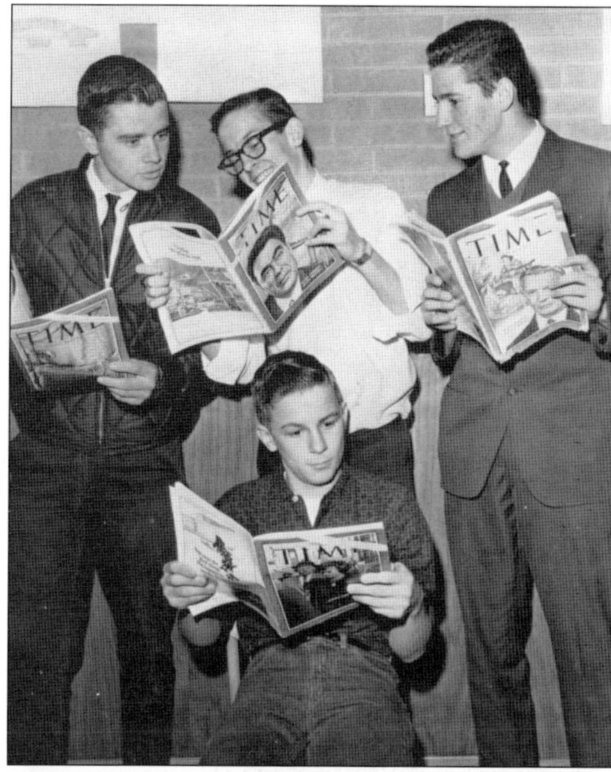

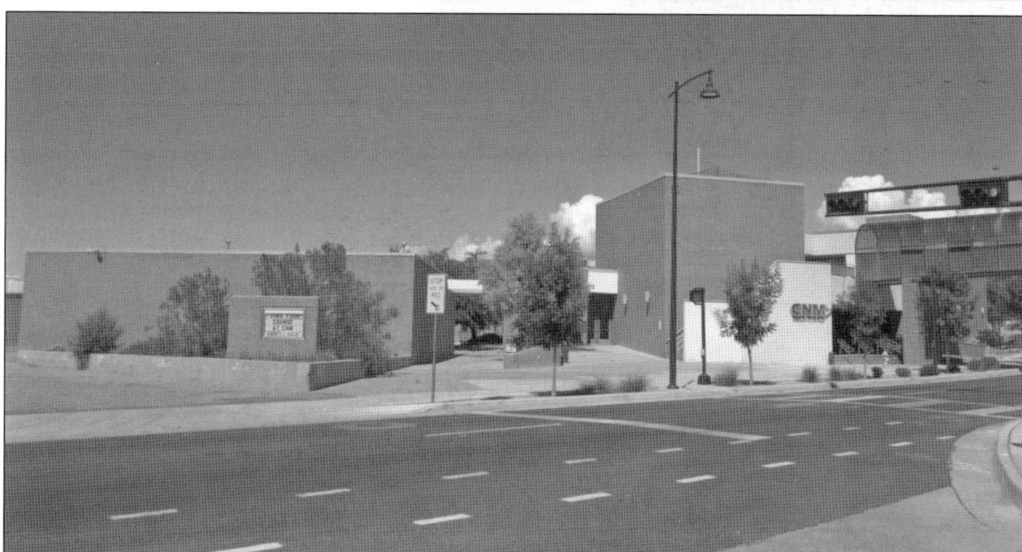

In 1964, APS opened a school to train older students in technology and trades—the Technical Vocational Institute. By 1986, the school was authorized to grant degrees, and in 2006 the institution was reconfigured as Central New Mexico Community College. By 2009, CNM was the largest degree-granting college in the state with an enrollment of over 24,000 students. Many well-known community leaders have served as CNM's presidents, administrators, and board members, creating a lively and rich history woven into the institution. Above, CNM is a proud gem in Albuquerque's educational cache. (Author's collection.)

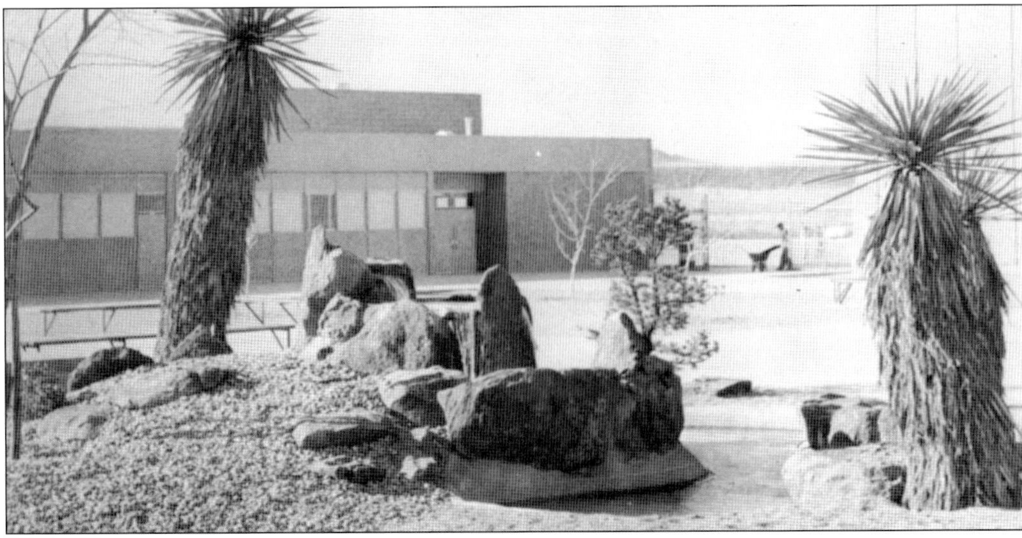

West Mesa High opened on the city's far west mesa in 1966. Visible above is a slice of the campus featuring a fountain given to the school by the class of 1969. The school's dedication was held November 6, 1966, and the speakers at the dedication included superintendent Robert Chisholm, Robert Evans, principal, S.Y. Jackson, from the school board, and Father Spellman of Holy Rosary. The first coaches were Fred Romero, basketball, and Jimmy Juarez, football. This image appeared in the 1966 West Mesa yearbook.

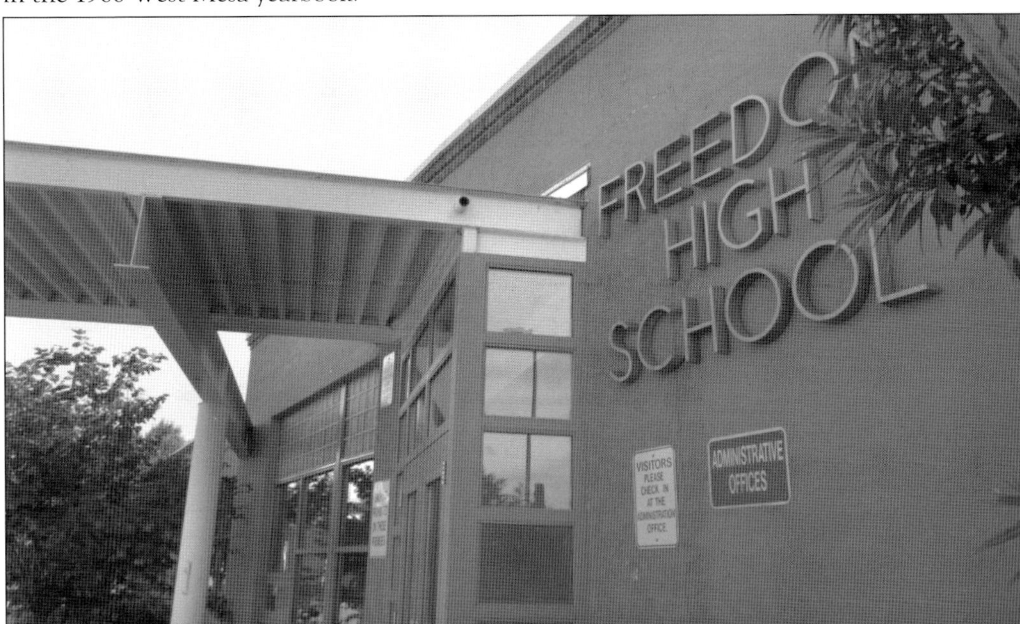


Freedom High, pictured above, opened in 1970, as did School on Wheels. Both schools set their mission's targets on reclaiming at-risk students who might not graduate without personalized intervention. Freedom was formerly Cortez Elementary, and today the school is nestled in the northeast corner of Interstate 40 and Cutler. Other APS schools opening in the late 1960s to early 1970s include John Baker, Navaho, Apache, Chelwood, Osuna, S.Y. Jackson, and Onate. (Author's collection.)

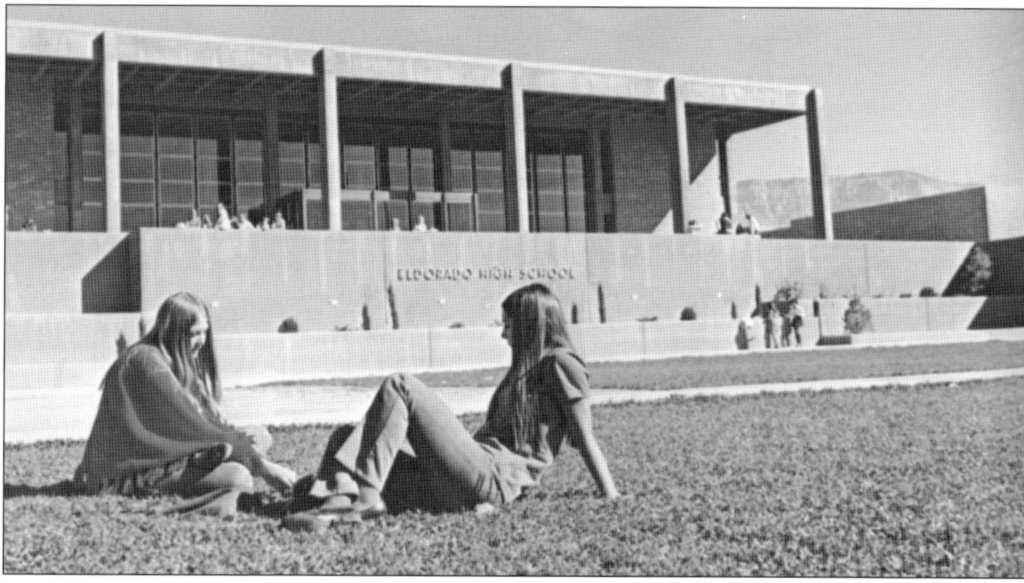


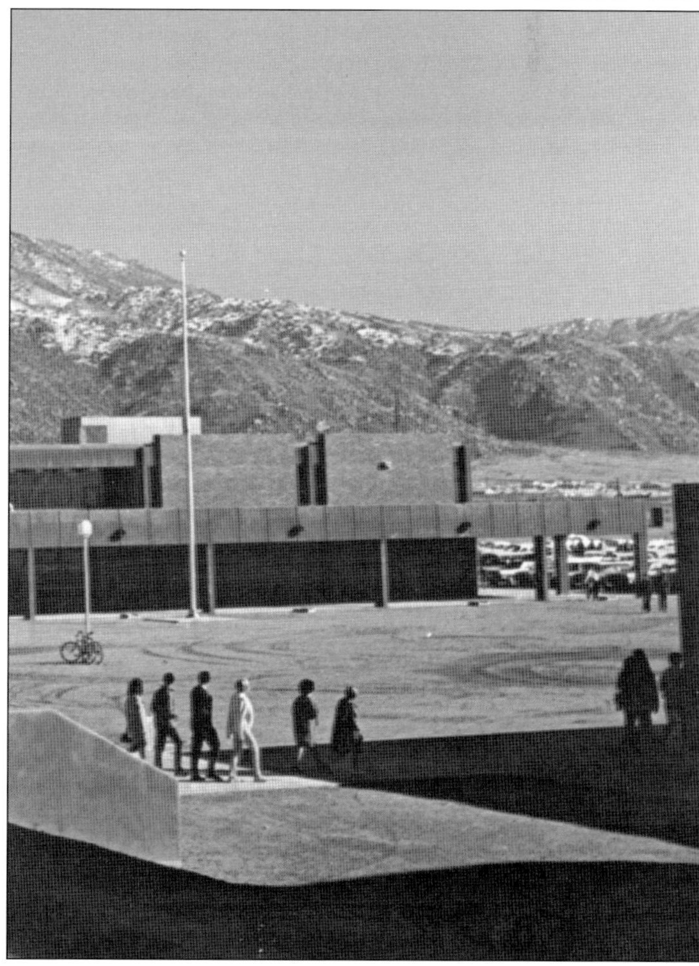

Eldorado High opened under first principal Elmer Bass. Though public sentiment was skeptical concerning the new school's chances of winning at football, first coach Bill Hayes pulled out a win in the Eagles' opening games against St. Pius. Construction on Eldorado was slowed by a plumbers' strike, but the school opened August 31, 1970, with an enrollment of 1,700 and 50 full-time teachers. The school experimented with contracted food services (returning to school-run food the next fall due to discontentment), and plans called for a swimming pool that never materialized. Above, students at Eldorado sit and enjoy the sunshine. At right is a 1972 look at the campus from west to east. These Eldorado yearbook images appeared in the 1971 and 1972 editions, respectively.

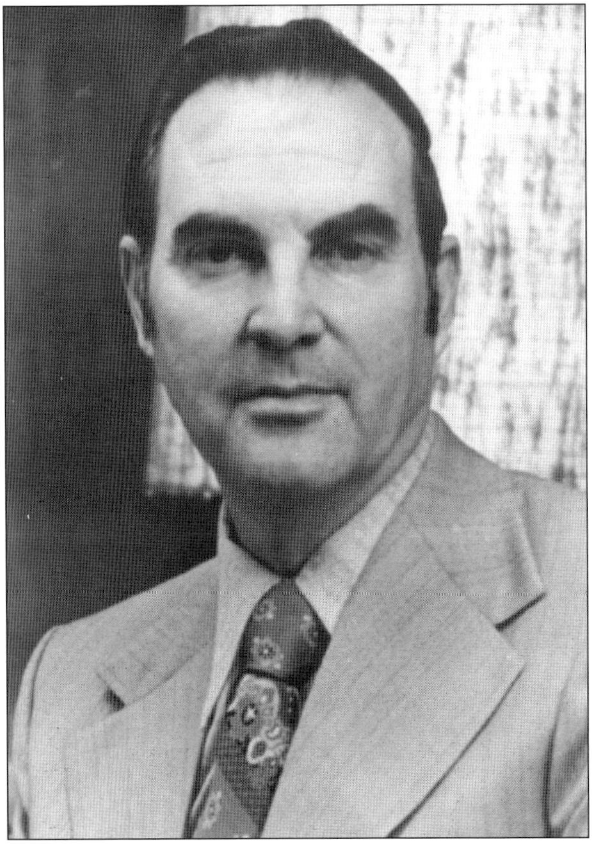

Dr. Ernie Stapleton took the helm as APS superintendent from 1971 to 1977, opening nearly 20 schools and overseeing the transition as city schools added a new district to the northwest, Rio Rancho. Surely Ernie's expertise at living through the consolidation of the county and city schools in 1949 contributed to his steady head, and the transition was and continues to be a successful partnership. (Courtesy APS.)

Even though Albuquerque had enacted a groundbreaking city ordinance in 1952 banning discrimination on the basis of race in public places, sentiments ran tight in the early 1970s in the city and the nation. On a hot June night in 1971, tensions broke and a race riot erupted on the south edge of UNM's campus, spilling over into the weekend to Roosevelt Park. Below, National Guard soldiers stand near the burned ruins of a UNM administration center. (Courtesy CSWR PICT 000-885(1)-0094.)

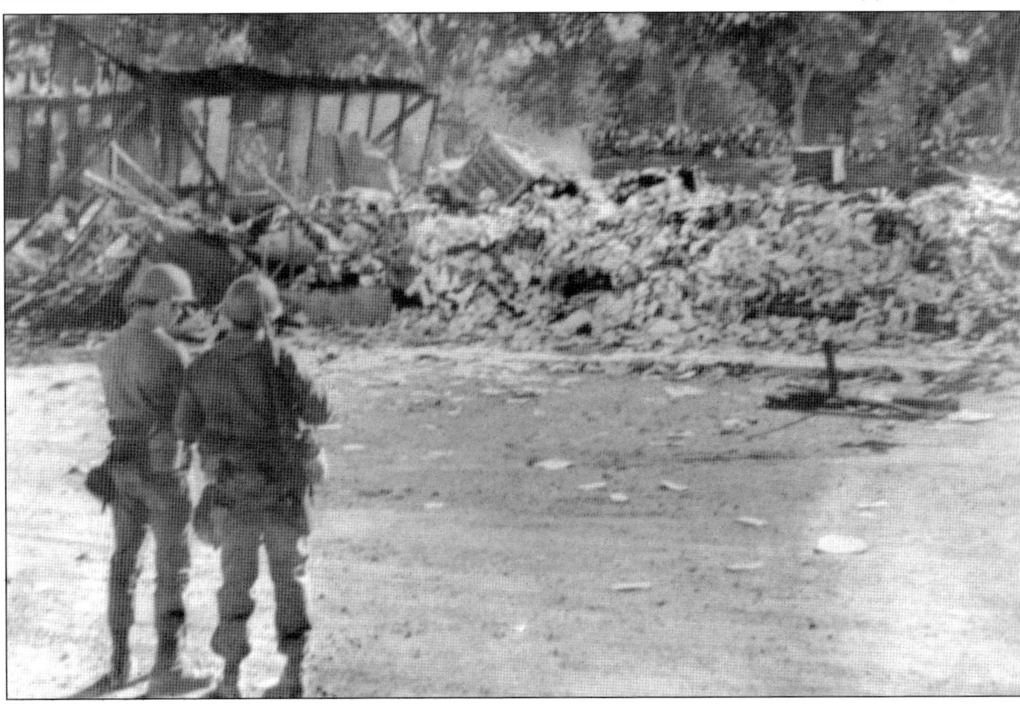

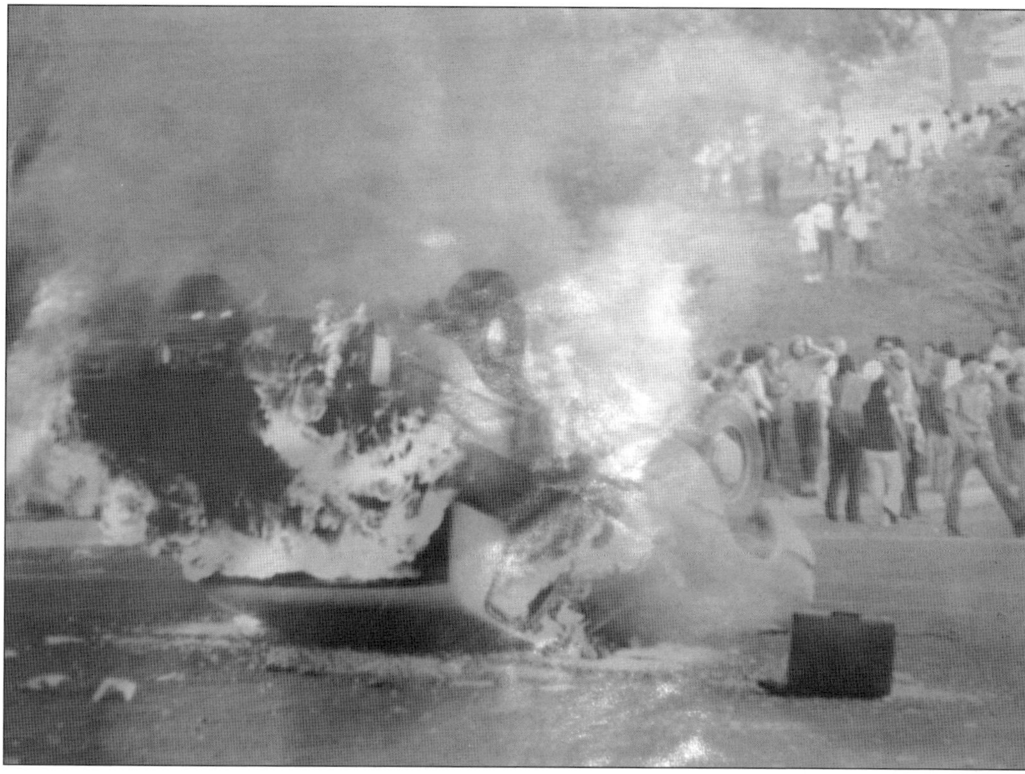

The June 14–15, 1971, disturbances protesting racial inequality, staged from "Chicano Hill" at the university, continued for two days. They caused millions of dollars of damage, hundreds of arrests, and resulted in 15 people being shot but not fatally injured. Above, the ruins of an overturned car flare while protesters stream up the hills into Roosevelt Park. Below, looters rampage near Central Avenue and Cornell. (Courtesy CSWR PICT 000-885(1)-0097 and PICT 000-885(1)-0099.)

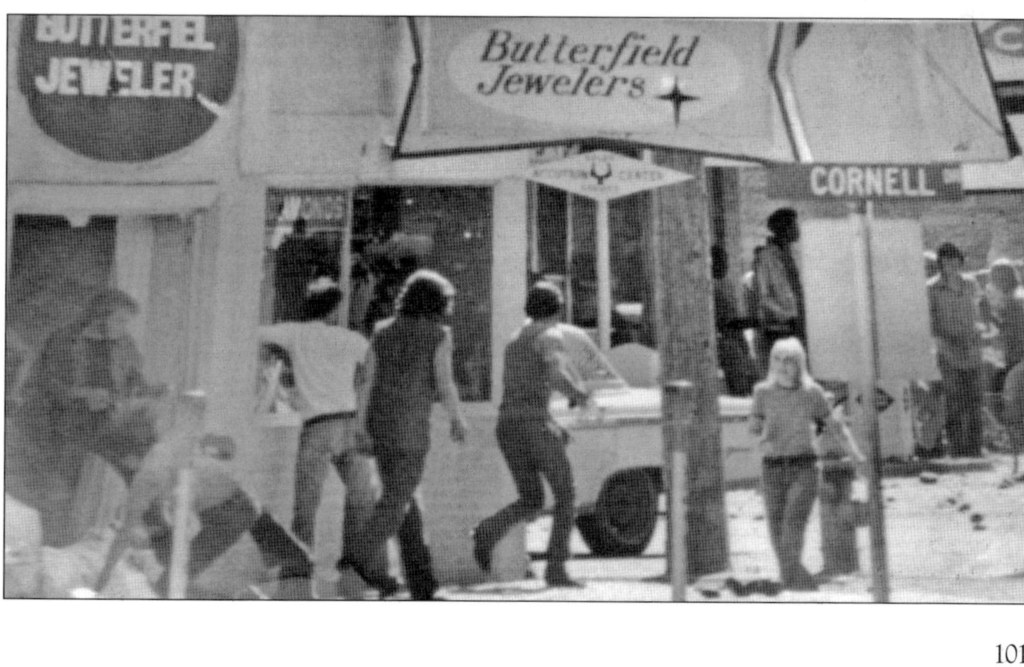

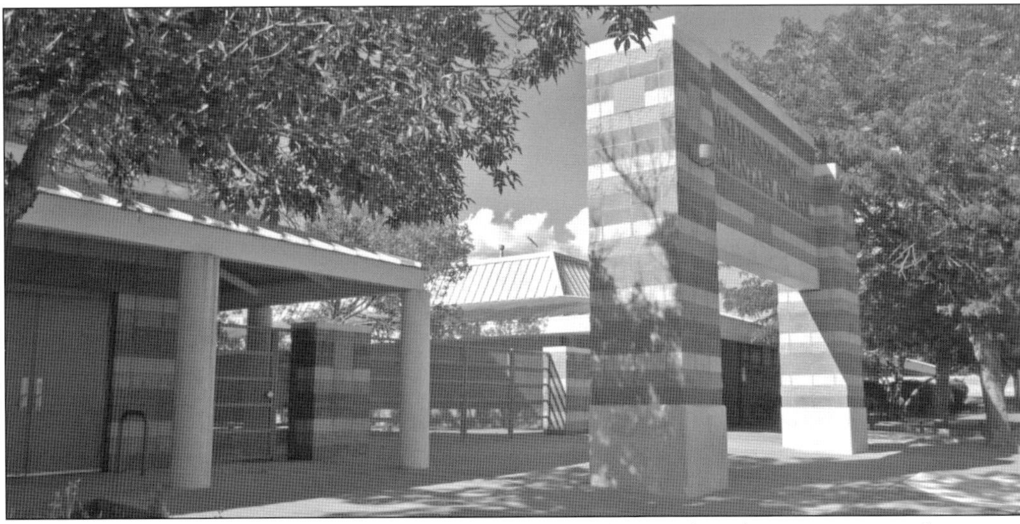

Opened in 1967, Matheson Park Elementary continued the trend in the city to name elementary schools after nearby streets or landform features. While quiet neighborhoods continued to be rapidly developed by builders, and wide dirt streets were graded for future paving, the assassinations of John F. Kennedy in 1963 and Martin Luther King Jr. in 1968 combined with the unending Vietnam War created covert and overt waves of stress politically, socially, and economically throughout the nation. (Author's collection.)

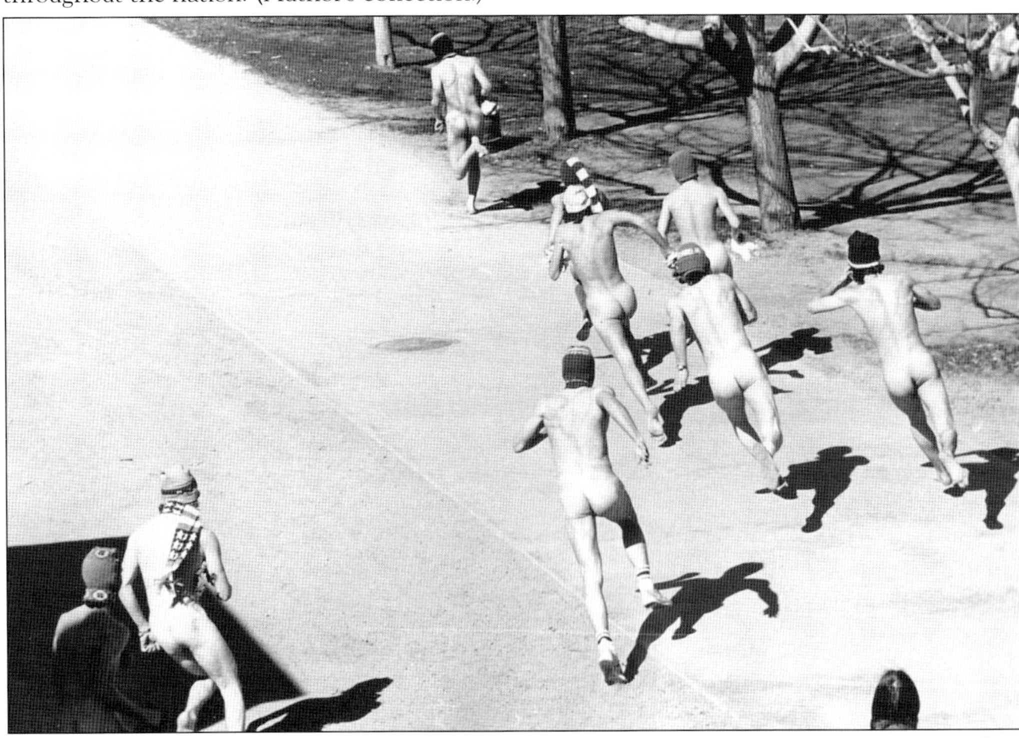

By the early 1970s a fad swept through America as the cultural stress began to ripple into a release of humor—television shows such as *Laugh-In* and *The Smothers Brothers* began to encourage a new irreverent rebellion. The phenomenon of streaking briefly swept the nation, and this c. 1973 image was captured from the upper story of Highland High. (Courtesy Al Kaplan.)

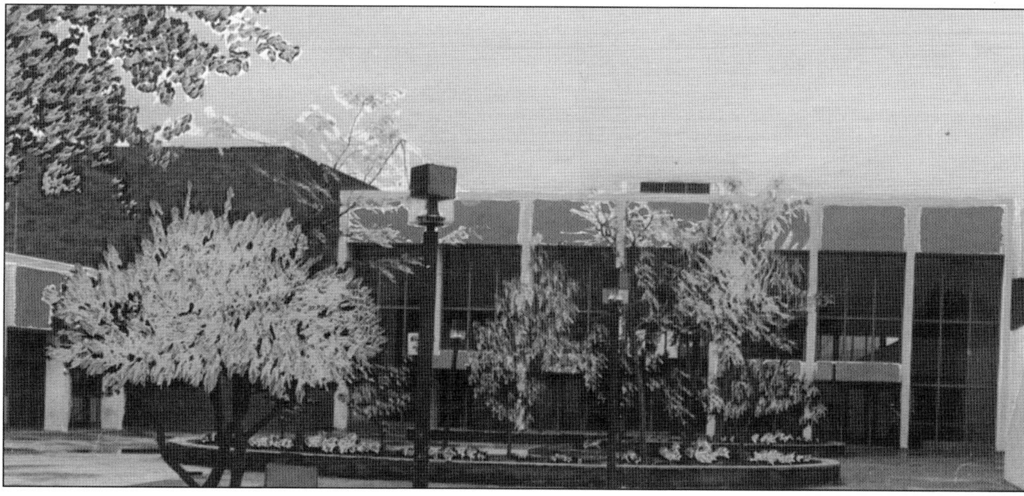

In 1974, Cibola High opened on the far northwest mesa of the city in a somewhat isolated setting. Nearly 40 years later, the school is very urban, surrounded by housing divisions, several major shopping malls, police and transit stations, and a Sam's Club. Above is a sketch of Cibola's entry. Other APS schools whose doors swung open in the mid- to late 1970s are Eisenhower, Rio Rancho Elementary, Truman, Dolores Gonzales, E.G. Ross, Hubert Humphrey, and Marie Hughes. This photograph appeared in the 1984 Cibola yearbook.

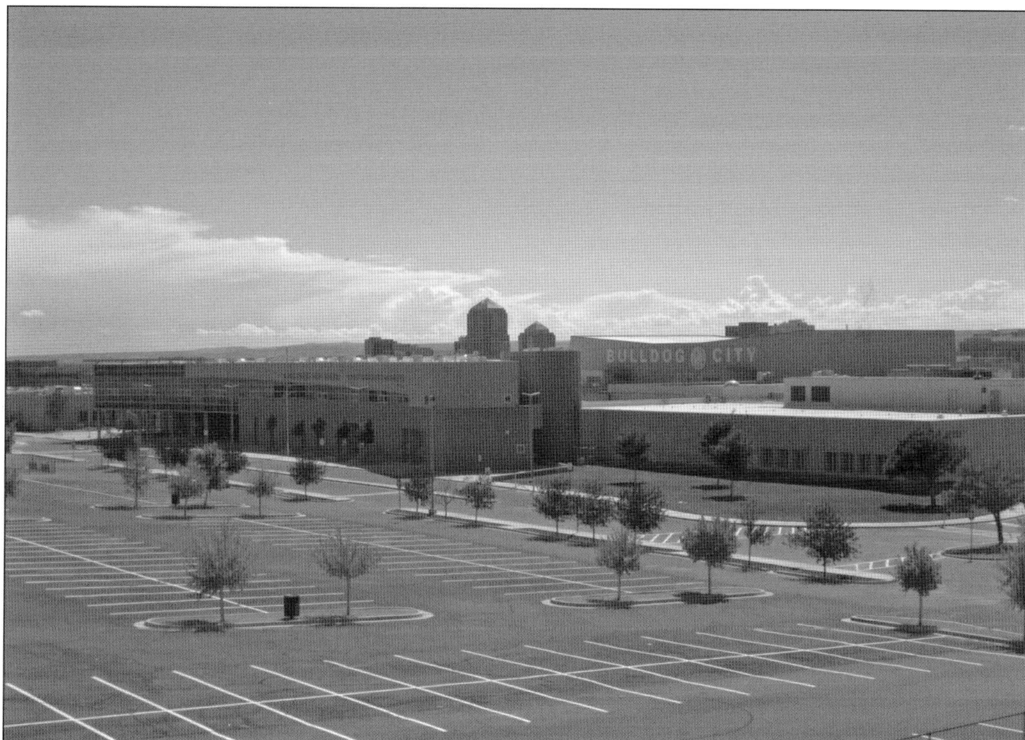

1974 was a big year for the city's public schools—old Albuquerque High reopened north of its nearly 60 year permanent location to a new building, pictured above. Additionally, the schools transitioned under Dr. Ernie Stapleton's calm leadership from junior high to middle schools that scooped up the sixth graders and passed their ninth graders to the high schools. (Author's collection.)

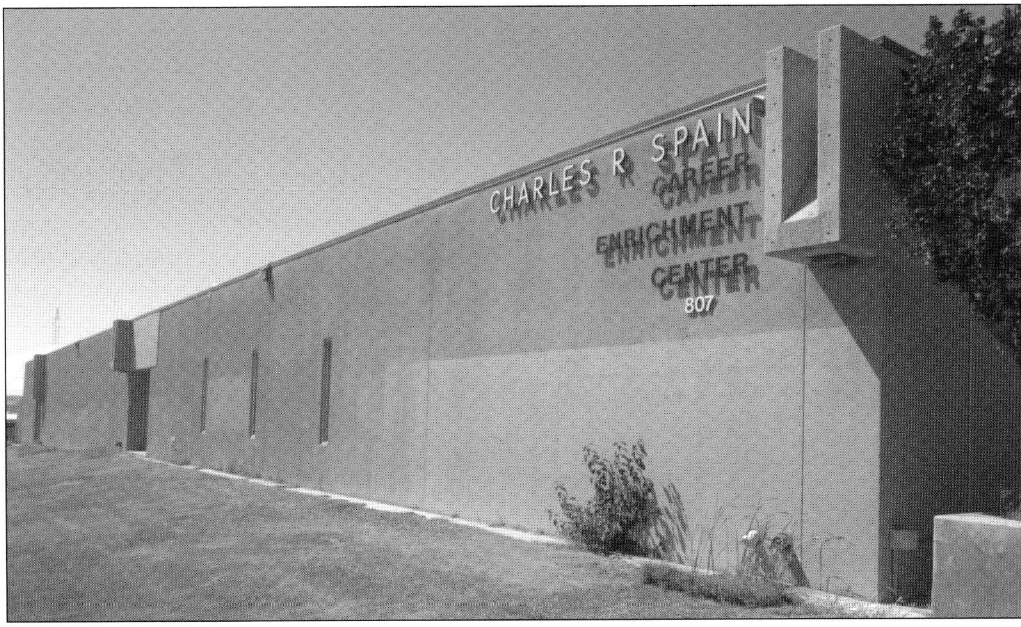


In 1975, APS opened the Career Enrichment Center, above, on the south edge of the new Albuquerque High. Named after former superintendent Charles Spain, the center focused on creating vocational and advanced academic paths for the district's high school juniors and seniors. That mission continues today, and has expanded to include concurrent college enrollment and a variety of other options for students, including advanced language learning. (Author's collection.)

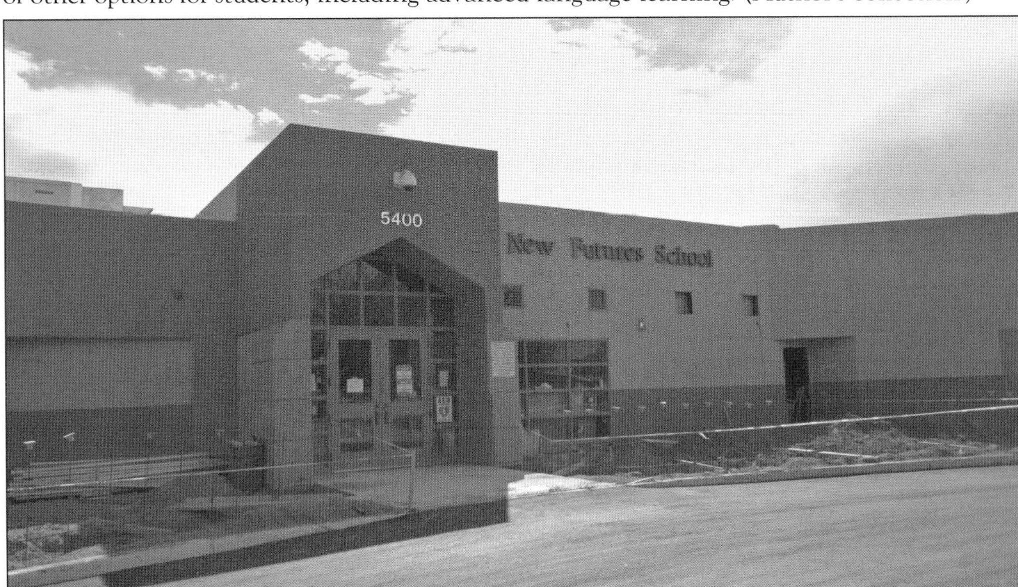


Another school of choice opened by APS in 1976, New Futures High School, is pictured above. Created in 1976 as a safe, nurturing, and educationally enriching environment for students who have children, New Futures serves as a model for districts around the county. The school emphasizes post-secondary choices, whole family wellness, and has recently welcomed fathers to enroll, as well as mothers. Comprehensive services are available, and the future is emphasized for all, with childcare available and parent skills emphasized. (Author's collection.)

# *Seven*

# Schools in Albuquerque 1990–Present

The 1990s shed a new slant of light on education and government throughout the nation. Slowly but surely, education in the United States acquired more and more responsibilities as Bill Clinton's policies morphed into Goals 2000, which George W. Bush picked up. A huge shift in how America viewed local control of education versus federal control had slowly evolved including gender equity in education and sports (Title IX, 1972); family rights and protection concerning educational records (FERPA 1974), federal protections for students with physical or learning disabilities (IDEA 1975/1990/2004), and regulations concerning those with physical, emotional, or behavioral disabilities (ADA 1990).

Schools scrambled under the increasingly litigious legislations from both federal and state governments, while concomitantly states began the charter schools movement, providing means for individual groups or entities to propose, finance (with public funds), and run (usually) small schools that—while not at the outset of the movement, but increasingly—met a niche market. APS, always on the forefront of movements, wrote and was granted one of the first five charter approvals in the state of New Mexico when Highland High became a charter school for a few years beginning in 1993.

By the late 1980s, school growth and building in Albuquerque had slowed, but the pace picked up again after the year 2000 when the city's west side experienced another growth spurt—so all eyes turned west. The area's colleges made plans to open west side campuses, and over 20 new APS schools opened since 1990.

Public schools wrestle to find a balance of accountability between schools and family. The dialogue will be ongoing, but meanwhile, families' neighborhood schools are pledged to serve their students' and community's needs. APS continues a tradition of offering a wide menu of schools from which families can choose: comprehensive traditional schools, smaller schools, or schools with magnet or targeted foci. Church schools and private options are available throughout the city, as well as a wide array of charter school options. Albuquerque's educational menu is rich, diverse, and—most would agree—satisfying.

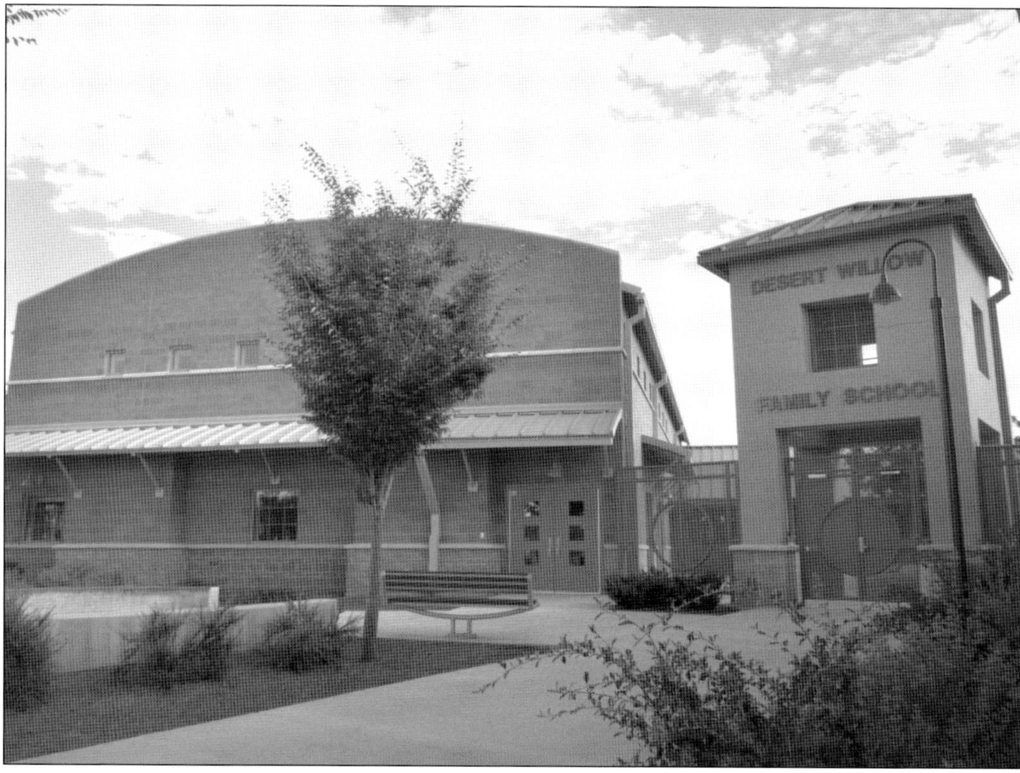


Desert Willow Family School continues to wow the city with its innovation and continued academic success. (Author's collection.)

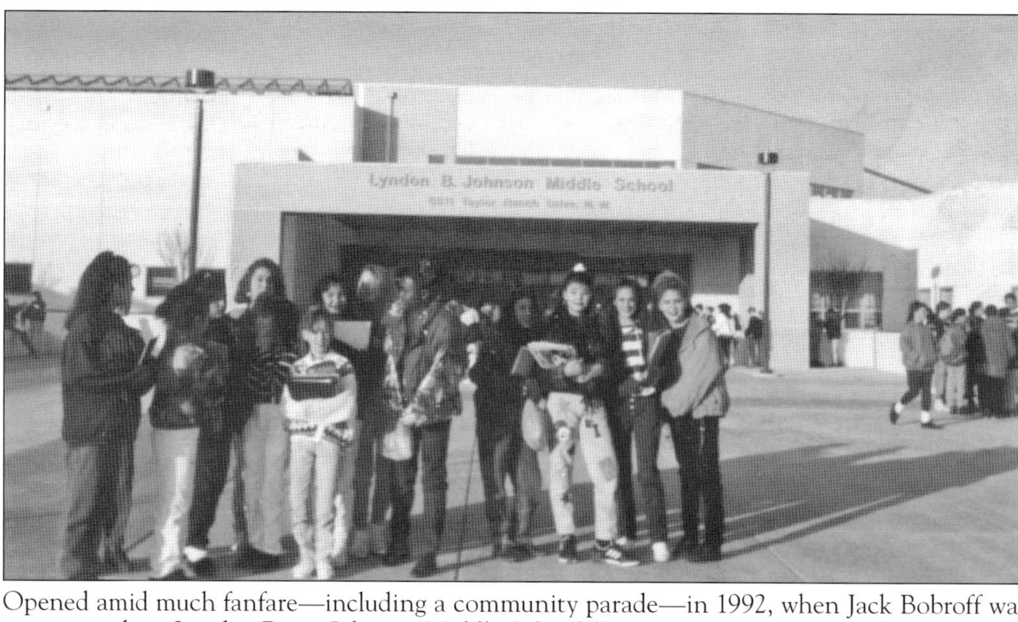


Opened amid much fanfare—including a community parade—in 1992, when Jack Bobroff was superintendent, Lyndon Banes Johnson Middle School (known in the city as "LBJ") continues to serve a large population on the west side of the city. Pictured here from the school's first yearbook, published in 1993, are students near the school's main entrance.

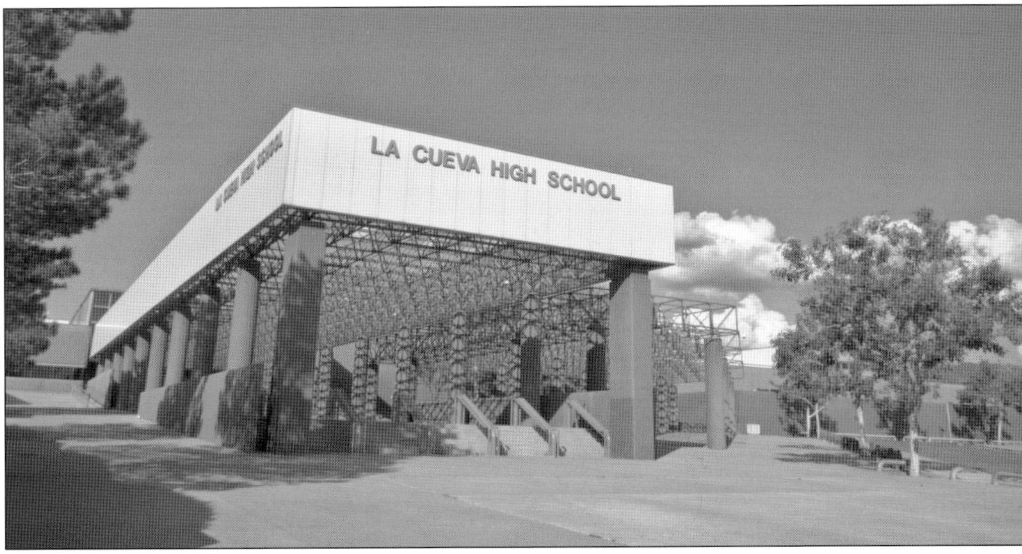


La Cueva High proudly opened its doors in 1986 under the leadership of principal Sue Griffith. The first new high school in the city since the new Albuquerque High had opened in 1974, La Cueva was state of the art, demonstrating the can-do attitude of Albuquerque. Quickly creating a tradition of academic and athletic success, La Cueva continues a proud tradition. Other APS schools that opened in the 1980s include Puesta del Sol, Mary Ann Binford, Martin Luther King, Georgia O'Keeffe, and S.R. Marmon. Many of these were moved to the Rio Rancho School District when it opened in 1994. (Author's collection.)

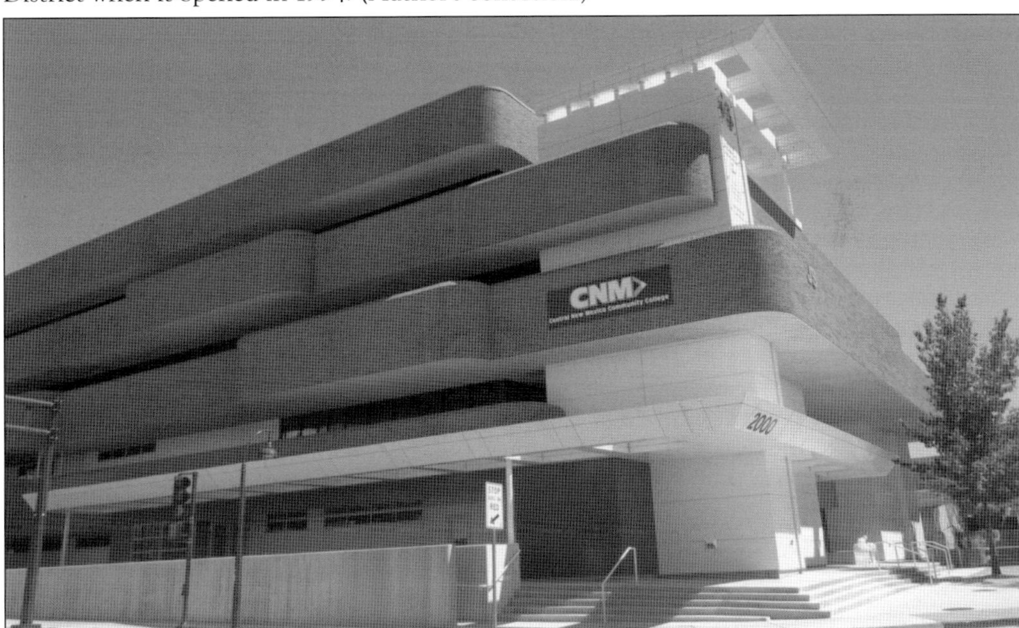


In 1979, the Technical Vocational Institute moved from the governance of APS to its own publicly elected seven-member governing board. In 1986, the institution was granted degree-giving power, and in 2006, the school became Central New Mexico Community College—currently serving nearly 30,000 students. Visible above is Jeanette Stromberg Hall, renovated in 2009, and named for long time APS librarian and school board member. (Author's collection.)

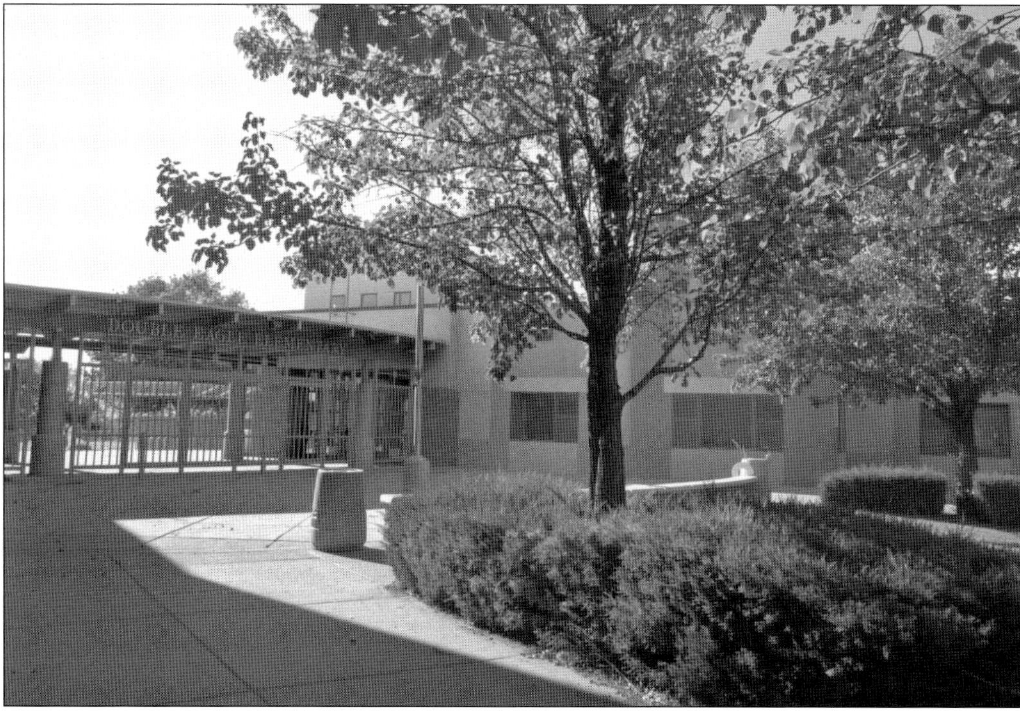


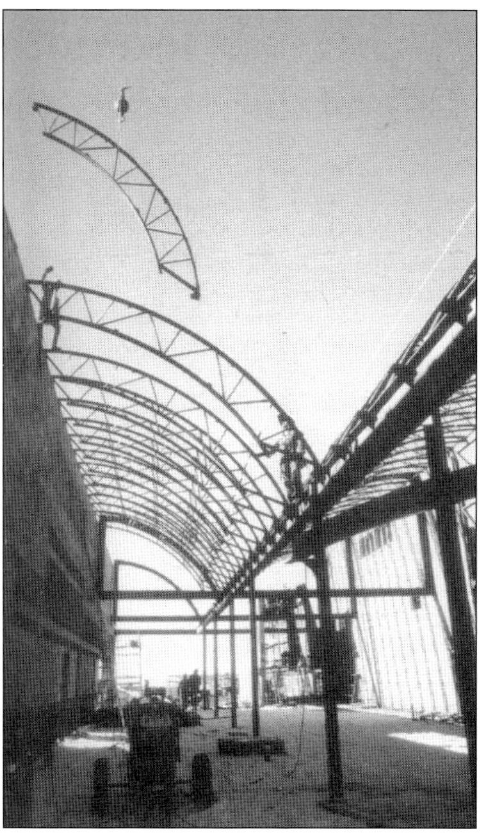

Double Eagle Elementary opened in 1996 and broke with the APS tradition of naming elementary schools for nearby landmarks or for famous people. Instead, it was named after the multiple series of balloon adventures undertaken by the Double Eagle balloon teams anchored by Ben Abruzzo and Maxie Anderson. The *Double Eagle II* successfully crossed the Atlantic in 1978, and the *Double Eagle V* spanned the Pacific in 1981. (Author's collection.)

Desert Ridge Middle School welcomed its first students in 1997. The school is pictured here under construction. After much community input, Desert Ridge was the first middle school in decades to break the tradition of naming middle schools after former US presidents. APS schools not pictured but that opened in the 1990s are Ernest Stapleton Elementary, Petroglyph, Chamiza, and Painted Sky. This image appeared in the 1997 Desert Ridge yearbook.

Jimmy Carter Middle School continues to house one of the largest APS middle school populations, even though it opened in 2000 on the city's growing west side. Right, excited students arrive at their school. The 2000s also saw these APS schools (that are not pictured) open: Seven Bar, Edward Gonzales, Ventana Ranch, and Sunset View. (Courtesy Jimmy Carter yearbook, 2003.)

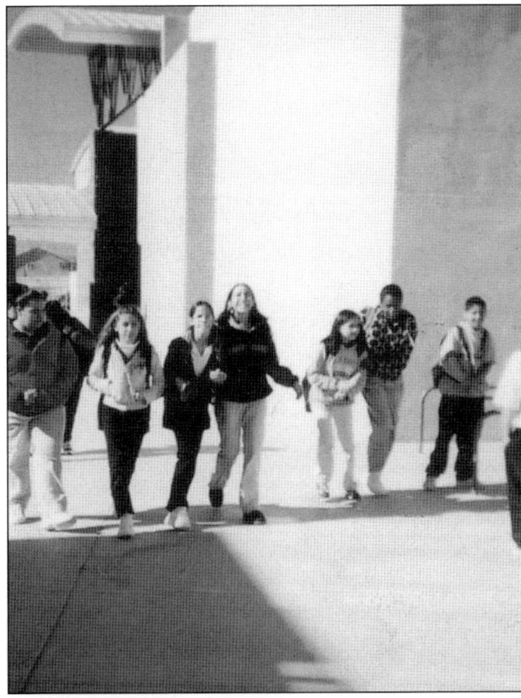

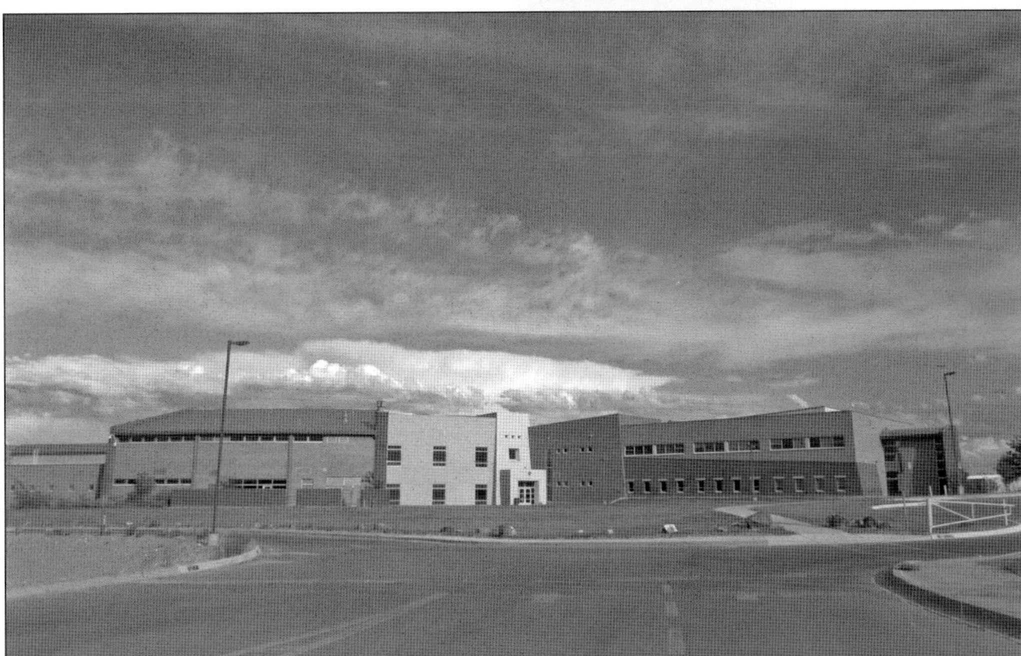

James Monroe Middle School was reborn on the far west side of Albuquerque in 2001. The first Monroe (see page 69) near today's Interstate 40 and Louisiana Boulevard was closed and razed to make way for Winrock Shopping Center. The new Monroe was one of APS's first true efforts to create a cutting-edge green building, and awards soon followed. Monroe's first principal was Vernon Martinez, and the school has matured and recently has welcomed a contiguous elementary school into its nearby and ever-expanding neighborhood. (Author's collection.)

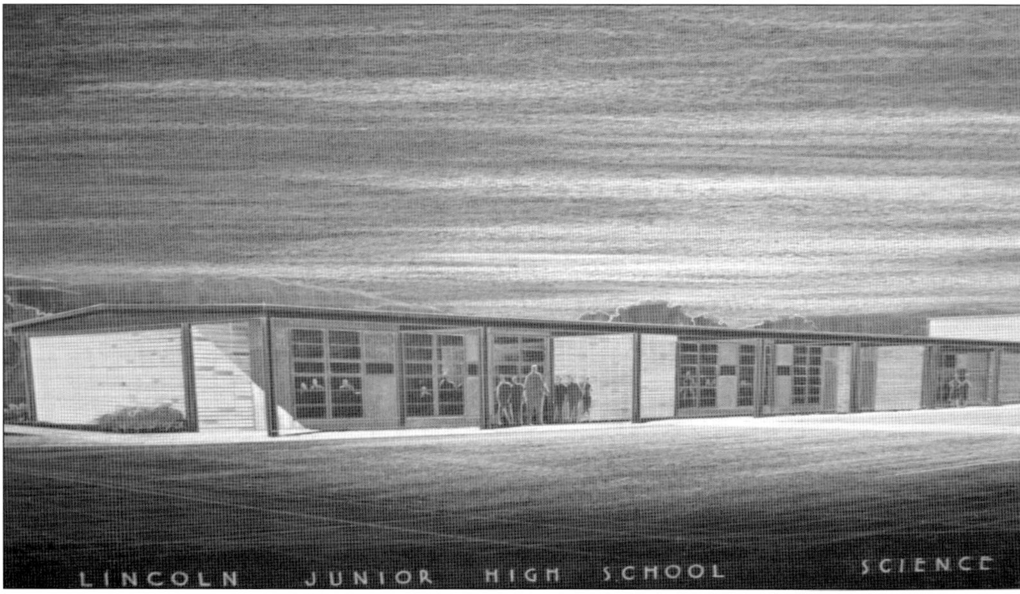


This sketch made for architect Louis Hesslden's firm shows a renovation to be made to Lincoln Middle School. Lincoln, like Monroe, was reborn on the city's west side, opening in 1985 and moving to Rio Rancho's school system, which formed in 1994. The original Lincoln still stands southeast of Coal Avenue and Interstate 40 and houses APS's district maintenance, operations, and facilities offices. (Courtesy CSWR.)

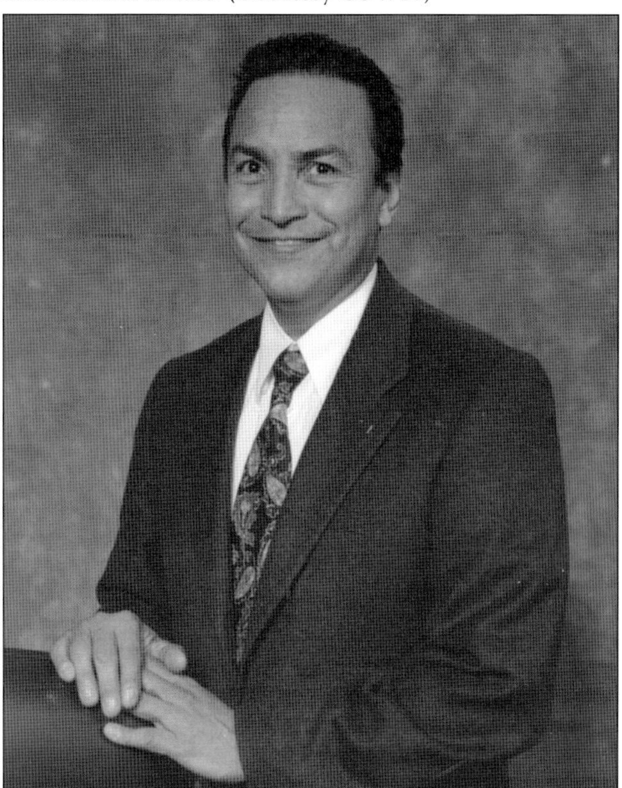

The city's public schools suffered a great loss when Joe Vigil, pictured left, died in a car accident in late July 2003. Vigil had emerged as a leading superintendent for APS more than a year before his death, following a brief period in which the district experimented with a four-person superintendent office. Vigil had been reappointed lead superintendent just days before his death, and he had been studying at Harvard in a doctoral program. Many believe his vision, passion for collaboration, and trust in principals held great promise for APS. (Courtesy APS.)

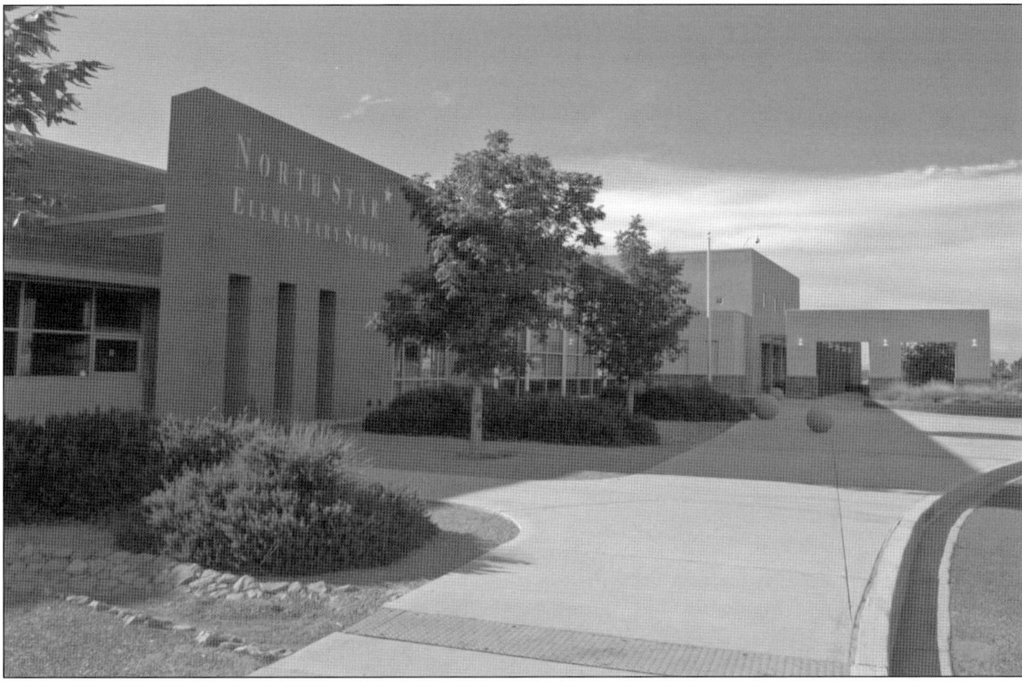


Pictured above, North Star Elementary opened in 2005 in the far northeast heights of Albuquerque. The school serves a largely well-to-do population, but the neighborhood is curiously mixed in its residential versus rural aspects. (Author's collection.)

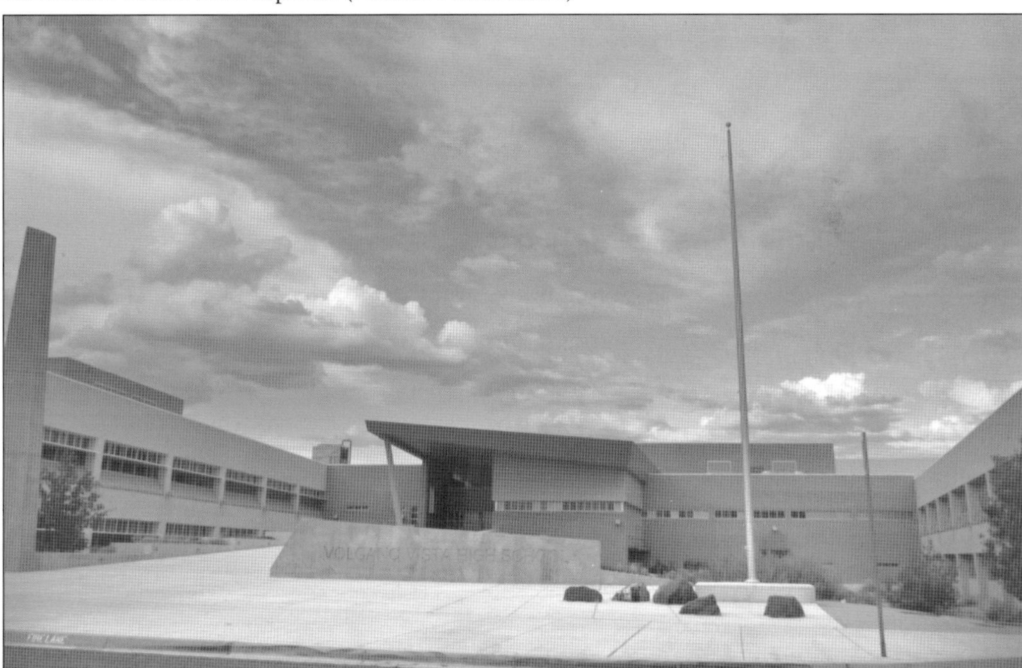

Volcano Vista High scraped the dust off its far west mesa doors and welcomed students in the fall of 2007. Another green-designed school, this comprehensive high school campus will serve the growing neighborhoods well for many years. (Author's collection.)

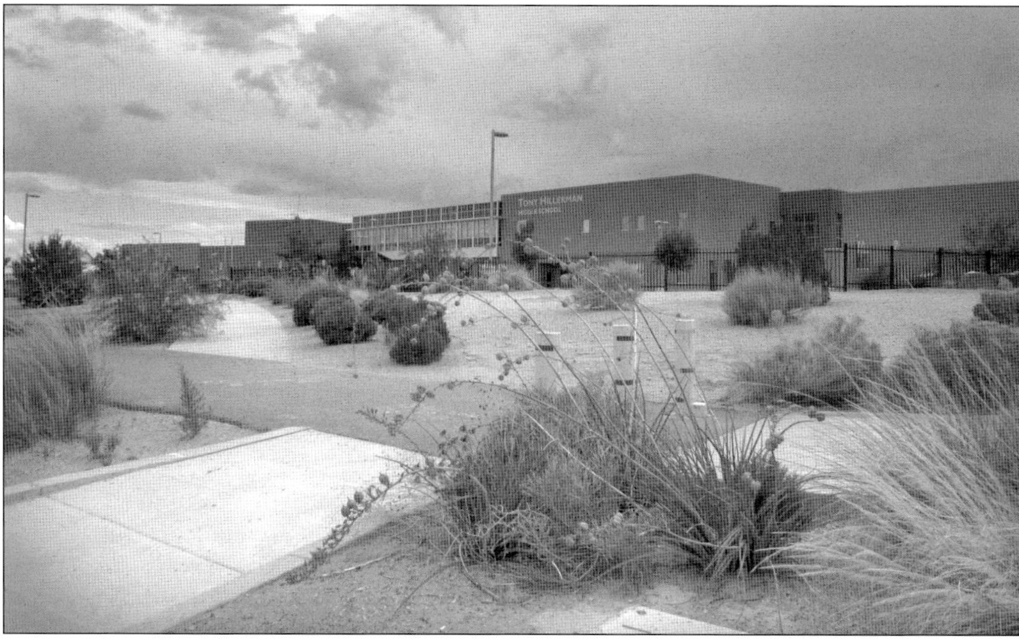

Contiguous to Volcano Vista High, Tony Hillerman Middle School opened in 2009 and is named after the renowned New Mexico author. Renee Garcia was the school's first principal. (Author's collection.)

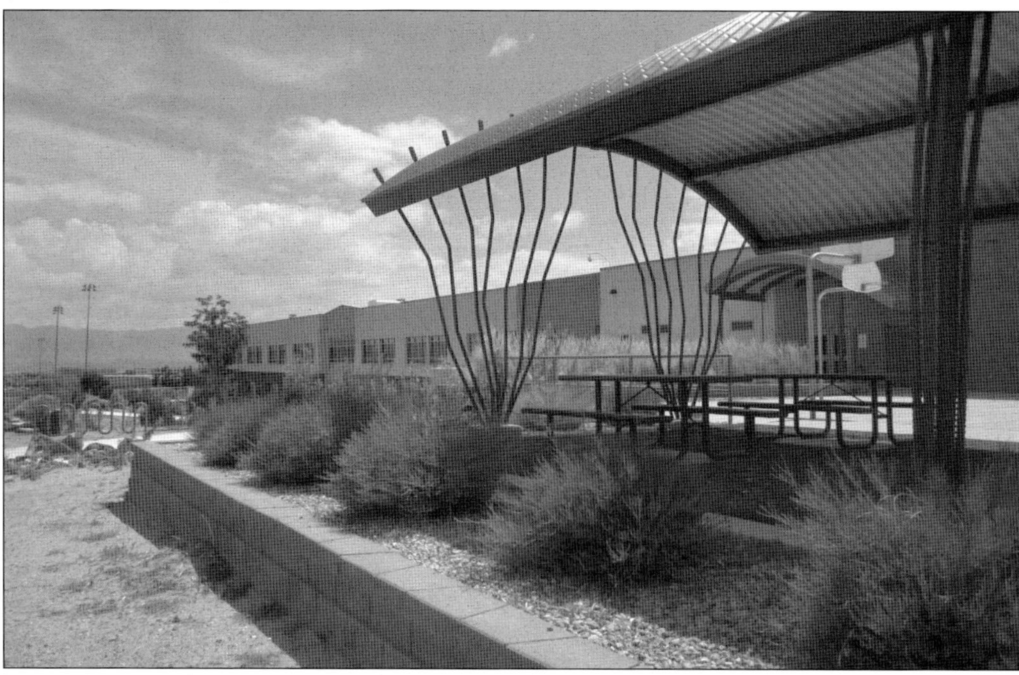

Tierra Antigua Elementary, opened in 2009, is nestled behind Volcano Vista High, and can be seen from Tony Hillerman Middle School. All three schools combine in an orchestrated tribute to the landscape from which they sprang, emanating colors, shapes, and angles that mimic the surrounding natural landscape. Even though the combined populations of the schools comprise over 3,000 students, the complex is visually soothing and calm. (Author's collection.)

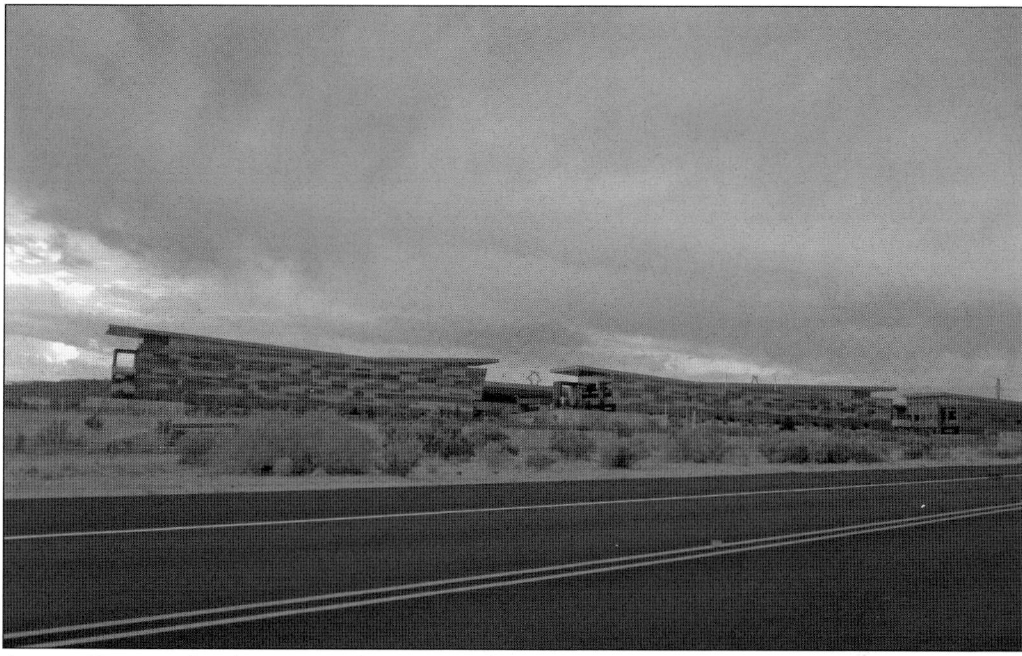

Atrisco Heritage Academy opened in 2008 under first principal Karen Sanchez Griego. Continuing APS's commitment to green and landscape-friendly schools, AHA greets the person arriving from the east with an Anasazi-type appearance—but then as the visitor rounds the curve to the south, the huge silver and glass structure meets the eye. (Author's collection.)

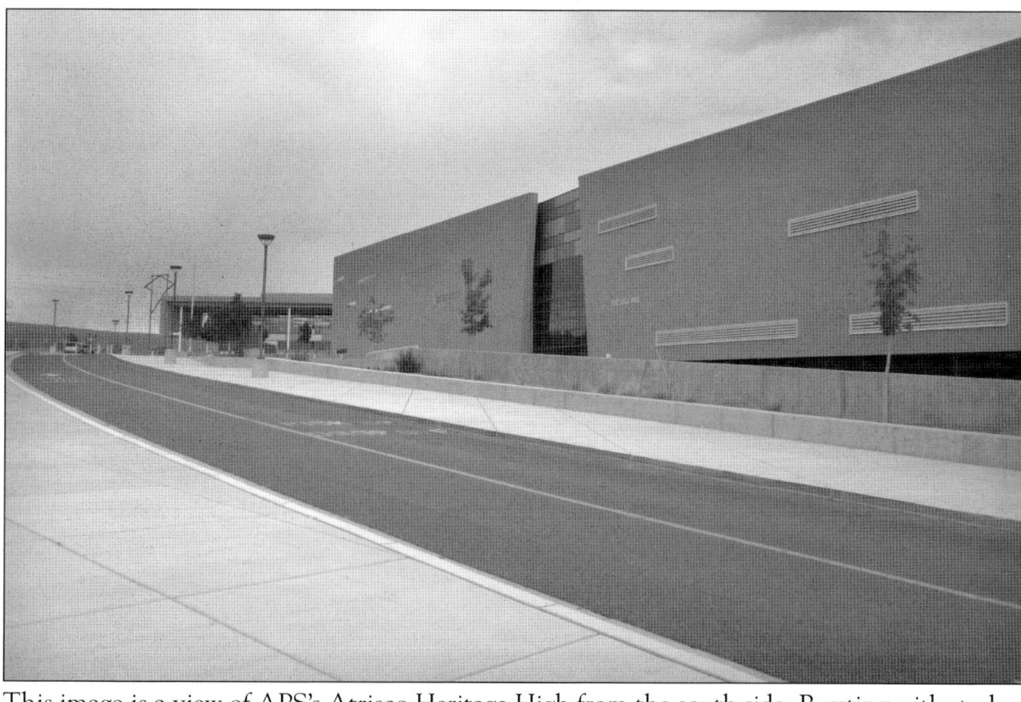

This image is a view of APS's Atrisco Heritage High from the south side. Bursting with student enrollment, AHA's designed facility was at capacity in 2013, and principal Antonio Gonzales juggles the many diverse needs of the surrounding communities. (Author's collection.)

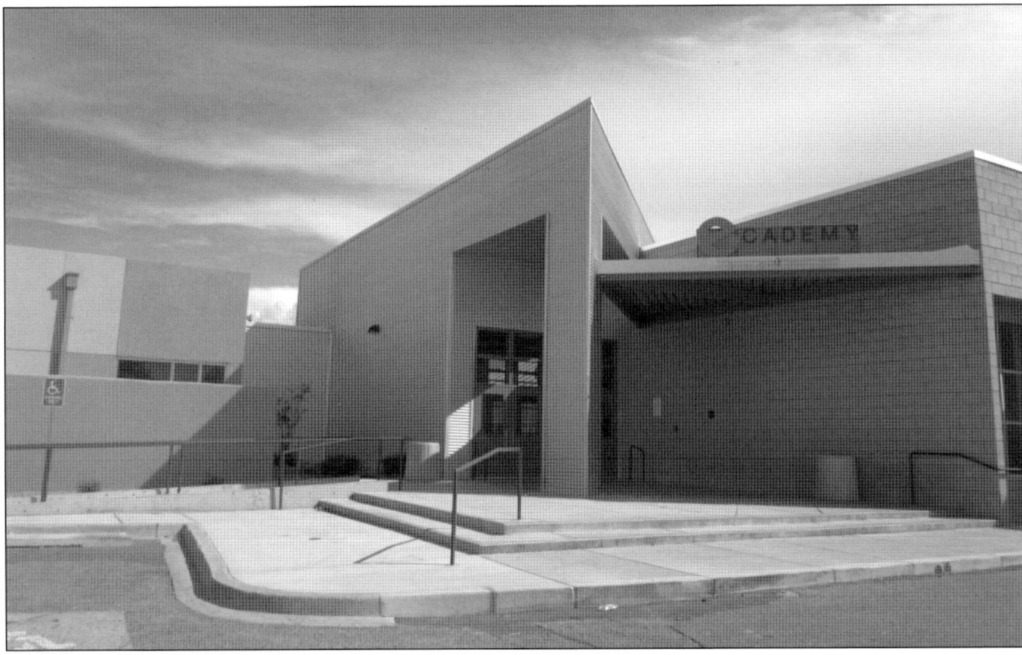

eAcademy opened in 2010 to serve a growing interest for APS to offer more online and computer-based options for student learning. Located contiguous and just north of Del Norte High, this gleaming new facility promises a host of opportunity's for APS high school students. (Author's collection.)

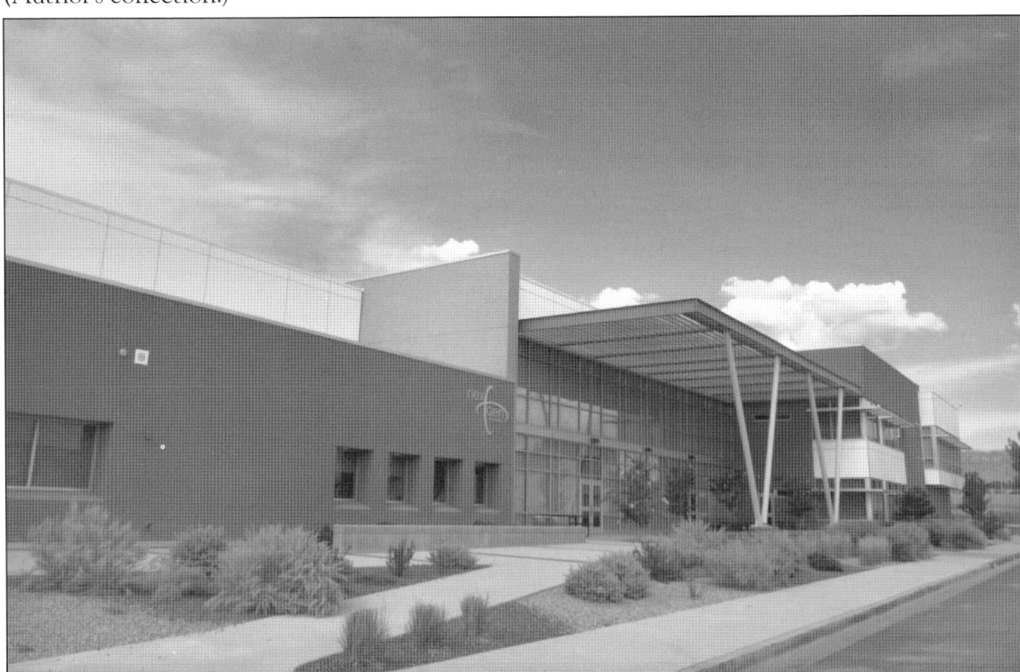

Another APS school of choice is Nex+Gen, opened in 2010. Offering independent learning options for a small group of students (up to 400 in enrollment), Nex+Gen centers on project-based learning and collaboration via technology. (Author's collection.)

# *Eight*

# Albuquerque Schools' Diversity, Acceptance, and Coexistence

Albuquerque is like no other place—that is an easy statement, but a fair one for those who know the area. Invaded by Europeans nearly 100 years before the Pilgrims landed at Plymouth Rock, the Albuquerque area began embracing outsiders over 300 years ago. That rich tradition of accepting others has colored the Albuquerque community with an inclusive paintbrush. Today, Albuquerque—a progressive leader in the western states—in general welcomes the entire spectrum of people and their assumptions, values, cultures, and beliefs.

A moonscape of sand and rock was carved up the hill from Old Town to New Town in 1881 when the railroad came through. The populace of the city trailed after, up the rise from the river, devising ways to port the water along with them. Various diverse cultures lived side by side—Germans, Greeks, African Americans, Italians, English, Native Americans, Mexicans, Spanish, and more—all collectively staked out a space on the rising east mesa, pledged to financially support school systems, and then shoulder to shoulder did the good work to build those schools.

The city continued to spread, particularly north and west, building schools for all ages and interests, adopting architectural styles that consider and reflect the landscape, while utilizing energy-efficient techniques. APS, CNM, and UNM continue to thrive, as do the city's church, private, and charter schools. Albuquerque's schools say thank you and welcome!

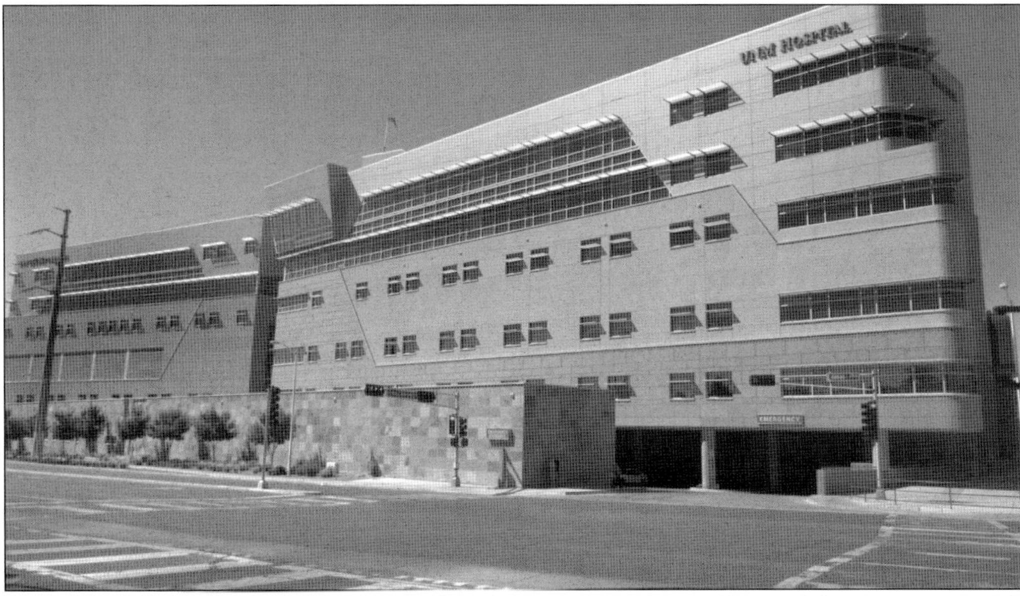


The University of New Mexico Hospital is the primary teaching hospital for the area. In July 2014, UNM's School of Medicine will celebrate the 50th anniversary of its first entering class. In 1994, UNM combined its many medically related schools into one entity, the Health Science Center, one of the largest health related educational entities in the western states. UNM's School of Medicine consistently ranks among the top nationally for its rural medicine, family medicine, and primary care medicine programs. (Author's collection.)

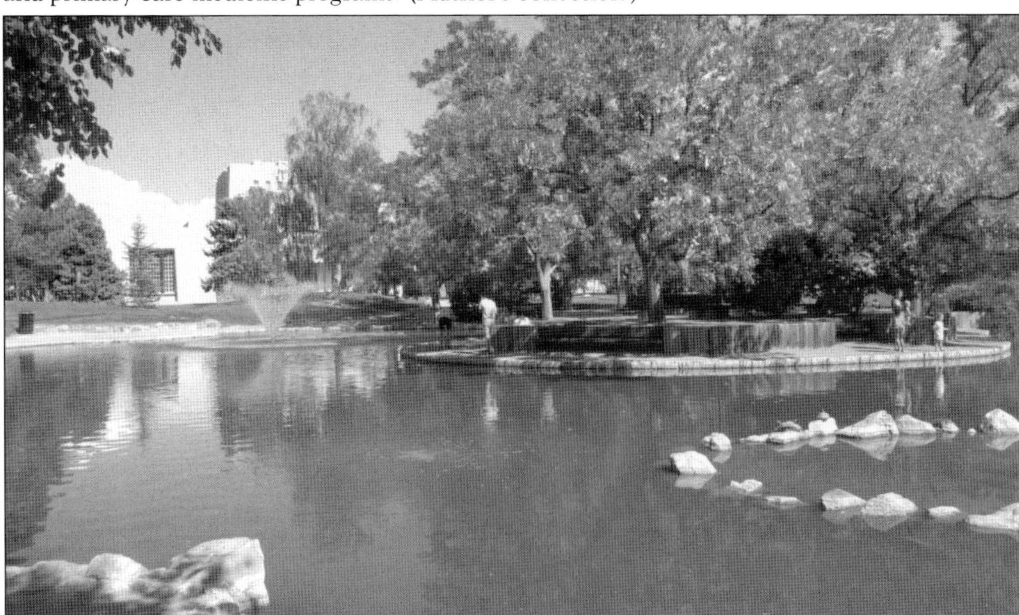

Almost all schoolchildren in Albuquerque make their way at some time in their youth to the University of New Mexico's duck pond. The pond and its surrounding green lawns, located in the center of UNM's main campus, form a backdrop perfect for relaxing, studying, and family outings. Zimmerman Library, built in 1937 and designed by John Gaw Meem, is in the background. (Author's collection.)

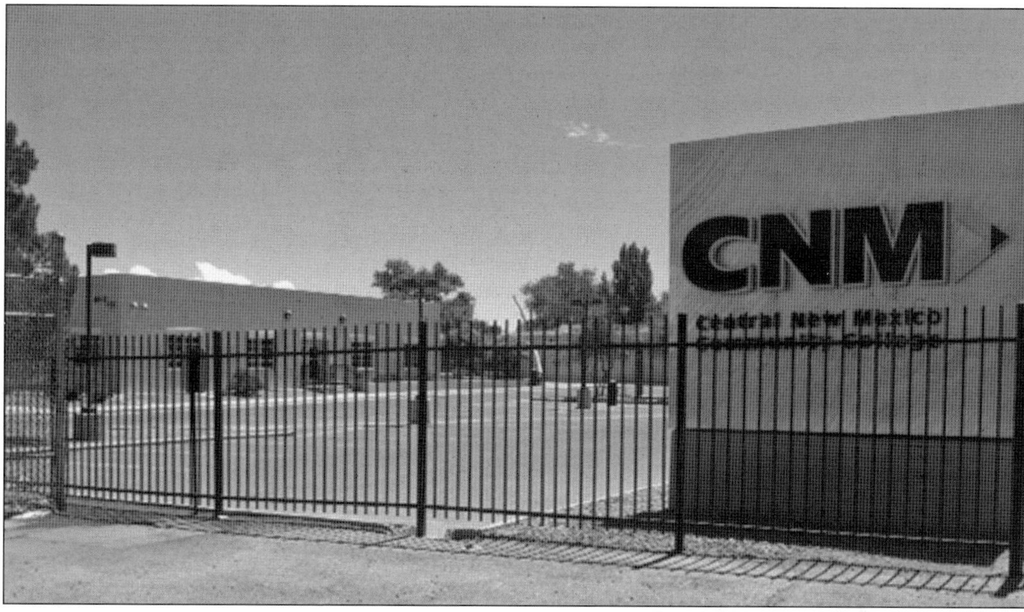


One of the educational jewels in Albuquerque is Central New Mexico Community College. Opened in 1964 by the Albuquerque Public Schools to teach trade skills to older youth and adults, the mission of the school zoomed ahead, and in 1978, the North Central Association accredited Technical Vocational Institute. In 1986, TV-I was approved to grant degrees in addition to certificates, and today (operating as CNM) the school provides a seamless and vital transition to students moving from high school (many gaining college credit in advance of graduating), to two-year degrees (many of which can be transferred to the university to continue), to serving as a bridge to four-year degrees and beyond. (Both photographs courtesy Beth Piper.)

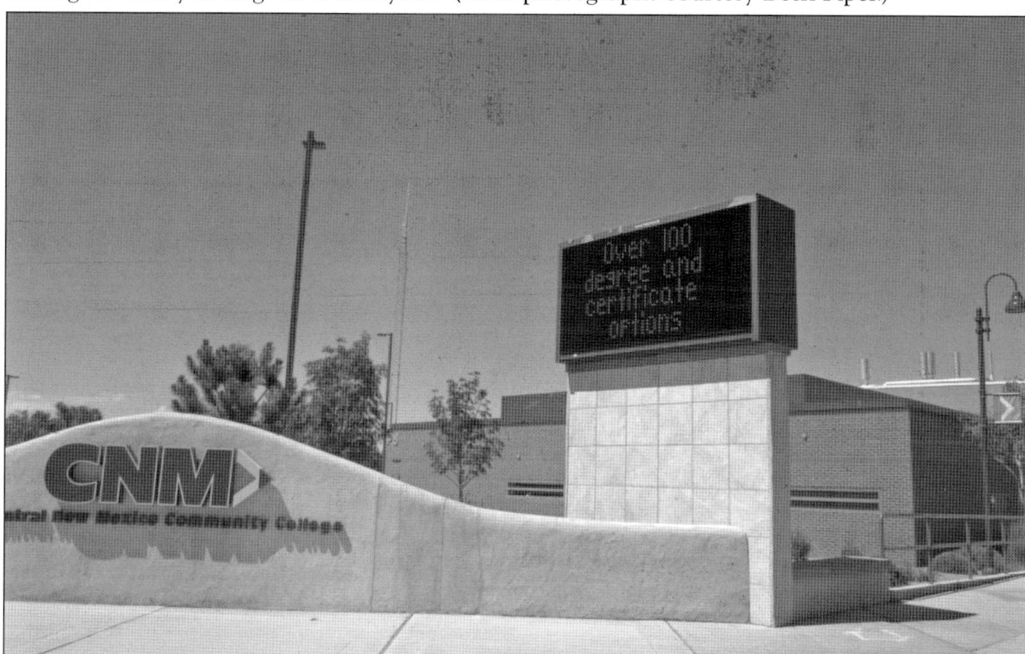

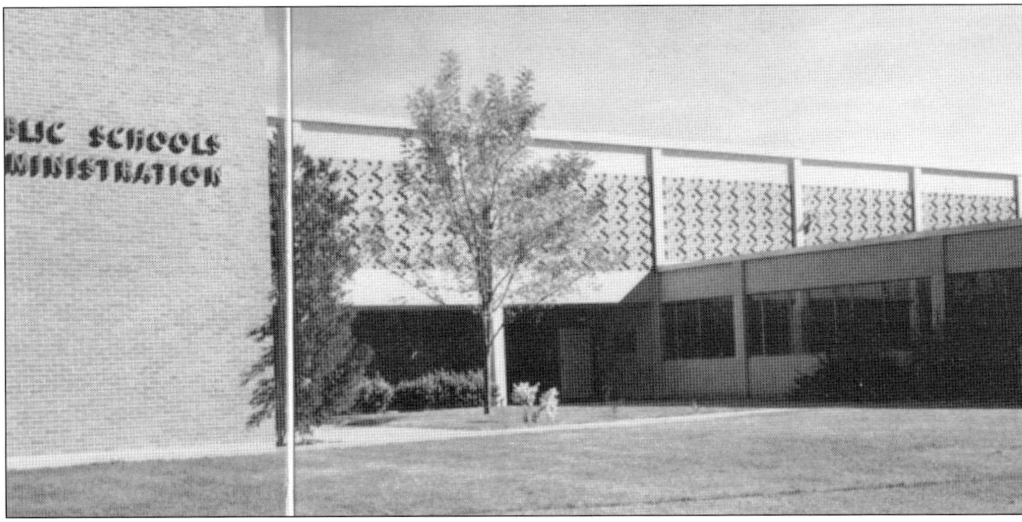

Above is the entrance to APS's central administrative offices, pictured around 1963 on University Boulevard south of Coal Avenue. Below is the City Center, the current administrative complex at 6400 Uptown Northeast. The contrast serves as a visual jolt, reinforcing the exponentially increased accountability, social expectations, human services requirements, state and federal mandates and regulations, litigious potential, and more that falls upon our pubic schools today in contrast to the days when John Milne reported to his eight-by-eight foot office at Third and Lead in 1911. (Above, courtesy APM; below, author's collection.)

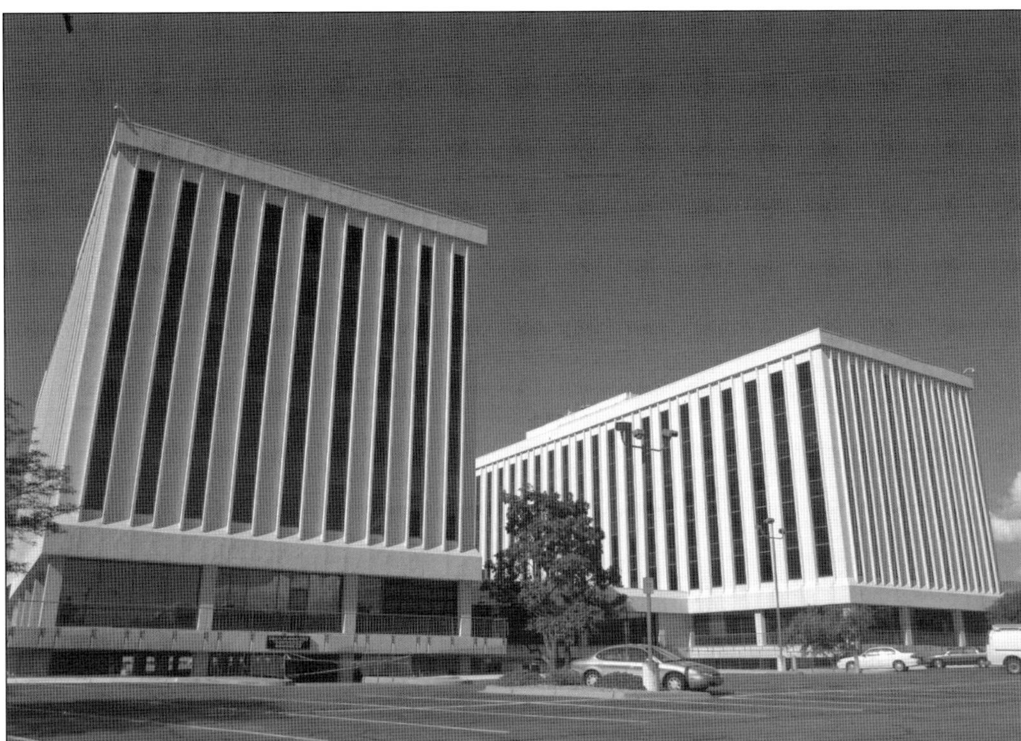

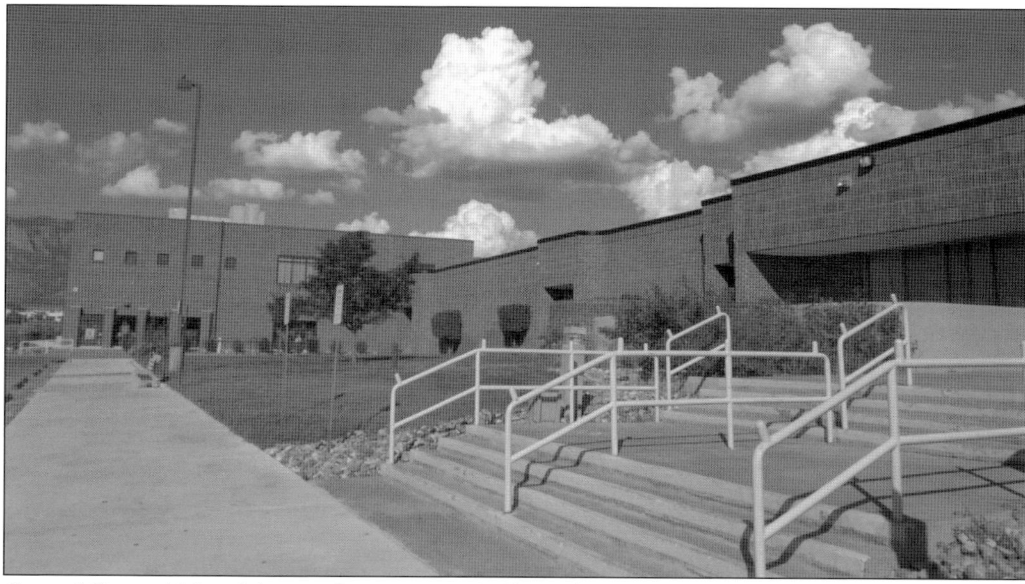

One of Central New Mexico Community College's branch campuses is the northeast heights Montoya campus. In order to serve its nearly 30,000 students, CNM has the main branch in central Albuquerque, and four other branches throughout a large geographical area that include Albuquerque's sister city to the northwest, Rio Rancho. (Author's collection.)

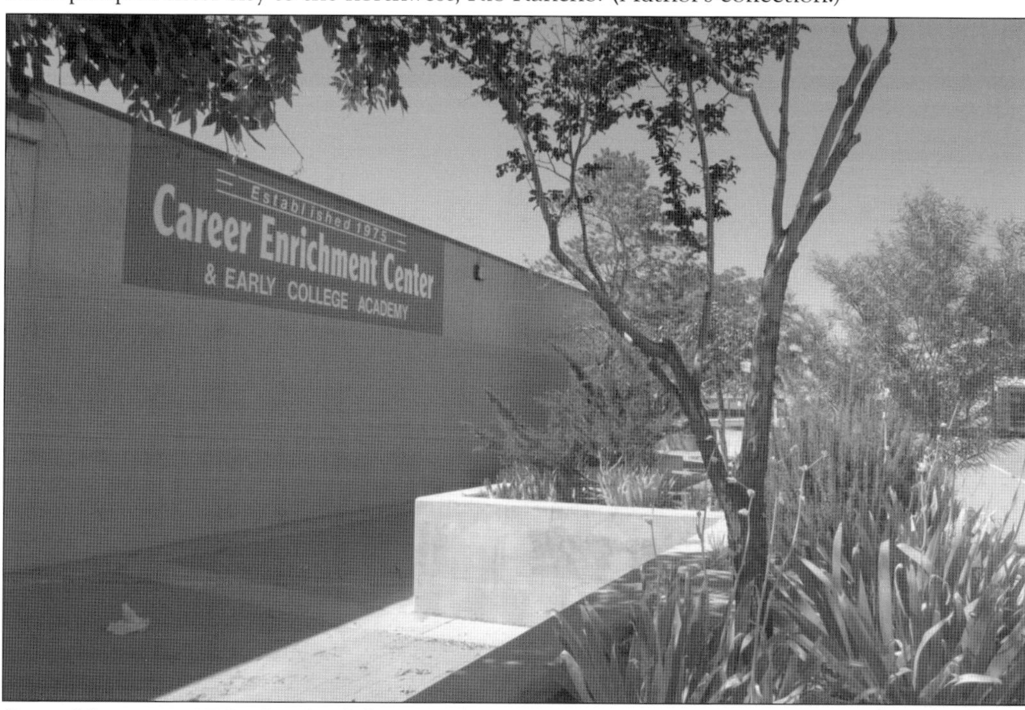


One of the many APS schools of choice is the Early College Academy. The leading "jump ahead" high school in the state for garnering high school students college credits while still in high school, ECA can start high school students on a fast track to a career in a variety of fields including nursing; emergency response; medical tech; language careers in German, Japanese, and more; and many other exciting fields. (Author's collection.)

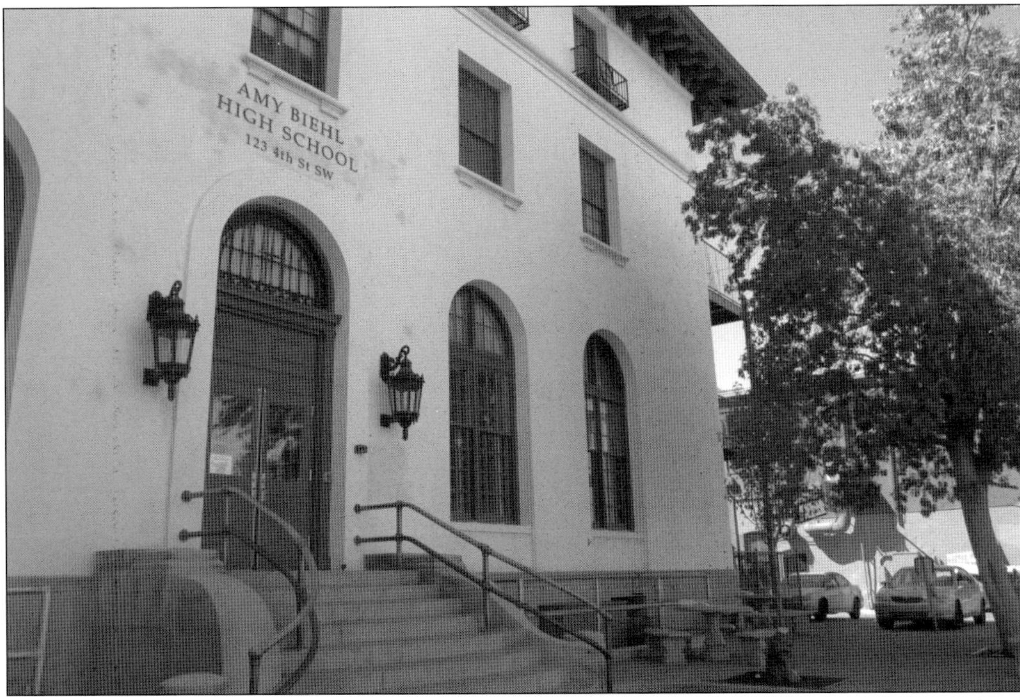


After Highland High (encouraged by APS) gained status as one of the first five charter schools in the state in 1993, New Mexico felt a lull—were charters a necessary transition? Highland relinquished its charter status within a few years, but in 1999 an energetic duo—one of whom was a former Highland teacher—were granted a charter to open Amy Biehl High School. The school has a high scholarship, service learning and community service focus, with an emphasis on collaboration and international relations exploration. Tom Siegel and Tony Monfiletto opened the school that was named after Amy, who died in South Africa, tragically mobbed and murdered by those for whom she championed. (Author's collection.)

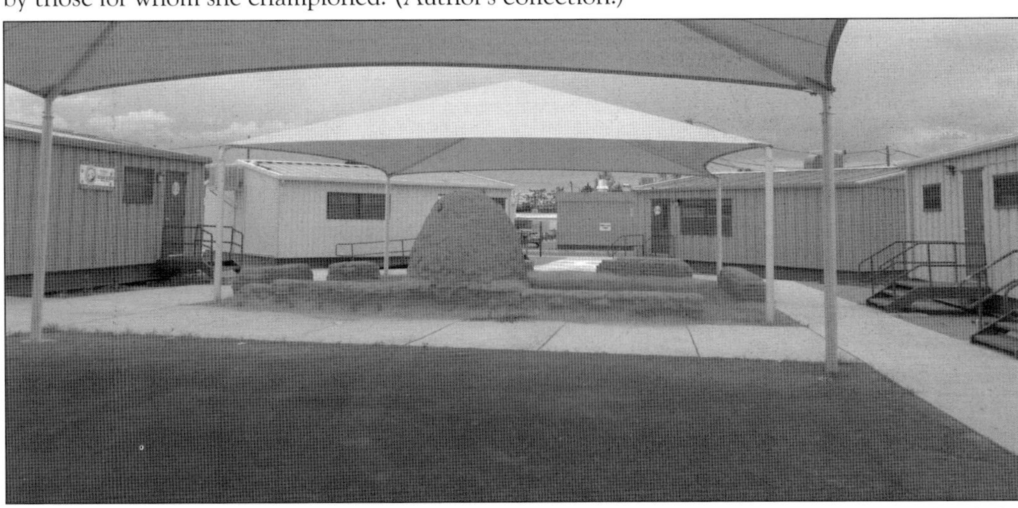

Above is the former campus of the Native American Community Academy charter school that relocated in the fall of 2013 from a portable building campus (at APS's Wilson Middle School) to the campus of the former Albuquerque Indian School. The principal of the school, Kara Bobroff, instrumental in its founding and opening, still serves. (Author's collection.)

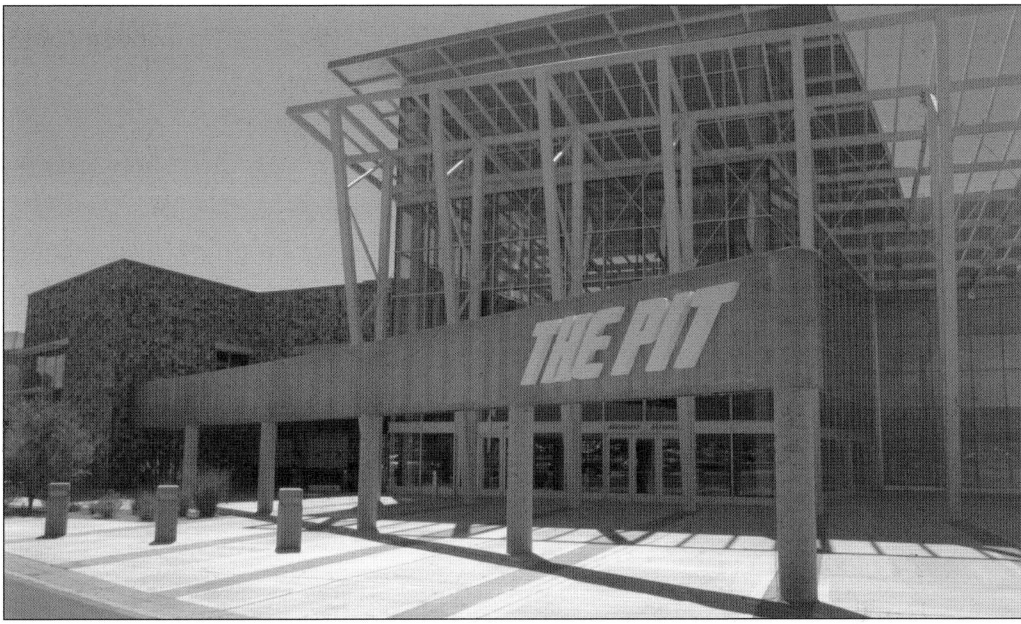


The University of New Mexico's portal to "The Pit"" is the school's basketball arena. UNM has a rich traditional of winning basketball teams and passionate fans, contributing to what makes Albuquerque as an educational community special. (Author's collection.)

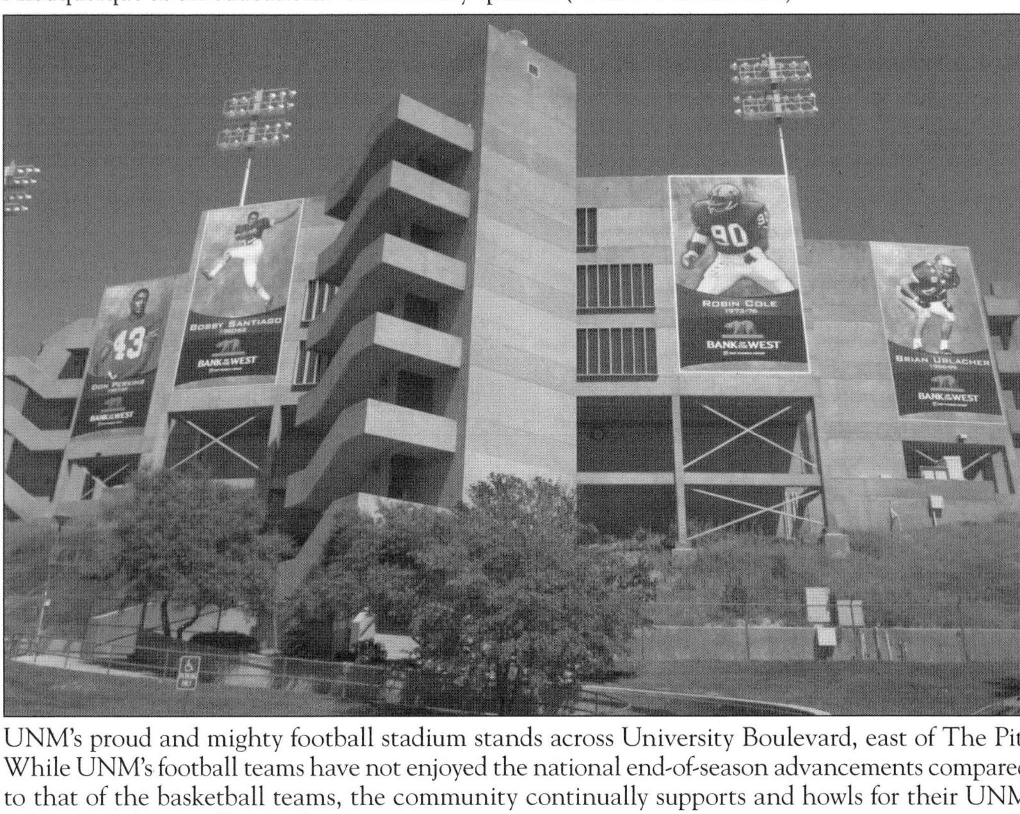


UNM's proud and mighty football stadium stands across University Boulevard, east of The Pit. While UNM's football teams have not enjoyed the national end-of-season advancements compared to that of the basketball teams, the community continually supports and howls for their UNM Lobos. (Author's collection.)

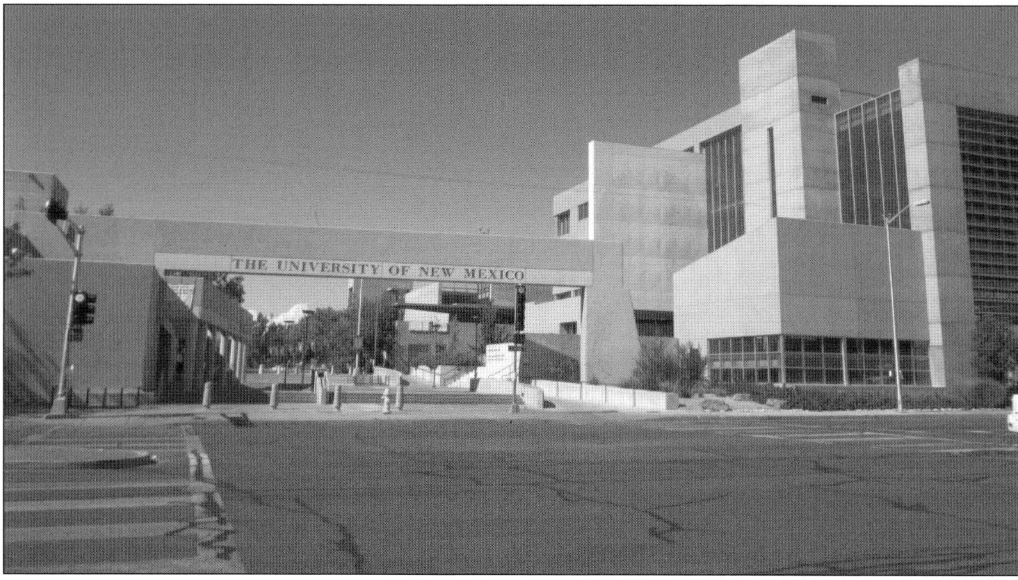


Relatively new buildings for the University of New Mexico are the George O. Pearl School of Architecture on the right, the decorative welcoming arch in the center, and a glimpse of the new UNM bookstore on the left. UNM contributes immeasurably to the vitality of the city's educational community. (Author's collection.)

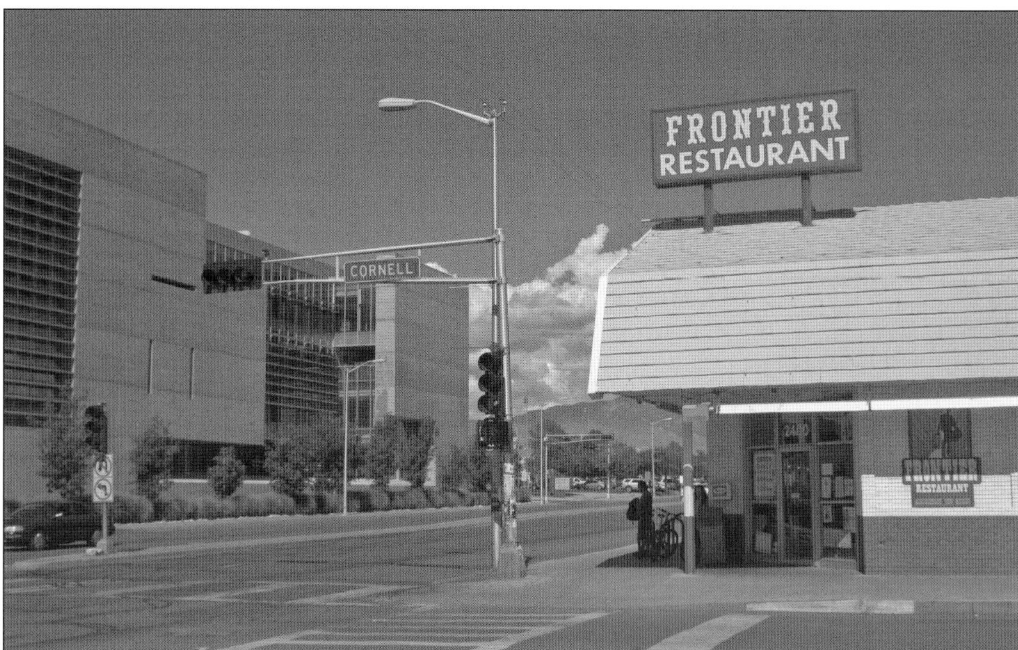


What University of New Mexico or city southeast heights resident does not frequent the Frontier Restaurant several times a month to study, eat a great meal, grab a famous sweet roll, or just generally watch the show that occurs daily? Owned locally for decades, the Frontier is an experience that must be savored. As local high school students unload from buses for various field trips to UNM, the Frontier is their common lunch stop and, in a sense, their gateway to their possible future as a UNM student. (Author's collection.)

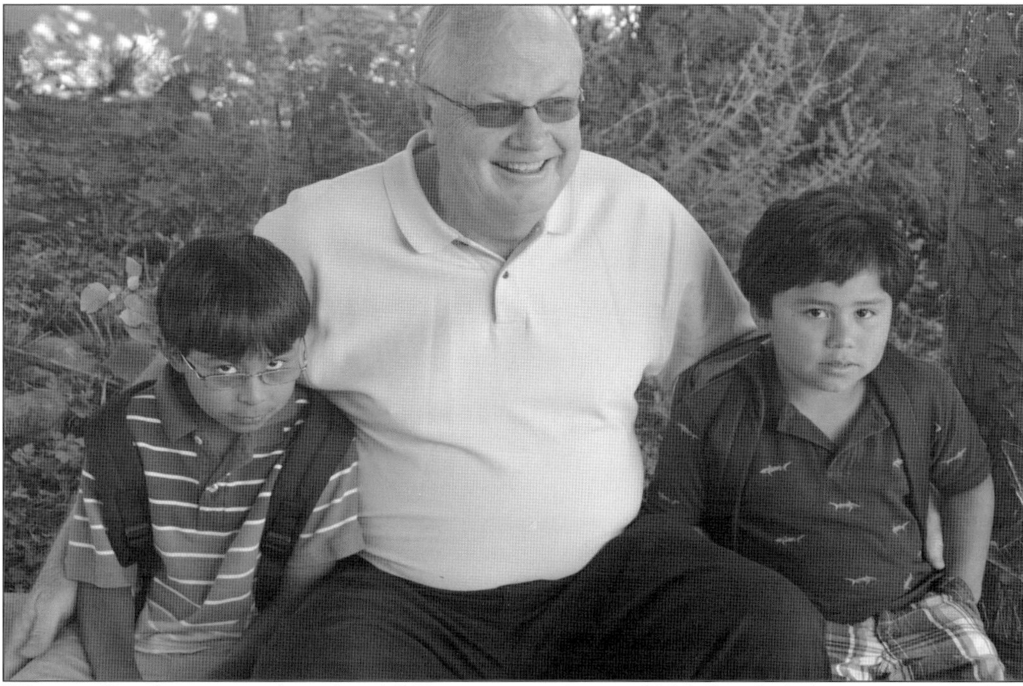

Winston Brooks came on board as APS's superintendent in 2006. Brooks believes passionately in the mission of public schools, and has worked to increase communication between himself, the Board of Education, students, and parents. He has strived to increase school choice in the city's school system, and reaches a hand across to set up dialogues with post-secondary institutions and grant-potential entities. Further, Brooks has maintained a positive relationship with the Board of Education and the teachers' union. (Courtesy APS.)

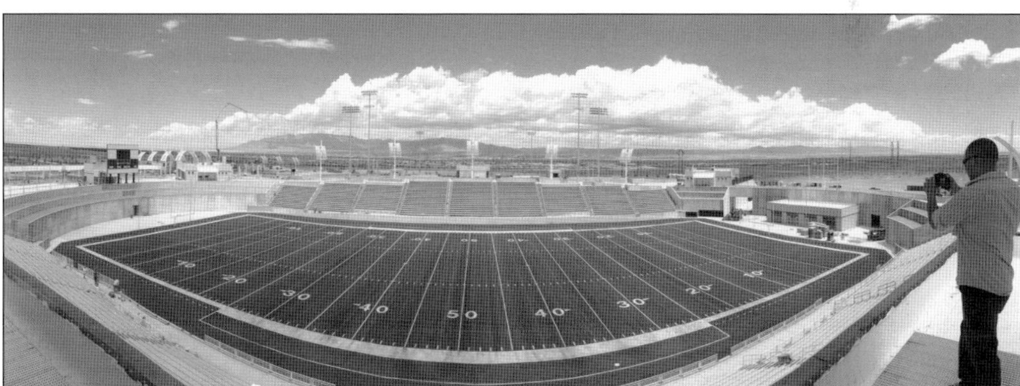

"Bulldog" Stadium was built for the city's only high school to utilize in 1940. In 1963, a second city school stadium, Wilson Stadium, opened on the east side of town. A new APS stadium was on its way in 2013. Community Stadium (above) hosted its first event on August 28, 2013, as Manzano High took on Volcano Vista High in a historic football game. Located on the city's west side, the facility has 7,000 seats, and utilizes new technology to keep lights and noise from disturbing area neighbors unduly. (Courtesy APS.)

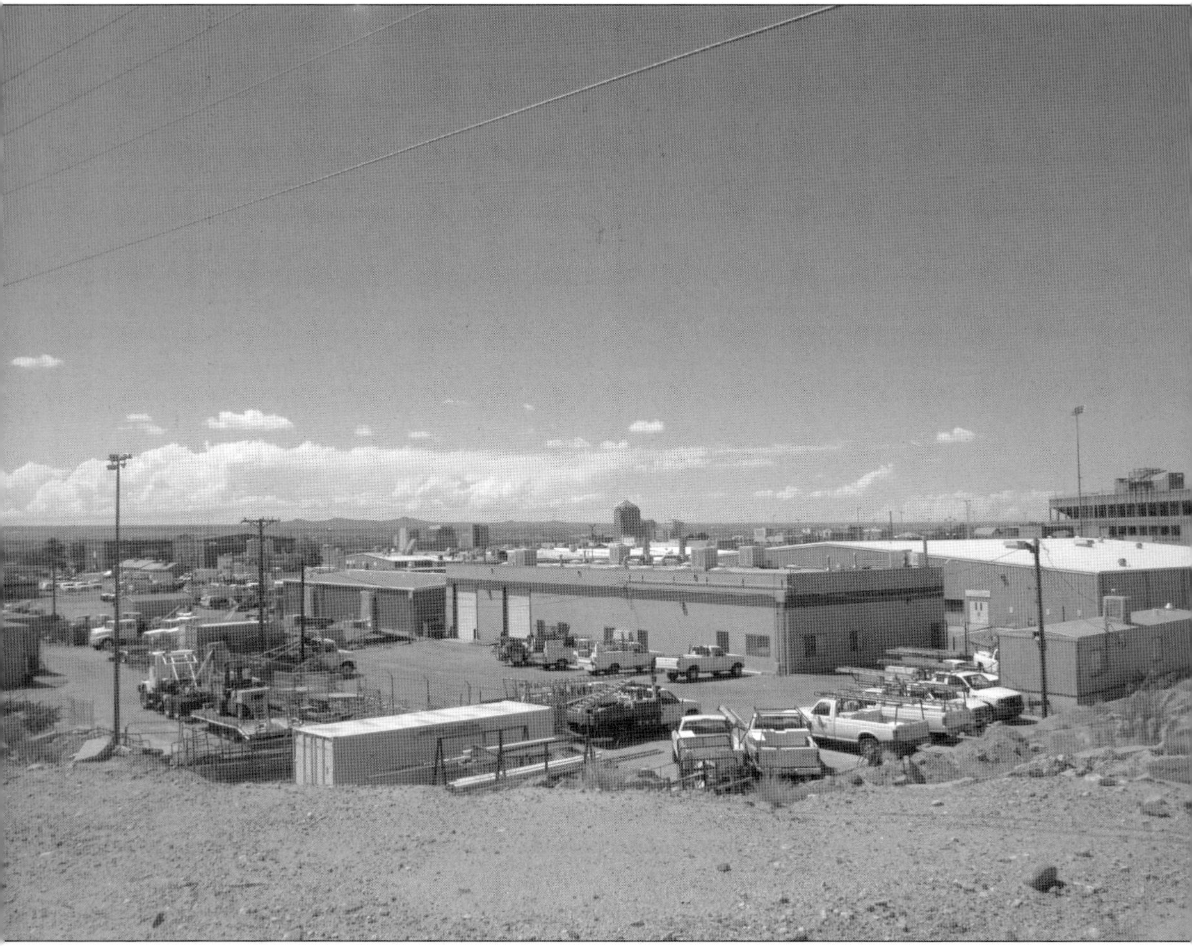

This view shows the bustling maintenance, operations, technology, library services, food services, and facilities design yards that APS maintains in order to run its approximately 80,000-student school district. To the back (west) and left center the profile of former redbrick Lincoln Middle School stands out. The teamwork that APS's staff exhibits makes APS a great work community. (Author's collection.)

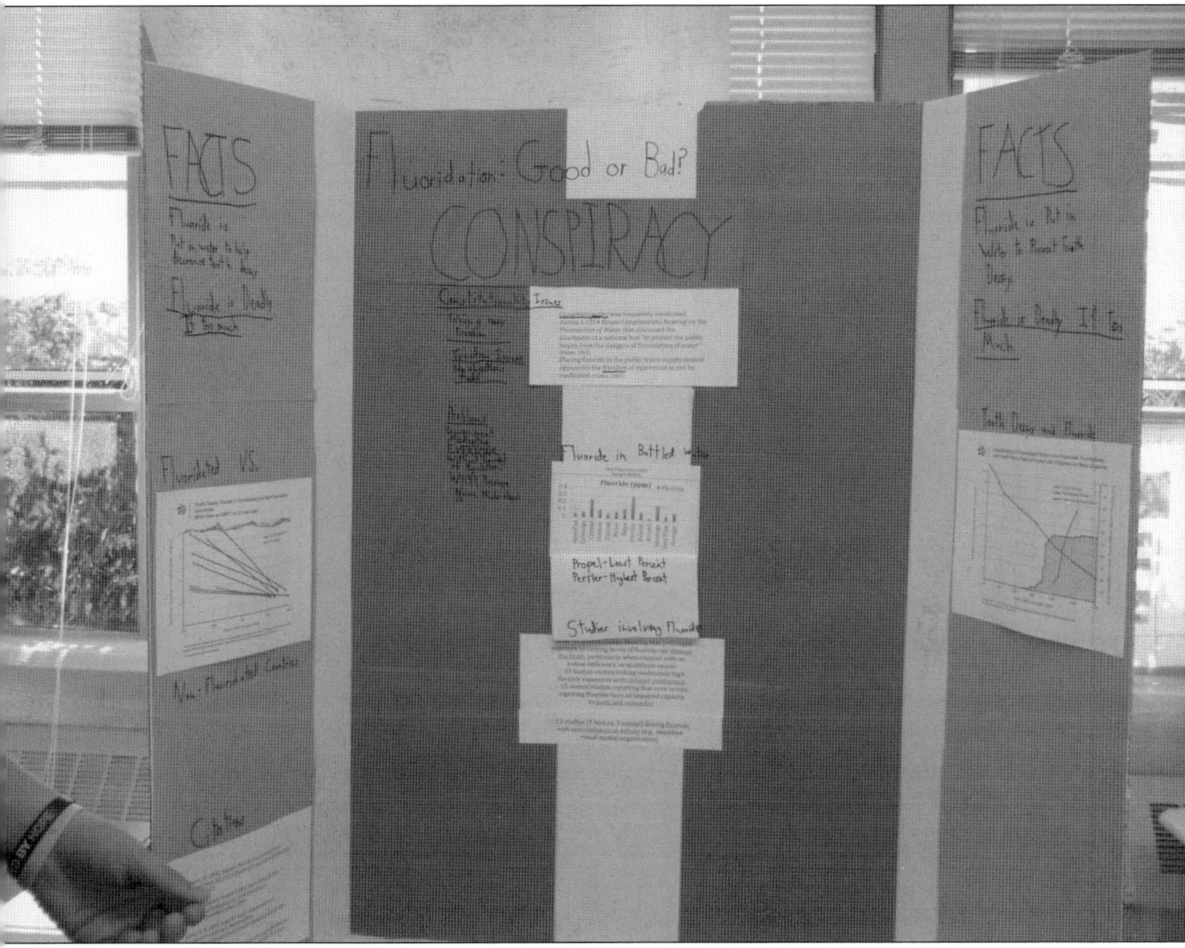


Pictured here is an example of the type of project that the APS Foundation supports. APS is very fortunate to have an outreach group that advocates for students, supplying myriads of programs, supplies, and services. This book is a collaborative partnership between the author and the APS Foundation, and a portion of the author's royalties benefit the APS Foundation. Thank you! (Author's collection.)

# Bibliography

Biebel, C.D. *Making the Most of It: Public Works in Albuquerque during the Great Depression 1929–1942*. Albuquerque: The Albuquerque Museum, 1986.

Davis, C. *From the Grain of a Mustard Seed*. Albuquerque: Footprints from the Bible, 2008.

Davis, W.E. *Miracle on the Mesa: A History of the University of New Mexico 1889–2003*. Albuquerque: University of New Mexico Press, 2006.

Flores, Steve. *Ghost Town Basketball*. Albuquerque: New Mexico Starline Printing, 2006.

Liberty, L. *Constant Possum: the History of Sandia Preparatory School*. Albuquerque: Sandia Preparatory School, 199.

Harrington, E.R. *History of the Albuquerque Public Schools*. Albuquerque: Albuquerque Public Schools, 1963.

Harrington, E.R. *A Pictorial Tour of the Albuquerque Public Schools*. Unpublished, in the possession of Robert Milne: c. 1944.

Mahoney, J. *Albuquerque's Huning Castle Neighborhoods*. Charleston, SC: Arcadia Publishing, 2013.

Mondragon, J.B. & Stapleton, E.R. *Public Education in New Mexico*. Albuquerque: University of New Mexico Press, 2005.

Pamonis, K.M. *Uncovering the History of the Albuquerque Greek Community 1880–1952*. Santa Fe, NM: Sunstone Press, 2012.

Piper, A. *A Line in the Sand: The Opening of Albuquerque's Second Public High School, Highland High*. Unpublished dissertation. Albuquerque: The University of New Mexico, 2013.

Sandweiss, N. *Jewish Albuquerque 1860–1960*. Charleston, SC: Arcadia Publishing, 2011.

Shunny, J. *The Sandia Peak and La Madera Ski Patrol: A History 1937 to 1986*. Albuquerque: Adobe Press, 1987.

Terry, R.H. *Light in the Valley: The McCurdy Mission School Story*.

# About the Author

Ann Piper grew up in Columbia, Missouri, and attended Hickman High there, Truman State in Kirksville, Missouri, and the University of New Mexico where she earned both master's and doctoral degrees in educational administration (1993 and 2013, respectively).

Piper has taught high school English at Albuquerque's Rio Grande, West Mesa, and Highland High Schools, years 1979–1993, and was activities director at Highland High 1993–1995. For five years, she was assistant principal at Albuquerque's Jackson Middle School, and following that served a stint for 13 years as the principal of Jackson. In her first year as principal of the city's Wilson Middle School, Piper is excited to put her collaborative leadership skills to use at the middle school in her own neighborhood where her three children, Beth, Michael, and Laura, attended public schools.

Piper's husband, Blair Kaufman, is also a city school's principal. He has served at Mark Twain, Chaparral, Sandia Base, and is currently at Matheson Park. Kaufman is the longest-serving and proudest member of the New Mexico Central Community College governing board. When this term of elected service is up, he will have served for 18 years.

Kaufman and Piper are pleased to be a part of Albuquerque's inclusive, vibrant educational community. Piper plans to continue mining the history of the Albuquerque Public Schools. Send facts, stories, and a blend of both her way!